Two prominent New York dealers of eighteenth- and early nineteenth-century European furniture recently approached the author independently of each other to express an interest in Art Deco furniture and the availability of top-quality pieces. Both realized that the increasing shortage of important works in their own field necessitated a search elsewhere. The nineteenth century beyond Charles X provided no ready solutions; the Louis Philippe and Napoleon III eras were, in most part, derivative, a pastiche of earlier styles. Nor did either of the antiquarians find Art Nouveau a viable alternative; its profuse organisms were too radical for their traditional taste and training. Both, however, discovered in Art Deco furniture the goal of an odyssey through one hundred years of French furniture-making history: an identifiable style of great refinement and vitality, and one that met the traditional dictates of good taste and virtuoso cabinetry. A fine Printz or D.I.M. commode can stand proudly alongside a Riesener or Oeben forebear, its elegant contours and decoration an irrefutable continuation of the finest French tradition. Both dealers were delighted not only because they had discovered a field in which to expand their inventory, but also because they felt an immediate affinity and respect for the style.

Art Deco furniture has, in fact, had a meteoric rise in popularity when measured by its auction prices in recent years. Several works by Süe et Mare and Ruhlmann have approached the $200,000 mark, with examples by Chareau and Dunand following close behind. And prices such as these for works which are hardly sixty years old, well short of the hundred-year limit which is generally accepted as the age at which an item qualifies as an antique! One can only speculate on the future spiral of prices. Art Deco furniture will continue to gain ground on its eighteenth-century predecessors for two reasons: first, some of the very finest examples are not yet in permanent museum collections; and second, its twentieth-century genesis gives it a broad appeal to collectors of modern art, a field also in its infancy.

Art Deco and modernism

In the mind of the public, however, the term 'Art Deco' continues to create confusion. It is used widely, often incorrectly, to embrace anything from a 1930s New York skyscraper to the smallest piece of Bakelite bric-a-brac or kitsch. In furniture, this confusion is compounded by the fact that everything 'modern' – whether in wood, metal, or a synthetic material – is often labelled by the uninitiated as 'Art Deco'. The intention of this introduction is to unscramble these misunderstandings by outlining the difference between Art Deco and other contemporary styles – most particularly, that now known as 'modernism'.

The term 'Art Deco' is of recent coinage, and is a contraction of the full title of the celebrated 1925 Exposition Internationale des Arts Décoratifs et Industriels Modernes, at which the style was extravagantly displayed.

Art Deco furniture drew its inspiration from the French *ancien régime* and its legacy was the late-eighteenth-century cabinetmaker. In this heritage lay the proven roots of a continuing rich French tradition. Ruhlmann, for one, actively encouraged a comparison with Riesener and Weisweiler, and in the Paris of the 1920s no accolade could be greater.

The need for a rebirth was felt particularly strongly after the exuberant Art Nouveau era, which history had already judged a grave and mercifully brief transgression against good taste. Drawn from the furniture of the Louis XVI period were purity of form and refinement, transformed in the 1920s by the new dictates of functionalism and a taste for splendour. Beauty lay in the graceful proportions of a chair leg or the understated ivory banding along its apron. The turn-of-the-century promulgators of functionalism – in particular Adolf Loos and Francis Jourdain – had been right from the start in their prognosis that the prevailing fashion for ornamentation was an aberration which would soon yield to a more rigid architectural discipline.

The First World War is generally seen to be the dividing line between the Art Nouveau and Art Deco furniture styles, but the latter was in fact conceived in the prewar transitional years of 1905 to 1910. Many pieces of furniture now accepted as pure Art Deco – especially pieces by Gray, Ruhlmann, Iribe, and Follot – were designed before the outbreak of war, and several more before 1920. The movement cannot therefore be rigidly defined within the years 1920 and 1930, as it usually is. Its inception was earlier, as was its decline.

By the mid-1920s the 'pure' or 'high' Art Deco style had reached maturity. Its first tenet, that form must follow function, later remained unchallenged by all succeeding twentieth-century schools of design, but its second, which related to decoration, proved its undoing. Ironically, it was the Art Deco proponent himself who had recoiled against the superfluous ornamentation of the *fin-de-siècle* movement, claiming that mouldings, whiplash or scrolled protrusions, and, simply, all sculpted excess performed no practical function whatever and must therefore go. Decoration, it was reasoned, must be contained within the piece's fundamental shape. Therefore marquetry, carved and cast bas-reliefs, and contrasting parquetry panels were permitted, all, of course, in the best materials that money could buy. The veneered landscapes and flamboyant ormolu mounts on Majorelle's 1900 cabinets had disappeared; in their place quiet lozenge-patterned ivory banding and lightly scrolled *sabots*.

Decoration remained an integral part of Art Deco furniture and its proponents argued that beauty in the home was essential to people's psychological well-being. Paul Follot, a

strict traditionalist and Art Deco adherent, later defended this stance in a speech at the opening in Paris in 1928 of an exhibition by the London firm of Waring and Gillow: 'We know that the "necessary" alone is not sufficient for man and that the superfluous is indispensable for him . . . or otherwise let us also suppress music, flowers, perfumes . . . and the smiles of ladies!'

Opposition had begun to build from the early 1920s, Le Corbusier speaking out strongly against Ruhlmann's remark that 'if only the very richest can afford to pay the price of innovation, they are also the only ones with the power to sponsor it'. The future of furniture (or anything else) did not rest with the rich, and even less with their decorative preferences. An object's greatest beauty lay, rather, in its perfect adaption to its usage. To reduce furniture to its basic elements was not a regression, but a rebirth of everything espoused by Josef Hoffmann and the Wiener Werkstätte, Hermann Muthesius and the Deutsche Werkbund, and Walter Gropius and the Bauhaus.

By 1926 the loosely knit band of modernists – whose most vocal publicists were Jourdain, Chareau, Le Corbusier, Mallet-Stevens, and Herbst – had become increasingly outspoken in their criticism of Art Deco furniture designers who still catered only to select clients and produced only *pièces uniques* or limited editions. They argued that the new age required nothing less than excellent design for everyone and that quality and mass-production were not mutually exclusive. Each epoch must create a style in its own image to meet its own specific needs. For furniture in the late 1920s and 1930s, this aim could best be realized through the use of metal and glass.

Both the modernists and the traditionalists claimed to be purists. Follot, in his Waring and Gillow speech, attacked the modernists' complete disregard for, and lack of under-standing of, people's basic needs: 'The theory of this school is that our Art ought to be inspired by the characteristics of our epoch: mechanism, speed, and business. In consequence the home it offers is directly inspired from the laboratory and the factory, with incomplete installations having only as furniture pieces of metal, glass tables, cold lighting, pink and faded colours, forms exclusively geometric and no ornament. Rather than reflect the bustle and speed of modern life, the machine or the factory, the home should provide spiritual equilibrium and serenity.'

The use of metal for furniture solved two problems. The first was that of cost. Whereas the socioeconomic status of the bourgeoisie had been marginally elevated in the seven years since the armistice, the cost of producing veneered furniture placed it beyond the reach of most. A huge section of the potential furniture market was denied the best modern furniture, as it had been traditionally. Metal, however, would redress the situation for it could be both fashionable and inexpensive to mass-produce. (The debt to Thonet's nineteenth-century bentwood prototypes was acknowledged by many 1920s/30s designers of metal furniture.) The second problem overcome by metal furniture was the growing use of central heating, which was proving disastrous to both antique and new wooden pieces.

Metal furniture was introduced at the 1927 Salon des Artistes Décorateurs to mixed reviews. Within two years, however, it was wood that was on the defensive, though controversy raged in Parisian circles for a considerable length of time. Metal furniture was said to be the most heated issue since the Dreyfus case! The critic Ernest Tisserand noted that it was more likely to arouse anger at a dinner table than politics, and that a well-bred woman who would not dream of criticizing the choice of paintings in a friend's house would, on seeing a tubular metal chair, lose all self-control and express her opinion so forcibly that further friendship between herself and its owner would be impossible!

André Lurçat, a strict modernist, felt it necessary to stress that even the new rationalism had its limits. He cautioned against excess in a 1929 interview published in *Art et décoration*: 'Ornament without purpose disappears, through the same happy transformation by which the higgledy-piggledy town of former times becomes the luminous habitat of today, bathed in air and light. The ideal is furniture for clinics and barracks; mere appliances, they count for nothing. You push them anywhere; as the situation requires they disappear into the wall, giving way to emptiness, to this vacancy which is becoming a mania. I know a study designed for modern man, composed of four walls, two chairs, and a table. Everything is bare. There is nothing to see. The modern man pushes a button or turns a key and the table reveals a typewriter, just like every other typewriter. The walls open revealing cupboards stuffed with books and papers no better organized than anywhere else. The passion for order has become so urgent that order itself had to be transcended.'

The battle, however, had been won by the proponents of mass-production. French Art Deco survives today as the last great sumptuous style, a legitimate and hugely fertile chapter in the history of world furniture.

The U.A.M.

The revolution in metal furniture was consecrated in 1930 through the formation of the Union des Artistes Modernes, whose five founding committee members were Hélène Henri, René Herbst, Francis Jourdain, Robert Mallet-Stevens, and Raymond Templier. The group's charter was basically no different from the philosophy its leaders had espoused since 1925, simply updated to encompass the new decade.

The U.A.M. members underlined their independence by exhibiting under their own banner at the 1930 Salon des Artistes Décorateurs, a tactic that earned considerable attention from the press. But the schism between long-standing Salon members seemed arbitrary and unnecessary to many critics. Léon Werth, for example, felt that the U.A.M.'s remedies did not address themselves directly to the fundamental problems of furniture design. He wrote: 'We have here some sober pieces of furniture, some plain pieces. They are descendants, offspring, of Francis Jourdain, the modern guru whose spirit inspires our physicians of furniture. Before him, we had only old wives' herbal remedies. But furniture was far too sick to be cured by such simples.'

At the 1931 and 1932 Salons the U.A.M.'s displays received equal coverage, but after that interest waned. Louis Chéronnet drew up the union's first manifesto in 1934, by which time the group's goals had largely been achieved, its battle with wood and *le goût antiquaire* undeniably won.

The scope of the book

This book was initially intended to provide a survey of French Art Deco furniture between the years 1920 to 1935. But, as already mentioned, many pieces of furniture which are accepted today as 'pure' Art Deco, were conceived before or during the First World War. In addition, it became increasingly more difficult after the war to distinguish between a mature Art Deco style and the evolving modernist one.

Included, therefore, are biographies of eighty-five furniture designers who embraced either the Art Deco or modernist styles, or both, and whose furniture was made between 1910 and the mid-1930s. Selection was based both on the relative importance afforded the designers by contemporary critics, and reappraisal today with the perspective of time. Omitted are a host of Art Nouveau cabinetmakers and designers whose work after the First World War appeared tired and commercial. Among these were Henri Bellery-Desfontaines, Charles Plumet, Pierre and Tony Selmersheim, Abel Landry, Louis Bigaux, Georges Nowak, Mathieu Gallerey, Théodore Lambert, and Edouard Asseur.

Absent also are three prominent Art Deco designers whose talents lay primarily in other fields, despite the design for an occasional piece of furniture or ensemble: Desny and Jean Perzel (lighting) and Rose Adler (bookbindings). In addition, Lucie Holt le Son, Sornay, and Jean Prouvé do not appear – even though the last-mentioned is now recognized as an immensely powerful force in contemporary architectural and furniture design – because their talents came to fruition in the 1930s rather than the 1920s. Finally, the survey is limited to designers who were based in Paris, the hub of the 1920s/30s furniture movement. For this reason, Gio Ponti

and Félix Delmarle have not been included.

That Art Deco furniture was quintessentially French, and specifically Parisian, becomes increasingly evident as examples from the period are analysed. Almost nothing of comparable design or quality was produced in the 1920s outside France. The London retailers Heal and Son and Waring & Gillow offered a range of unexceptional, lightly decorated imitations. In the United States, there was no identifiable furniture style at all until the late 1920s when a tubular, modernist style was introduced by the department stores to meet the depression's austerity budgets. In Germany the Bauhaus, founded in 1919, came to full bloom in the mid-1920s, but its influence was not nationally pervasive.

The 1920s/30s furniture designers

It seems astonishing that only a handful of Paris's Art Deco furniture designers had more than a smattering of technical knowledge. Yet of the eighty-five individuals and firms discussed in this book, there are only five who appear to have been professionally qualified as cabinetmakers: Leleu, Léon Jallot, Chanaux, Mercier Frères, and the aging turn-of-the-century *maître*, Majorelle. And of these only one – Chanaux – emerges as a complete master of the entire range of fashionable 1920s materials: exotic veneers, *galuchat*, ivory, and vellum.

The furniture designers of the period can be grouped loosely into three categories: traditionalists, modernists, and individualists.

The traditionalist took as his point of departure France's eighteenth- and early nineteenth-century cabinetmaking heritage. This unimpeachable legacy provided the inspiration for a host of 1920s designers; most particularly, Ruhlmann, Follot, Groult, Leleu, Süe et Mare, Dufrène, and Chauchet-Guilleré.

Under this same heading were cabinetmakers *per se*, who were located in the 1920s where they had been since the days of the Bourbons, in Paris's bustling Faubourg Saint-Antoine quarter. Most cabinetmakers limited their output to slavish reproductions of fashionable styles, from Louis XIV to the present day. Only one of them, Mercier Frères, is included in this book, though many others, who have often remained anonymous, produced Art Deco furniture of more than passing quality. (It should be remembered that Ruhlmann, for one, had his furniture manufactured in the Faubourg Saint-Antoine for many years.)

The modernist rebelled against the tightness of the neoclassical harness, bringing his or her own blend of individualism – defiant or understated – to the project at hand. Metal was *de rigueur*. The most notable modernists were Adnet, Arbus, Block, Pierre Petit, Prou, Sognot, Dufet, and Dupré-Lafon. They were joined in the early twentieth

century by the architect, who moved increasingly into the field of furniture design. In the 1920s Herbst, Mallet-Stevens, Burkhalter, Chareau, Lurçat, Le Corbusier, Perriand, and Moreux, to name only the most prominent, extended their architectural designs to the building's interior space and furnishings, giving prestige and authority to the modernist philosophy.

The third group is reserved for those furniture designers whose brilliant individualism defies ready categorization. Only four qualify: Legrain, with his bizarre blend of tribal African and modernist influences; Gray with her lacquered Orientalism, whimsy, theatricality, and ultramodernism; Printz, whose distinctly personal and kinetic designs were constructed in the traditional manner; and Coard, whose innovative spirit was allowed only infrequent escape from the harness of traditional commissions.

Furniture materials

Ebony was Art Deco's premier wood, its jet black surface buffed repeatedly to draw out its innate majesty (its preference by France's seventeenth- and eighteenth-century monarchs led to the adoption of the word *ébéniste* to describe cabinetmakers). Although rare and therefore costly, it had by tradition been used as entire sections in furniture construction – legs, drawers, and even the entire carcase – in the same manner that mahogany was later employed in the Art Nouveau era. This profligacy soon led to a shortage which persisted into the 1920s. Cabinetmakers had to make do with ebony veneers, as Gaston Varenne explained in a 1927 article on cabinetry in *Art et décoration* which traced the history of cabinetmaking: 'The scarcity of this wood means that it is used very rarely at its full thickness, only for the feet, columns, or pilasters of furniture. It is spread in thin leaves of veneer.'

The 1920s cabinetmaker could draw on a wider range of sumptuous veneers than any of his or her forebears. Many of these were exotic. Most popular, because of its distinctive parallel grain, was macassar ebony, indigenous to the Ile de Celebes, an Indonesian island off Java. Another imported tropical veneer, favoured particularly by Printz and Legrain, was palmwood (*palmier*), its coarsely textured surface impervious to the voracity of North Africa's termites. Because of its rich grain, Brazilian jacaranda (*palissandre de Rio*) was also a favourite with numerous cabinetmakers. Zebrawood and calamander were used more sparingly as their grains were felt to be overpowering.

Nearer home, selection could be made from a wide range of traditional veneers: amaranth, amboyna, mahogany, violetwood, and sycamore, to name only a few of the more popular. These were often used in juxtaposition with a

panelled burl wood, such as maple or ash, whose contrasting cellular structure offset the former's single colour. The range of decorative effects was infinite, limited only by good taste.

The revival in popularity of Oriental lacquerware in France prior to the First World War was sustained throughout the 1920s. Gray was the first (*c.* 1910) to utilize it successfully in modern furniture design, through her association with the Japanese master Sougawara, followed some years later by Dunand, Jallot, and Hamanaka. The lacquer's bright tactile finish brought opulence to the furniture's wood (or, later, metal) framework. Its exponents adhered strictly to the time-honoured, and time-consuming, technique of lacquer application, described by Maximilien Gauthier in a 1925 article on Dunand in *L'Art vivant*: 'Twenty-two stages are necessary for the building up of a lacquered surface. Stage one: you apply to the wood which has previously been sanded down a coat of natural lacquer (a special resin, imported from Japan). Stage two: tautly stretched linen is applied to the prepared panel; a mixture of natural lacquer and of a clay also imported from Japan serves here as an adhesive. Stages three to ten: coats of pure lacquer and clay which are left to harden in a humid atmosphere, and then sanded, this being done eight times in succession. Stage eleven: the hardening of the whole by means of a coat of natural lacquer. Stages twelve to seventeen: six coats of lacquer mixed with an extremely fine Japanese clay. Stage eighteen: the first coat of black lacquer (natural lacquer oxidized by iron). Stages nineteen and twenty: two further coats, each preceded and followed by meticulous sanding. Stages twenty-one and twenty-two: decoration, inlay of eggshell, mother-of-pearl etc., necessitating two or three coats.'

By 1930 lacquer, like wood, faced the challenge of mass-production and modernization. Industrial synthetic varnishes were developed which gave, to the inexperienced eye, an identical high-gloss finish known today as 'japanning'. Lacquer was suddenly seen as a relic of a bygone era, its onerous method of application an anachronism in the new age.

Another material to enjoy a great vogue – this time after a lapse of some two hundred years! – was shagreen, known as *galuchat* in recognition of its noted eighteenth-century exponent, a M. Galuchat, who used it in his sheath-making business. *Galuchat* is the skin of the small spotted dogfish *roussette*, to this day a culinary delight awaiting the unsuspecting holiday-maker in France's coastal resorts. Cut into sections of roughly 20 × 30 cm, the skin was steeped in a chlorine solution which bleached it. It was then scrubbed with a wire brush and filed before being cut and glued into position on the piece of furniture, often a dressing-table or desk top. It could be left in its bleached state, or varnished, or tinted blue or green to accentuate its granular surface pattern.

Interchangeable with *galuchat* was snakeskin, its different cellular structure allowing a subtle change of effect. In the same category were animal hides, such as ponyskin, favoured by Dufet, Le Corbusier, and Legrain. In the late 1920s vellum was introduced into interior design, principally as wall panelling.

Ivory, absent in furniture design at the turn of the century, replaced *ormolu* as the period's foremost furniture mount and decorative fillip. It was used to lend grace and refinement in drawer pulls, *sabots*, or in the slender *chute* which outlined the curve on a cabriolet leg.

Wrought-iron also underwent a surge in popularity. Largely overtaken by bronze in the Art Nouveau years, its 1920 exponents brought it to a technical pinnacle not seen since Emile Robert had resurrected its decorative potential in the 1880s. In the deft hands of Brandt, Subes, Piquet, Poillerat, and a host of now unsung *ferronniers*, iron's unyielding mass became as malleable as putty. It was widely used for furniture, light fixtures, and architectural elements, its motifs changing from stylized flowers to sunbursts and zig-zags as the medium's traditional tools – the anvil and hammer – yielded to injection-moulded machinery in the late 1920s.

Rarely used, but today immediately identifiable as a product of the period, was straw marquetry. The technique's lavish effect far exceeded its modest costs. Bales of rye straw were softened in water, then individual tubes were slit with a razor and flattened with a burnishing tool. An artisan glued and positioned the individual pieces on to a wood base on which the design had been sketched. Trimming and varnishing followed, the resulting fan or sunbeam design emitting a honeyed glow. Jean-Michel Frank used the medium to such a degree that his competitors quipped sourly that the staggering cost of his most recent glamorous commission had been the 'last straw'.

The Paris department stores

Throughout the 1920s, Paris home-owners could select their furniture from four major department stores – Au Printemps, Le Louvre, Au Bon Marché, and Les Galeries Lafayette. A fifth, Trois Quartiers, was established in 1929. The function of these stores was that of arbiter of taste, especially in the promotion of up-to-date household furnishings.

This had not always been the case. From 1912, when the first store, Au Printemps, was established, department stores had by convention been a conduit for the manufacturer, merchandising as best they could, and with narrow profits, the range of commodities presented to them. In the early 1920s they began to realize that matters might be otherwise, and established their own art studios in which to design and manufacture what the customers wanted, rather than what they had been forced by lack of choice to accept. The studios for Au Printemps, Le Louvre, Au Bon Marché, and Les Galeries Lafayette were Primavera, Studium Louvre, Pomone, and La Maîtrise, respectively.

Thus, the manufacturers effectively separated from the marketplace, the department stores moved smartly into the vacuum and assumed the role of trendsetter. The cream of France's bright young designers – Sognot, Prou, Block, and Kohlmann – were brought in to direct the studios and their modern furniture was presented to a public easily persuaded that it was, at long last, getting what it wanted.

Competition between the department stores spread to smaller firms, such as Joubert et Petit's D.I.M. and La Compagnie des Arts Français. Furniture benefited by the conflict: designs and materials were modernized, the stores' pavilions at the 1925 Exposition drew enthusiastic audiences and praise from the critics.

Thérèse and Louise Bonney wrote in *Buying Antique and Modern Furniture in Paris* (1929) that the art studio of Au Printemps, Primavera, 'has a large group of artists working exclusively for it, including Sognot, Guillemard, Madeleine Sougez, Claude Lévy. The artists, however, retain all rights to design and execute work for individual clients, having at the same time a unique opportunity to experiment and bring their work before the greater public at a large store.... For some time now, artists connected with Primavera have gained considerable recognition at different expositions and in the world in general. Guillemard has won prizes at expositions, as has Sognot; Madeleine Sougez and Claude Lévy have been awarded gold medals; and Lévy has been honoured with the Blumenthal fellowship for 1928. So you will be buying works of value from recognized artists.'

There is a phenomenon here which was quite new to furniture design. Cabinetmakers had never before collaborated, if only as members of a team, while maintaining separate individual careers. The *métier*, from Boulle and Cressent to Majorelle and Gallé, was by tradition fiercely individualistic. No record survives of an Ecole de Nancy collaboration beyond the superficial unity necessitated by a shared Exposition pavilion. And it is unthinkable that the opinionated Hector Guimard should share his celebrity with anyone. Yet suddenly, in the 1920s, tradition was put aside, if not reversed. When called upon to do so, everyone was prepared to collaborate, most especially in the Ambassade Française, the pavilion of the Société des Artistes Décorateurs at the 1925 Exposition. It was a rare and precious moment in furniture history, one that was not to be repeated after the Second World War. The Appendix to this book shows numerous examples of unprecedented collaboration between major designers.

The Exposition Internationale des Arts Décoratifs et Indus-triels Modernes was a long time in the making. Conceived as early as 1907, it was scheduled and rescheduled as the First World War came and went. Planning was begun again in 1919 for 1922, then for 1924, and finally for April to October, 1925.

In a furniture context, the Exposition came at the moment when the 'pure' or 'high' Art Deco style was approaching its end. The extravagant exhibits launched by individual interior designers and department stores actually brought the curtain down, rather than up, on the movement. Yet few furniture designers felt confident enough to bypass such an event, if only because their competitors would not.

The principal furniture designers and manufacturers were spread out along the Alexander III bridge, the rue des Boutiques, and the Esplanade des Invalides on the Left Bank. The only major exceptions were Poiret, whose theatrical interiors were housed on three barges moored at the Quai d'Orsay, and Le Corbusier, whose L'Esprit Nouveau pavilion was banished by the Exposition's organizing com-mittee to the Right Bank. Represented was the pride of France's modern furniture movement, from the cabinet-makers of the Faubourg Saint-Antoine to the country's top designers.

The major French exhibits were lined up along the Esplanade des Invalides, a park in front of Les Invalides. The exhibition visitor could stroll from one pavilion to another, each with its own expanse of lawn and garden statuary. Pride of place went to the top department stores – Bon Marché, Au Printemps, Galeries Lafayette, and the Louvre – whose art studios designed and furnished their own pavilions. Inter-spersed with these were the private exhibitors, quite unawed by their larger neighbours. The critics were unanimous in their choice of Ruhlmann's Hôtel du Collectionneur as the Exposition's most spectacular event. After that, in varying order of preference, came Süe et Mare's Un Musée d'Art Contemporaine; the Salon des Artistes Decorateurs' pavilion – L'Ambassade Française; and René Lalique's pavilion.

The impact of the Exposition both on the general public and furniture critics was enormous. Many of its major pieces of furniture were immediately recognized as masterpieces and purchased directly by the Musée des Arts Décoratifs and the Metropolitan Museum of Art in New York. Others are now in private collections worldwide.

Contemporary collectors

Francis Jourdain, one of the period's foremost decorators, stated in 1920 that 'one should not lose sight of the fact that antique furniture when new was nothing else than modern furniture. There are periods when little that is new is created, when we must live on the contributions of the past. Today is decidedly not one of these.'

Who were the collectors of this modern furniture? The biographies in this book chronicle a wide range of royal, state, commercial, and private commissions, underlining the widespread response to the new modernism.

Some names stand above the rest, however, for their connoisseurship and staunch patronage of individual artist/designers, often when the latter were at a crossroads, torn between their desire to pursue their chosen profession and their inability to earn a living doing so. Such a patron was Jacques Doucet, whose protégés included Iribe, Gray, Legrain, Coard, Miklos, Mergier, Rousseau, and Adler. Legrain, in particular, remained indebted to Doucet for the 1917 commission to design bindings for his renowned library, a job specially created for the destitute Legrain and one which launched him on a career that established him by the mid-1920s as the craft's undisputed leader.

Doucet was a noted couturier whose commissions punc-tuated the period from 1913 until his death on 30 October 1929. In 1912, he sold his collection of eighteenth-century furniture and *objets d'art* at auction, furnishing his new apartment at 46 avenue du Bois with contemporary art. The following twelve years were spent adding to the initial purchases. By 1924 the new collection – consisting of a *mélange* of modern paintings, Oceanic and African tribal art, and furniture – warranted its own space, and Doucet engaged the architect Paul Ruau to design a studio for it on the rue Saint-James in Neuilly. A 1930 article by André Joubin in *L'Illustration* included views of the interior which confirmed both Doucet's great vision and his enormous wealth.

David David-Weill, the National President of French Museums, was a vehement publicist of modern furniture, not so much by his one or two purchases of Ruhlmann pieces (he was not an especially wealthy man), as by his unbridled enthusiasm and influential position.

Another celebrated patron was Jeanne Lanvin, the fashion designer, who limited herself largely to the interiors of Rateau, as did the prosperous New York couple, George and Florence Blumenthal.

The United States could boast of one other avant-garde collector, Templeton Crocker. A member of the prosperous California Crocker railroad and banking family, he commis-sioned Jean-Michel Frank in 1927 to decorate his San Francisco apartment. A February 1927 article in *Vogue* shows an interior that matched closely that of Frank's Parisian client, the Viscount Charles de Noailles, the previous year. Packed up, stored, and forgotten after Crocker's death, the collection was discovered when Art Deco came back into fashion in the late 1960s.

A string of luxury vessels was launched in the 1920s, starting with the *Paris* in 1921. Described variously by an ecstatic and jingoistic press as floating palaces or museums of decorative arts, 'dream machines', or, in a Le Corbusier context, 'machines à habiter', the ocean liners afforded France's foremost interior designers an excellent international showcase. They therefore became, as the critic Paul Sentenac pointed out in a 1921 review, an extension of the annual Salon: 'One goes round the rooms of the *Paris* rather as one visits the furniture section at the Salon d'Automne or the Salon des Artistes Décorateurs.' The interior of the *Paris* was, in fact, organized by the Société de l'Art Français Moderne, the furnishings of the cabins and public areas parcelled out to Tony Selmersheim, Le Bourgeois, Lalique, Prou, Süe et Mare, Follot, Dufrène, and others. Boasting of its essentially French and feminine attributes, the advertisements for the *Paris* also offered the 1921 American traveller bored with Prohibition the added attraction of his choice of alcohol.

After the *Paris* came the *Ile-de-France*, *La Fayette*, *Le Champlain*, and *Le Colombie*, each in its turn heralded as just that much more splendid than its predecessor. The race for the North and South Atlantic was on and the French government both sponsored and subsidized these emblems of national pride.

In several instances, however, reality hardly survived the dream. The *Atlantique*, launched from Bordeaux in September 1931 to service South American ports with its sister ships, the *Massilia* and *Lutétia*, was gutted by fire within fifteen months. A substantial amount of the finest of modern French decorative arts was lost, in particular, four giant lacquered Dunand panels inspired by Kipling's *Jungle Book*, the designs by Jouve and Schmied. Also destroyed were restaurants and de luxe cabins by Follot, Montagnac, Prou, Leleu, Bouchet, and D.I.M. Dunand was so shaken by the loss of the indestructible *Atlantique* that his later ocean liner commissions were executed on inflammable stucco, rather than on wood.

The next in France's proud line of 'largest, fastest, grandest, and most modern' was the *Normandie*, even more unsinkable, its promoters promised, than the ill-fated *Atlantique*. The reams of literature published at the time bear testimony to the designers' claim that the *Normandie* was incontestably the most luxurious vessel ever conceived. It made its inaugural voyage on 29 May 1935 from Le Havre, gaining the New York harbour on 3 June, a transatlantic record at an average speed of over thirty knots per hour. Paul Iribe underlined some of the contradictions in the literature published by the vessel's parent company, La Compagnie Générale Transatlantique, in an imaginary dialogue published in his satirical newspaper, *Le Témoin*:

'This boat really is the fastest in the world?'

The officer on the *Normandie* bowed, 'Undoubtedly, Sir.'

'Very good. And also the most luxurious in the world, isn't it?'

'Yes, Sir . . .'

'Well then, try and explain something to me . . . Why is it that the more pleasant and comfortable a ship is, the shorter the journey it makes?'

'I don't know, Sir.'

The *Normandie* arrived for the last time at her New York berth on 28 August 1939. Four days later Germany's invasion of Poland precipitated the Second World War, preventing her return to Le Havre. In 1941, after Pearl Harbor, the United States Government commandeered the ship for use as a troopcarrier. Conversion began on 24 December 1941 and the furnishings were to be stripped and stored. On 9 February 1942, however, a welder's acetylene torch ignited a pile of burlap-wrapped life-jackets, setting the *grand salon* on fire. Firefighters pumped in so much water that the vessel capsized. Eighteen months later the hull was towed to Newark and sold as scrap. The rest, including the surviving furnishings, were sold by the government in a series of public auctions in 1942/43. Lost or dispersed were major decorative works by Dunand, Dupas, Ruhlmann, Sabino, Leleu, Süe, Dominique, Prou, and many more. In recent years several pieces have reemerged at auction, generating great nostalgia, the weighted feet on the chairs and the gimbal shelves on mobile dumb-waiters poignant reminders of France's golden era of ocean liners.

COLOUR PLATES 1-12

1 *Arbus:* bed with lacquer by Jean Dunand, the feet in *galuchat* (shagreen), 1930s (Collection of Warren Cresswell and George Matheson Gerst)

2 *Chareau:* desk and stool designed in sycamore for Hélène Henri. A similar desk with wrought-iron feet, illustrated in *Art et décoration*, Jan. 1927, was offered in the sale of Karl Lagerfeld's collection at the Hôtel Drouot, Paris, 21 Nov. 1975. The lacquered panel is by Jean Dunand (Collection of Galerie Lamouric)

3 *Chareau:* (foreground) desk in wood and metal with roll-top metal cabinet. Illustrated in *Mobilier et décoration*, Nov. 1928, p. 216; and *Pierre Chareau*, Paris 1954, p. 29. (Rear) linen-chest in sycamore and wrought-iron with pivoting door, illustrated in *Nouveaux Intérieurs français*, Paris, pl. 13; *Ensembles nouveaux*, Paris, pl. 14; *Art et décoration*, Jan. 1927; and *Encyclopédie des métiers d'art*, Paris (Collection of Jean-Claude Brugnot)

4 *Chareau:* ensemble including three armchairs upholstered in brown velours, a metal centre table with three-sectioned swivel top, a wrought-iron and wood bookcase, and a metal plant stand. The bronze sculpture by Gustave Miklos. The table illustrated in *Pierre Chareau*, Paris 1954, p. 40; the plant stand illustrated in *Pierre Chareau*, p. 101; *Ensembles mobiliers*, 3rd series; *Intérieurs VI*, Léon Moussinac, Paris, pl. 48; and *Art et décoration*, Jan.–June 1932, p. 5; the chairs illustrated in *Pierre Chareau*, p. 25; and *Les Arts de la maison*, Summer 1926 (Collection of Jean-Claude Brugnot)

5 *Chareau:* ensemble, including a stool illustrated in *Art et décoration*, Jan.–June 1932; and *Mobilier et décoration*, Nov. 1928, p. 222; a floor lamp in metal and alabaster, illustrated in *Pierre Chareau*, Paris, 1954, p. 70; *Le Mobilier français d'aujourd'hui (1910–1925)*, Pierre Olmer, Paris 1926, pl. 32; *Ensembles mobiliers*, 3rd series; *Les Arts de la maison*, Winter 1924; and *L'Art décoratif français 1918–1925*, Léon Deshairs, Paris 1926, p. 14; the table exhibited at the 1925 Exposition and illustrated in *Art et décoration*, Jan.–June 1925, p. 155; *Les Arts de la maison*, Summer 1926; and *Ensembles mobiliers*, 3rd series (Collection of Jean-Claude Brugnot)

6 *Cheuret:* silvered-bronze and alabaster floor lamp, exhibited at the 1925 Exposition. Illustrated in *Le Luminaire I*, Guillaume Janneau, Paris 1926, p. 46 (Photo: Christie's, NY)

7 *Coard:* settee in palisander with ivory and caned basket-weave borders, on block feet, the original mohair upholstery replaced by leather. Commissioned by Jacques Doucet, 1930. Illustrated in *L'Illustration*, 3 May 1930, p. 17; *L'Oeil*, Dec. 1961, p. 47; and *Maison et jardin*, Dec. 1961, p. 110 (Collection of Sydney and Frances Lewis)

8 *Coard:* canoe-shaped double bed in palisander, silvered-metal, ivory, and bakelite, *c.* 1930 (Collection of Anne-Sophie Duval, Annie Partouche, and Rodolphe Perpitch)

9 *Da Silva Bruhns:* wool rug, *c.* 1925. Similar models are illustrated in *Les Echos des industries d'art*, Dec. 1930, p. 25; *Répertoire du goût moderne II*, 1928, pl. 33, and *V*, pl. 40; and *Paris 1928*, Antoine Roche, Paris 1928, pls. 54, 55 (Photo: Christie's, NY)

10 *Dominique:* cabinet in black lacquer with gold-leaf applications, the central handle in ivory carved with the signs of the Zodiac. Illustrated in *Plaisir de France*, Jan.–Feb. 1941, p. 13

11 *Dufet:* desk and chair in palmwood and burl ash with chromed metal feet and python skin upholstery, marketed by Le Bûcheron; the vase by Claudius Linossier, oil painting by L. H. Tutundjian. The chair illustrated in *Art et décoration*, Jan.–June 1930, p. 183 (Collection of J.-J. Dutko)

12 *Dufrêne:* semainier in burl elm and calamander, exhibited by Les Galeries Lafayette in La Maîtrise pavilion at the 1925 Exposition. Illustrated in *Ensembles mobiliers*, 2nd series, pl. 21. Exhibited also in 'Art Deco and its Origins', Heckscher Museum, Huntington, NY, 1974; 'Benito Retrospective', NY Cultural Centre, 1974; and 'Deco 1925–1935', Rothmans Touring Exhibition, Canada, 1975–76 (Photo: Christie's, NY)

I

2

3

4

5

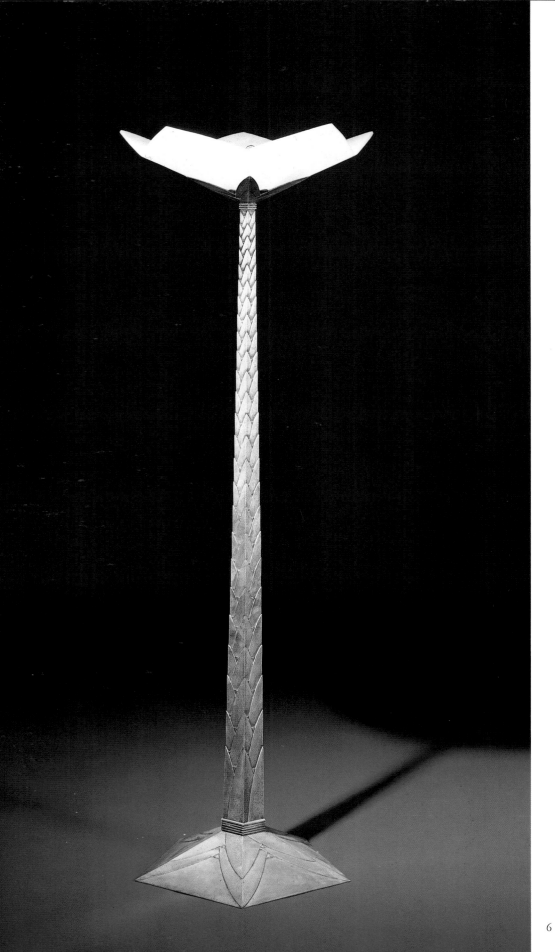

7

8

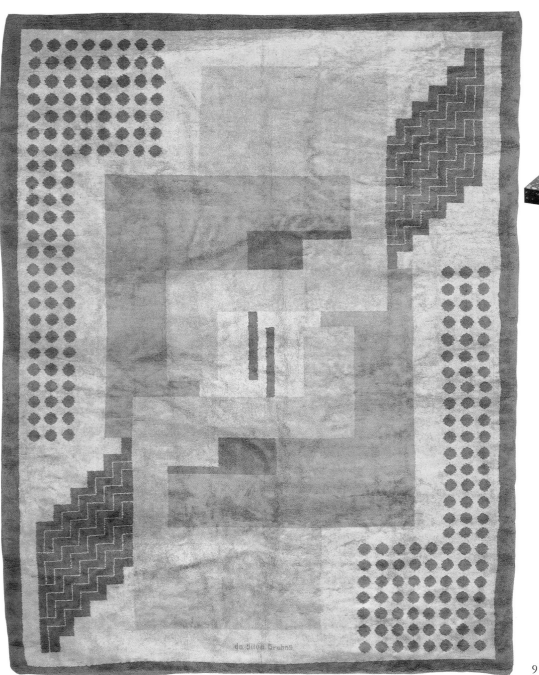

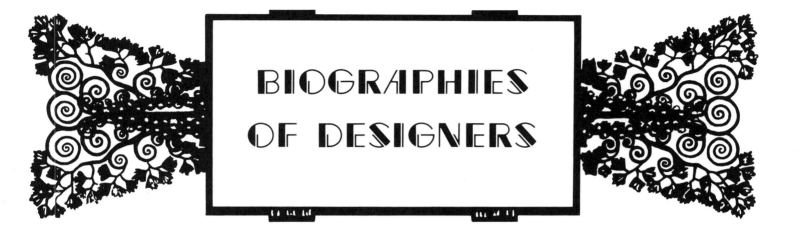

BIOGRAPHIES OF DESIGNERS

Adnet, Jacques:

The Adnet twins, Jacques and Jean, were born 20 April 1900 in Chatillon-Coligny, near Bourgogne. They spent their adolescent years in Auxerre, attending the Municipal School of Design, and in 1916 transferred to the Ecole des Arts Décoratifs to study architecture under Charles Genuys.

After graduation, Jacques worked briefly for Tony Selmersheim, perfecting his cabinetry skills. Demobilized after the First World War, the brothers joined La Maîtrise, where Maurice Dufrène became a mentor and close friend. From 1923 they worked together on numerous projects, sharing credit at the Salons under a joint name: J.-J. Adnet. In 1928 they parted company, Jacques accepting the directorship of La Compagnie des Arts Français, Jean remaining at La Maîtrise, where he became a sales manager for Galeries Lafayette.

La Compagnie des Arts Français was established in 1919 by Süe et Mare to promote 'Evolution dans la Tradition'. Adnet changed its charter, rejecting the past. As Louis Chéronnet stressed in his monograph, *Jacques Adnet*, published in 1948 by *Art et industrie*, 'His aesthetic preoccupations are different. Born with the century, he feels no nostalgia. His only thought is that this century, whose new beauty is slowly revealing itself in photography and the cinema, a century of the precision machine and of speed, a century of the aeroplane, electricity and steel, must discover in design meaningful analogies in greater harmony with its means and outward appearance.' Chéronnet continued: 'One aspect of the power of money today is that it is the basis of big industry; without hesitation, therefore, our designer will turn to industrial products. A true artist can ennoble whatever he touches. Adnet is among the first to expect metal and glass to integrate with the structure and decoration of furniture where they will complement the ample space and bare surfaces created by the reinforced concrete and, by their sparkle, the effects of electricity.' The firm provided Adnet with an ideal platform from which to promote his modernistic designs, by 1928 distinctly avant garde, even compared with the work of contemporaries such as Lurçat, Sognot, and Dufet.

Adnet's furniture incorporated woods – often exotic, such as peroba and bubenga – for the carcases. There was a sharp transition in 1930 to chromed metal, the shelves and doors embellished as before with a combination of mirror, leather, *galuchat*, parchment, and – Adnet's favourite medium – smoked glass. His furniture became increasingly streamlined, the earlier mounts, never pronounced, now barely visible. A rigidly functional aesthetic was pursued, with ornamentation pared away wherever possible. A 1930 quote summed up the battle being waged: 'What a lot of work to achieve simplicity!'

The brothers exhibited at the 1925 Exposition in their own stand on the Esplanade des Invalides, as well as in the Ambassade Française, and La Maîtrise. A spectacular feature at this time was the range of tubular glass light fixtures which adorned their interiors, the adjoining frosted tubes set at right angles or in zig-zag fashion. The effect was excitingly kinetic, heightened by the sparkle of the nickel mounts.

In the late 1920s Jacques exhibited at both Salons several interiors marketed by Saddier et ses Fils. It was at this period that his genius was most visible; within five years many decorators had adopted his *machinisme*, claiming it as their own.

The 1930s brought a wide range of prestigious commissions, including ministeries, universities, and ocean liners. Collaborators included Edouard Schenck (nickel and glass), Mme Léoné Huet (carpets and fabrics), Louis Gigou (furniture mounts), Jean Besnard (ceramics), and J. and L. Bernard (paintings). At the 1937 Exposition, Adnet collaborated with René Coulon on the Saint-Gobain pavilion, which had walls made of glass bricks.

Adnet remained at La Compagnie des Arts Français until it closed in 1959, at that point accepting the directorship of the Ecole Nationale Supérieure d'Art Décoratif.

Aguesse, Henri (see ills. 5, 6)

Alix, Charlotte (see Sognot)

Arbus, André-Léon:

Arbus was born 17 November 1903 to a family of Toulouse cabinetmakers. He attended the city's Lycée before entering the Ecole Militaire de Saint-Cyr to study law, his free hours spent in his father's workshop at 34 rue de Metz. Ill health forced him to switch from the military academy to the Ecole des Beaux-Arts, where he met the sculptor Henry Parayre, who became a friend and mentor. On graduating, Arbus joined his father, whom he succeeded on the latter's retirement. Arbus himself never practised cabinetry, content to leave the execution of his sketches and maquettes to the firm's journeymen furniture-makers.

Arbus made his début at the Paris Salons in 1926 and moved to the capital four years later, opening the gallery L'Epoque at 22 rue la Boétie.

He showed his work in both annual Salons, participating also in the Salon des Tuileries and La Galerie des Quatre-Chemins. Collaborators included Marc Saint-Saëns (a painter and fellow Toulousian), Androusof (sculpted decoration in wood, gesso, and terracotta), Paule Marrot (upholstery), Gilbert Poillerat (wrought-iron), Belmondo (bas-reliefs), and Baguès (light fixtures).

The 1930s generated countless commissions and an unexpected bonus, the Prix Blumenthal in 1935. Arbus seized every opportunity to exhibit: the Exposition de Bruxelles (1935), Exposition Internationale (1937), and the New York World's Fair (1939), among the most prestigious. The postwar period brought an even busier schedule, the Ministries of Agriculture and Armaments joining an ever longer list of clients.

In the March 1934 issue of *Formes*, Arbus published an article entitled 'Introduction à la technique et constantes de l'ébénisterie' in which he discussed in considerable depth all aspects of furniture-making. The critic Gaston Varenne provided a favourable analysis of his theories the following year in *Art et décoration*.

Arbus rejected painting and marquetry, preferring to decorate his furniture with a combination of finely grained veneers, parchment, lacquer, *galuchat*, or bleached animal hide. The furniture's carcase was often in sycamore, with key plates and mounts in metal. These materials generated the aura of sumptuousness that Arbus intended, and this was further embellished by Paule Marrot's tufted damask upholstery. Arbus's inspiration was classical; in most part, Louis XVI, First and Second Empire. His light, angular forms proved popular but not distinctive, and were often difficult to tell apart from those of coexhibitors Jean Prouve, Etienne Kohlmann, or Pierre Petit. Critics approved of his lavish upholstery, used, for example, in a *méridienne à bateau* at the 1930 Salon d'Automne, and made no mention of the whiff of Ruhlmann influence evident in certain tables, divans, and fall-front desks.

Arbus eliminated the firm's stock-in-trade eighteenth-century furniture styles, replacing them with a range of modern designs. Labelling himself both modernist and decorator, he immediately clashed with the philosophy espoused by the U.A.M.: Le Corbusier, Sognot, Herbst, Burkhalter, etc. Waldemar George analysed this late 1920s decorators' dilemma in his pamphlet, *André Arbus*, published in 1948 by *Art et industrie*, 'Arbus thinks that the French house does not have to be a faithful reflection of the century of iron and reinforced concrete. Instead, it should compensate for it. Although it is essential that the house satisfies the material comforts of the inhabitant, it must also satisfy his moral needs. It can help create peace and happiness by the size of the rooms and their general layout, and by the colour of the ceilings, walls and hangings.

'A house by Arbus is the home of a sedentary life full of humanity. Artistic skills, too often neglected, gradually find their place there. Carpets, tapestries, trimmings, gesso work, wrought-iron, and decorative bronzes are the usual ornaments which combine to create a total effect. Are these masterpieces of craftsmanship the leftovers of a bygone era? Not at all. They vouch for man's resistance to the machine.

They escape the downward pull of mass production, and the resulting poor quality. They perpetuate a civilization which is not only a judicial idea, but a way of life.'

Later in his treatise, Waldemar George returned to his subject's cause: 'This style fulfils a need. It seems to satisfy the aspirations of a public tired of the fanciful structures of primitive modernism. Its success is confirmed day by day. Its effect neither wearies the mind nor kills the imagination.'

A great deal of Arbus's finest furniture was created in the 1940s and 1950s. He remained in Paris until his death in 1969.

Athélia (see Block)

Bagge, Eric :

Bagge's early history is sketchy. Born in Anthony in 1890, he trained as an architect, presumably in Paris, and then lectured at the Ecole des Arts Appliqués. His participation in the two annual Salons began after the First World War.

Most of Bagge's early 1920s furniture was designed in collaboration with Bernard Huguet. Numerous ensembles or single pieces, despite their spartan Louis XVI provincialism, were reviewed favourably by the critics. Four gouache and ink sketches, dated 1921 and retained by the Musée des Arts Décoratifs in Paris, provide examples. Further furniture was created on occasion in partnership with René Prou, Fressinet, and Bastard. A marvellous Art Deco mantel clock, illustrated in 1921 in *Art et décoration*, was designed in collaboration with Peters.

Bagge's choice of woods included mahogany, oak, maple, ash, palisander, ebony, amaranth, sycamore, and violetwood, often inlaid with ivory or parchment. The furniture was executed in most part by the firm of G.-E. and J. Dennery and marketed through such retail outlets as Mercier Frères, Saddier et ses Fils, Contenot and Lelièvre, Les Etablissements Guinier, La Maîtrise, Léon Arbus, and, in the 1930s, L'Atelier des Champs-Elysées and La Maison P. Blache.

Diversification followed, Bagge introducing carpets, wallpapers, and fabrics into his Salon exhibits. Carpets were manufactured by Coupé and retailed by Lucien Bouix; wallpapers and fabrics were manufactured by Robert Bonfils or Leroy and sold by L. Bouix. Jacques Gruber or F. Chigot were commissioned to make stained-glass windows, a favourite decorative feature in Bagge's 1920s interiors. Contemporary magazines also show designs for light fixtures and wrought-iron radiator covers, plus jewelry sketches for La Maison Fouquet.

Bagge exhibited a wide selection of furnished interiors at the 1925 Exposition. A dining room exhibited by Saddier et ses Fils proved particularly successful. The chair backs were veneered with circles of ivory dots enclosing bunches of

grapes. The buffet and table top were similarly decorated with baskets of stylized fruit (recalling, inevitably, an earlier celebrated Ruhlmann motif), all charmingly set off against the room's matching wallpaper and curtains. Bagge exhibited a desk at La Société de l'Art Appliqué aux Métiers and, in collaboration with René Prou, a boudoir and adjoining bathroom in the Ambassade Française pavilion. The ensemble incorporated a recurring Bagge motif: fluted curved or block feet on chairs and commodes. There was a further ensemble at Le Pavillon de la Ville de Paris, this time in collaboration with Adrien Bruneau and René Prou.

Bagge also found time to remind the world that he was before all else an architect. The official Exposition catalogue lists many architectural commissions, including boutiques for the jeweler Henri Dubret, the publishers L. Rouart and J. Watelin, and the furriers Guèlis Frères. Larger projects included pavilions for the Viennese sculpture dealer Arthur Goldscheider and the perfumer Jacquet. Bagge also designed the large exhibition hall in which all the participating French schools of art were housed.

In the second half of the 1920s Bagge's style matured rapidly. Ensembles were neat and crisply executed. A 1927 dressing table in violetwood and sycamore, for example, caught the period's trend toward reduced ornamentation as did a lady's desk and chair entered the same year in a competition at the Union Centrale des Arts Décoratifs.

A 1929 article in *Mobilier et décoration* lists Bagge as the newly appointed Artistic Decorator of Mercier Frères. The interiors shown in the magazine, with their clean architectural lines, sober yet forcefully avant-garde, insist that Bagge's relative obscurity today is unwarranted.

Barret, Maurice:

Barret was born in Besançon (Doubs). Parental pressure forced him into medical school, but he withdrew after one year, arriving in Paris during the 1925 Exposition. Its impact was profound, Barret realizing instantly his true *métier* as he raced from one exhibit to another. Time was short and Barret made up for lost years by taking a crash course at the Ecole Nationale des Arts Décoratifs, followed by private research and instruction from the period's foremost decorators and architects. He later recalled these years: 'Francis Jourdain taught me that the art of furnishing a room is largely the art of taking furniture away. Maurice Dufrène taught me that you cannot buy elegance and distinction. Le Corbusier showed me that in mathematical terms architecture is everywhere – at the Acropolis in Athens, in this earthenware dish, in the engine of this Hispano. It was left to life to teach me that we are here on earth to earn our daily bread by the sweat of our brow.'

Barret displayed a range of kitchen and study furniture at the Salon des Artistes Décorateurs from 1932. Collaborators were listed as L. Lelièvre & Cie or Flambo. His first exhibit was a kitchen, the one room eschewed by nearly all other decorators. To Barret, it was 'the heart of a house: a miniature factory where everything is combined according to sound principles, science, and the organization of work. As the house lives by its heart, health must reign supreme there. There should be precise use of space, logical positioning of furniture, and an arrangement of utensils that avoids wasting energy, time, and space.'

Barret's furniture designs for a house's remaining rooms were no less analytical. A 1935 'study for an intellectual' spelled out his rationalism, each piece of furniture a standardized element within the unified whole. The relationship between a room's architecture and furnishings merged, their function interdependent. Warmth and comfort, where necessary, were instilled by coloured walls or, in the case of a man's bedroom, lacquered panelling. Busquet's celebrated rotative desk lamp in chromed metal was incorporated into many of the Barret interiors shown in *Nouveaux Intérieurs français*, its severe design in keeping with its surroundings.

Barret became a member of the Union des Artistes Modernes in the 1930s, and several of his ensembles are illustrated in the group's book, *25 années U.A.M.*, published in 1956.

Beaumont, Jean:

Little is known of Beaumont's upbringing beyond that he was born in Elbeuf. Two Parisian addresses were listed in the 1920s and 1930s: 214 rue du Château-des-Rentiers and 5 rue Sébastien-Mercier.

Beaumont produced tapestry, carpet, and fabric designs in the prevailing Art Deco idiom. His stylizations caught exactly the period's decorative mood: elongated animals and people among huge flower sprays. He used a muted palette in which greens, oranges, and reds predominated.

Beaumont's tapestry designs were manufactured in part by Aubusson, Hamot Frères, or Beaumont's wife. A 1927 article in *Les Echos des industries d'art* described a special weaving technique of his by which silk threads were embroidered on to a reticulated canvas pattern so that the detail stood out in relief. Beaumont's best known tapestry design, 'Grignon', was commissioned by Maurice Dufrène for a suite of seat furniture exhibited in La Maîtrise pavilion at the 1925 Exposition. The cabinetmaker Roumy manufactured wooden frames for Beaumont's own upholstered furniture.

A major work was a large panel, 'Les Phéniciens introduisent le vin en France', in 1935. At the same time he completed several designs for lacquered panels executed by Louis Midavaine.

La Maîtrise displayed a range of Beaumont's carpet and fabric designs at the 1925 Exposition alongside examples by Benedictus, Dufrène, Englinger, Bonnet, Adnet, and Lassudrie.

Block, Robert:

The Studio Athélia was inaugurated 15 December 1928 as an adjunct to the department store Trois Quartiers on the boulevard de la Madeleine. The Studio's function matched that of Primavera, Pomone, and La Maîtrise: to design and mass-produce items for Paris's middle- and upper-middle income groups.

The Swiss-born designer Robert Block was the Studio's first director, his address in Paris given as 60 avenue Malakoff. His association with Athélia appears to have been short-lived: by the mid-1930s various pieces of furniture designed by him were marketed by Gaveau (a lacquered piano), Waring and Gillow (a dining room), and Heal and Son (a desk executed by La Société Industrielle d'Art).

Block's furniture, several outstanding examples of which were illustrated in *Sièges contemporains* and *Petits Meubles du jour*, shows a strikingly fresh creativity at a time when tubularism had reduced much of what was new to anonymity. Although certain pieces recall the work of Sognot and Ruhlmann, Block's furniture was chic, functional, and quite simply a cut above much produced by his competitors. Emphasis was placed on modular furniture – *meubles transformables et juxtaposables* – for the city's small apartments.

Collaborators at Athélia were listed as P. Havard, J. Desnos, and Paul Delpuech, the last-mentioned assuming the firm's directorship when Block left.

Bouchet, Léon:

Born in Cannes, *c.* 1880, Bouchet's name appeared sporadically in furniture competitions reviewed by contemporary art magazines at the turn of the century. In 1913 he became a professor at the Ecole Boulle, joining the staff at approximately the same time as André Fréchet. Bouchet was primarily a cabinetmaker-turned-decorator. Early commissions in Paris involved the design of inexpensive furniture *en série* for manufacturers in the Faubourg Saint-Antoine. Demobilized at the end of the First World War, he first exhibited at the Salons in 1920. Early works were well proportioned and delicate, though largely unspectacular. Pierre Olmer provided an accurate evaluation in *Mobilier francais d'aujourd'hui (1920–1925)*, published in 1926: 'His most beautiful pieces of furniture are works of the most elaborate cabinetry marred only by some rare sculptural blemishes: bronzes or inlay appear infrequently in his solid, logical, and perfectly studied constructions.'

Bouchet displayed at both the Salon d'Automne and the Salon des Artistes Décorateurs. Early exhibits included a library in palisander with violet velours upholstery and lighting by Edgar Brandt (1920); a bookcase in macassar ebony and locustwood (1921); a commode in mahogany and amaranth and a bookcase in acacia and lemonwood; and a dining room in zebrawood with fabrics by Raoul Dufy and glassware by Jean Luce (1922). In all these the inspiration was distinctly Louis XVI. The feet on his furniture especially, with their short fluted *toupie* forms, showed unashamed Louis XVI influence.

The 1925 Exposition provided Bouchet with the means of exhibiting his work through various furniture retailers. Included was a dining room in *bois des îles* for La Maison Epeaux et Fils, in collaboration with Paul Brindeau de Jarny (light fixtures) and Laurent Malclès (sculpture); an ensemble for Soubrier in collaboration with Genet and Michon (lighting) and Jean Beaumont (carpets); a studio for Le Confortable in association with the lighting engineer, Georges Salomon, and several pieces of furniture for the *grand salon* in the Ambassade Française designed by Henri Rapin and Pierre Selmersheim with a host of collaborators. Bouchet offered his furniture through four retailers: Le Confortable, Epeaux et Fils, Soubrier and, most frequently, G.-E. and J. Dennery.

Unlike so many of his Art Deco contemporaries whose work deteriorated toward the 1930s, Bouchet clearly improved with time. His early work appears somewhat anonymous, indistinguishable from that of many other designers, but by 1930 his furniture was distinct and distinguished. Pieces exhibited in the Grand Salon de Collections at the 1930 Salon des Artistes Décorateurs, for example, are ultramodern, almost of today. The angular chairs are deeply padded and sleek; the desk has hinged side filing drawers which open outwards. Bouchet shared the Salon's decoration with, among others, Jean Dunand, da Silva Bruhns, Henry de Waroquier, and Jean Besnard. In the same year, *Mobilier et décoration* published an article on recent ensembles, including a house for a M. R. Ph—. The critic found an ample division of space and richness throughout; furniture in palisander and burl ash was enhanced by ochre wallpaper with silver trim. In 1931, a cabinet in burl thuyawood incorporated inlaid pewter banding on its cupboard doors. Again, the effect was extremely elegant and conceptually advanced, as was a walnut buffet shown at the Salon des Artistes Décorateurs the following year.

In 1935, again at the Salon des Artistes Décorateurs, Bouchet displayed a bedroom for a young mother, in unbleached silk with green seams and buttons. The Louis XVI influence was gone, in its place a slight touch of Second Empire.

Brandt, Edgar:

Born in Paris in 1880, the son of a director of a mechanical engineering firm, Brandt was educated at the Ecole Professionel de Vierzon. On graduating he established his own studio, laying the foundation of his subsequent emergence as the preeminent ironsmith of the 1920s/30s. At the turn of the century, while still in the shadow of the celebrated Emile Robert – to whom goes the credit of the nineteenth-century revival in metalware – Brandt began to exhibit through the annual Salons. He adopted the prevailing Art Nouveau style, designing wrought-iron and bronze furnishings and architectural elements with floral motifs into the mid-1920s, at which point he made an effort to introduce into his repertoire the sharply angular designs which heralded the coming decade.

Private commissions came quickly in the 1920s, a large number from architects who retained Brandt to create grillwork and fixtures for private houses and hotels. A notable public commission was a First World War monument, *La Tranchée des baïonnettes*, near Verdun, in 1921. Brandt maintained a fruitful collaboration with its architect, Henri Favier, for many years. Others with whom he worked were André Ventre and Bouwens de Boijen. Further prestigious commissions were afforded by ocean liners, in particular, the *Paris, Ile-de-France,* and *Normandie.* Between such commissions, Brandt exhibited regularly at both annual Salons, showing a seemingly limitless range of nonarchitectural metalware such as grills, radiator covers, lamps, and consoles.

The 1925 Exposition gave Brandt numerous opportunities to display his work, beginning with the exhibition's imposing point of entry, the Gate of Honour, designed by Henri Favier and André Ventre. Brandt's own stand on the Esplanade des Invalides offered a broad range of wares, while other works were dotted throughout: grills in the Hôtel du Collectionneur; gates in Le Pavillon National Monégasque, La Boutique de l'Illustration, and Le Pavillon de la Renaissance; and light fixtures in the Sèvres exhibit. The following year Brandt participated in the exhibition of Modern French Decorative Art at the Metropolitan Museum of Art, New York, returning in 1928 for both the Lord and Taylor exhibition and the exhibition at Macy's.

A 1926 firm's catalogue gives two Parisian addresses: 101 boulevard Murat (workshop) and 27 boulevard Malesherbes (showroom). Two overseas showrooms were listed, at 3 George Street, Hanover Square, London, and Ferrobrandt, 247 Park Avenue, New York. The catalogue illustrated a wide range of items ranging in price from Fr275 for an unpretentious table lamp, to Fr84,000 for the 'Oasis' screen, and Fr120,000 for 'L'Age d'Or' doorway, the last-mentioned a virtuoso work in pierced wrought-iron with bronze classical figures at its centre.

Brant's dexterity is amply shown in the facility with which he interchanged materials; most frequently, in the 1920s, wrought-iron and bronze, the more ambitious works enhanced with gilt-copper motifs that provided a light accent of preciosity and richness. Later came steel, aluminium, and, *c.* 1934, the alloy 'Studal'. Occasional collaborators were given ready recognition: the sculptors Max Blondat and Badory, and the metalworkers Pierre Lardin and Gilbert Poillerat. In rare collaboration, Dunand provided lacquer for two wrought-iron screens, 'Le Zodiaque' and 'Heracles', at the 1926 Salon des Artistes Décorateurs.

Ancillary materials were ordered from the period's foremost manufacturers: glassware from Daum, porcelain from Sèvres, and crystal from Pantin. Marble and alabaster were shipped from Italy.

Brandt's favourite motifs were the pine-cone, eucalyptus, gingko, roses, and, most theatrical of all, the serpent, reproduced in a wondrous series of 'Cobra' and 'La Tentation' lamps. The 1930s brought stark modernism: overlapping scrollwork and diagonal sunbeams.

The apparent ease with which Brandt transformed a bar of pig iron into the most ephemeral flower spray belied the material's innate lack of malleability. Yet he succeeded in taming it, making it at once robust and plastic, bold and frivolous.

In 1921 Jean Locquin wrote in *Art et décoration* of this talent: 'These small knick-knacks, made from the basest metal and transformed by the magic of the craftsman, are there to show, once again, that beauty is independent of the material from which it is wrought, and that the true artist has the privilege of ennobling whatever he handles.'

Bureau, Louis (see Dufet)

Burkhalter, Jean:

Burkhalter was born in Auxerre in 1895. He studied at the Ecole Nationale des Beaux-Arts, Paris, graduating during the First World War. His début at the 1919 Salon des Artistes Décorateurs was followed by employment at Primavera, where he proved himself a gifted and versatile designer of small household accoutrements, fabrics, endpapers, etc.

At the 1925 Exposition, Burkhalter took stand 66 on the Esplanade des Invalides and displayed a range of carpets, posters, and fabrics. He also collaborated in the furnishings of a studio and dining room in the Primavera pavilion, and the Pierre Imans' boutique on the Alexander III bridge, the latter with his brother-in-law, Joël Martel, and Edgar Brandt. A member of the Exposition's jury, he was awarded a first prize, *hors concours.*

continued on page 41

COLOUR PLATES 13-29

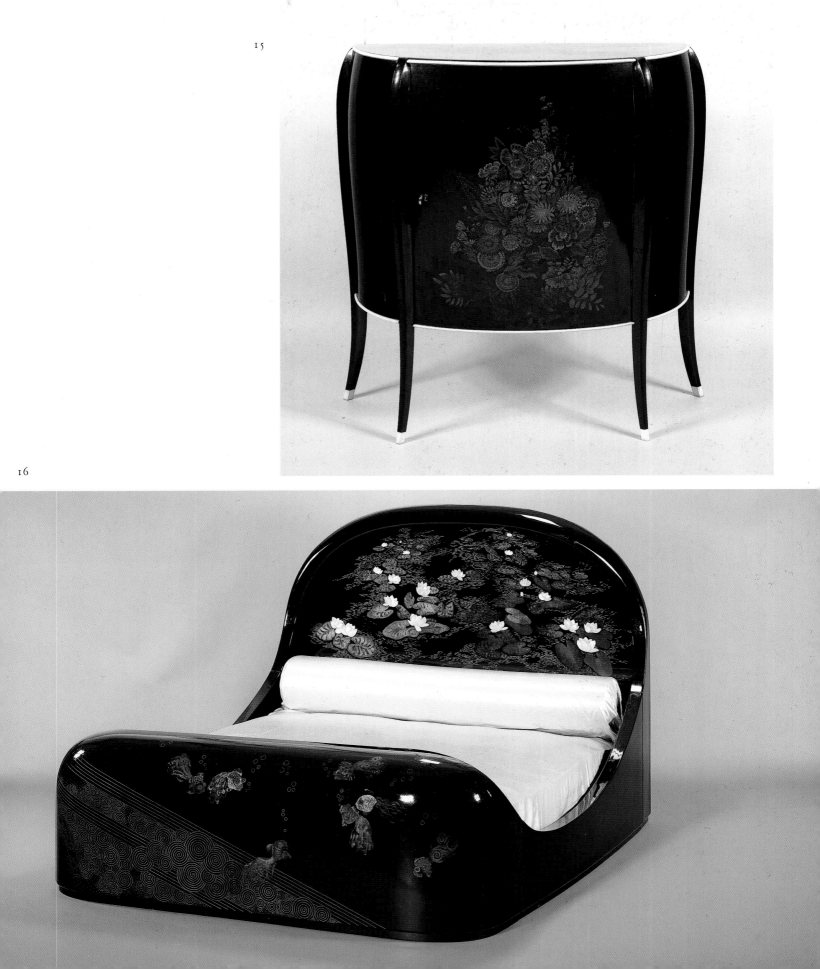

15

16

20

21

22

25

26

Burkhalter came to furniture design in the late 1920s, producing small items: kitchen tables, ladies' desks, chairs, and plant stands. His designs and choice of materials caught the immediate attention of the group of rationalists who founded U.A.M. in 1930. Tables and desks were in oak, their supports in chromed or galvanized tubular steel which twisted and curved back on itself gracefully in its path around the object. Forms were studied, light, and functional. Léon Moussinac traced Burkhalter's philosophy in a 1930 article in *Art et décoration*: 'His ideal would be to use building material in such a way that it goes beyond the practical in order to touch our feelings and thoughts. As he chooses to work with his hands he has come to love the materials he uses, and they form an element of visual and tactile pleasure. The metal tubing which supports a table or chair has only the briefest of contact with the ground, so to speak. It curves in a way which makes it seem unattached.'

Burkhalter became a founder-member of U.A.M., displaying four tubular tub chairs, marketed by Chareau, at its inaugural exhibition. In the following years his range widened, to include flower-holders, porcelain tableware, etc.

Burkhalter was appointed the director of the Ecole des Arts Décoratifs in Auxerre in 1935, transferring some years later to the Ecole Nationale des Arts Décoratifs in Limoges. He was still listed as an active member of U.A.M. in 1955.

Champion, Georges:

Champion was born in 1889 at Chaumont (Haut-Marne). A decorator by profession, he designed furnishings marketed in the middle and late 1920s by Le Studio Gué, the interior decorating firm of Georges and Gaston Guérin, of which Champion became a director in 1928. His furniture is characterized by its large proportions; its rigorous linearity; and its provocative interplay of contrasting colours, achieved either by juxtaposing light and dark wood veneers or by using high-gloss paints.

At the 1925 Exposition Champion exhibited a dining room for Le Studio Gué, in collaboration with Jules Coudyser (carpets), and La Maison Rouard (ceramics). The furniture was predictably chic, with square corners and high-gloss finish. Matching light fixtures and glazed windows completed the fresh, vigorous effect.

Champion exhibited at both annual Salons. A dining room at the 1926 Salon d'Automne showed his fiercely angular, avant-garde style. The legs on the chairs consisted of fluted vertical planks of wood supporting a curved backrest and cushion seat. The critics approved: 'It is really welcoming. . . . The furniture in light wood contrasts with the shades of blue and black in the carpets and cushions. I am less fond of the chairs, which are a little too upright, than of the little corner arranged so intimately in a semicircle.' Another,

undated, dining room from the period is arresting in its modernity, suggesting a strong de stijl influence: two-toned white and black furniture and a matching geometric carpet recall earlier works by Van Ravenstyn and Van Rietveld, and the contemporary designs of Delmarle.

At the 1925 Salon des Artistes Décorateurs, Champion displayed a *coin de repos* designed within a confined square space. A built-in couch running along three sides produced the intended feeling of intimacy.

Chanaux, Adolphe:

Information is gradually coming to light on Art Deco's unsung designer/craftsman, Adolphe Chanaux. Throughout his career Chanaux played a brilliant second fiddle to a group of designers who benefited hugely from his creativity. These included Groult, Ruhlmann, and Frank.

Chanaux was born in Paris in 1887. He studied painting at the Ecole des Beaux-Arts, and after the First World War joined Groult's atelier where he worked as a cabinetmaker. He is credited with at least the execution, if not also the design, of the celebrated *bombé* chest-of-drawers included by Groult in his woman's bedroom in the Ambassade Française at the 1925 Exposition. A prototype of the model, illustrated in *Le Mobilier français d'aujourd'hui (1910–1925)*, was manufactured in 1921, while Chanaux was still in Groult's employment.

Chanaux's importance lay in his mastery of the period's most exotic and fashionable furniture materials – *galuchat*, parchment, vellum, ivory, straw marquetry, and hand-sewn leather – and the refined manner in which he used them. A pair of chairs by Groult in the 1924 competition organized by David-Weill and de Camondo were executed by Chanaux, the tapestried upholstery designed by Laurencin. The Jury was lukewarm, awarding Groult the second of two third prizes!

After Grout's atelier, Chanaux's trail narrows. We know that he worked briefly for Ruhlmann in the mid-1920s because some of the latter's furniture bears both branded signatures. And it is likely that the association was an unhappy one, for not only does no record of Chanaux's employment exist in Ruhlmann's Salon entries, but Chanaux is quoted as saying that he found the renowned cabinetmaker's style unadventurous and – far indeed from its intended market – excessively bourgeois. By 1927 he had formed an association with the cabinetmaker, Pelletier, leaving him within three years to join Frank, whose taste in materials and design matched his own more closely than any of his previous associates. By 1931, they were partners, supervising the La Ruche workshops on the rue Montauban. Several contemporary photographs of the firm's furniture bear two stamps: that of *Frank, 140 Faubourg Saint-Honoré* and *Chanaux et Cie, 7 rue Montauban, Paris XVe*.

Chanaux's responsibility in the partnership must have been primarily to oversee from beginning to end the execution of the approved designs. After a foreman or draughtsman had measured the room to be decorated, including furniture and objects, installment plans were drawn up. Scale models followed, each offered under Chanaux's supervision for the client's approval. The furniture was then made in the La Ruche workshops.

In 1940, Chanaux left Paris for Arcachon, returning after Frank's death in 1941 to close the La Ruche works. In 1943 he joined Jean-Pierre Guérlain, by whom he was retained as an artistic advisor until his death in 1965.

Chareau, Pierre:

Chareau was born 3 August 1883 in Bordeaux into a family of Le Havre shipowners. On completion of his architectural studies, he joined a Paris-based English firm, leaving in 1914 to enlist. In 1919 he made his début at the Salon d'Automne, displaying a bedroom and office for Dr Jean Dalsace, for whom he undertook ten years later his most celebrated architectural commission, the 'Maison de Verre'.

Chareau established himself in the 1920s. From his studio/showroom at 54 rue Nollet he participated in the annual Salons, 'Les Cinq', and, as a cofounder, the U.A.M. exhibitions. He received both private and public commissions, including interiors for Mme Thérèse Bonney, Mallet-Stevens, Edmond Fleg, Mme Reifenberg, and Mme Kapferer. His most important works came toward 1930: in 1927 a golf club at Beauvallon on the Riviera; in 1929 the Grand Hôtel in Tours; and, two years later, his 'Maison de Verre' for Dr Dalsace at 31 rue Saint-Guillaume. The latter, in collaboration with the Dutch architect Bijvoet, was of revolutionary design, with walls made of glass bricks and an interior with sliding room partitions.

Chareau participated in the 1925 Exposition as both an architect and decorator. On the Esplanade des Invalides he designed the furniture manufacturers' gallery, in which he retained a boutique to display a range of wrought-iron plant stands. His office/library in the Ambassade Française received wide attention for its palmwood panelling and desk, the latter a double construction that incorporated extra filing space. Collaborators were listed as Dalbet (wrought-iron), Jean Lurçat (a carpet), Jacques Lipchitz (sculpture), Hélène Lantier (textiles), and Pierre Legrain (a furniture garniture and bookcovers). Elsewhere Chareau designed a dining room in Gabonese *bilinga* for a colonial habitation.

From 1932 to 1938 Chareau continued his research, concentrating on the development of mobile room partitions and screens. In 1937, for Djémel Anik, a dancer and friend, he designed a small country house which included a new system of heating ducts and in the same year participated in the U.A.M. pavilion at the Exposition Universelle. In 1938 he designed an office for M. Marx, minister without portfolio.

When war broke out Chareau tried to move to London, but ended up eventually in New York. Here he received an important commission from the young American painter Robert Motherwell, who asked him to build him a house in East Hampton from surplus army sheet-iron. Chareau added sections of glazed glass panels from an abandoned greenhouse, and the house stands today as a triumph of architectural expediency. The commission generated another challenging project from Motherwell's neighbours, Germain Monteaux, a pianist, and Nancy Laughlin, a writer. The two shared a home in which they also worked. Chareau applied himself to the acoustical problems of sealing the music room from the rest of the house. He remained in New York after the war and died there in 1950.

Chareau provided logical architectural solutions to furniture design. Models consisted of basic components which with slight modification could be adapted to multiple needs. Linen cupboards, bars, filing cabinets, hearth fenders, and desks incorporated the same fundamental structure, additional elements extending their usage. No attempt was made to mask the item's functionalism: the contours of wood and metal were left brazenly undisguised. Chareau's style was discussed by Léon Deshairs in a 1927 article in *Art et décoration*, the accompanying illustrations showing a wide range of furniture with rigid wrought-iron supports terminating in short inturned feet. Most furniture was made of a combination of wood and wrought-iron. Woods were warm and highly buffed to offset the coldness and austerity of the metal – palisander, *amourette*, walnut, sycamore, and violetwood. The iron supports, cast in broad sheets, were treated with a light patina and bolted together. Chair upholstery was in velours, pigskin, or, rarely, sable fur. Cushions were credited to Chareau's English wife, Dollie, who administered his business.

Perhaps Chareau's most successful furnishings were his light fixtures, the shades constructed of overlapping slices of alabaster placed at angles to each other. The design was repeated in floor, table, wall, and hanging models. Everyone seems to have approved except Léon Deshairs, who wrote in a 1924 article in *Art et décoration*: 'Why this obsessive geometry, in light fittings, bristling with weirdly interlocking pieces of glass, on carpets, in paintings, and in sculpture?' The carpets, paintings, and sculpture to which Deshairs referred were designed by Jean Lurçat, Marcoussis, and Lipchitz respectively, Chareau's regular collaborators. Many Chareau interiors were illustrated in contemporary reviews, such as *Les Arts de la maison, Intérieurs français*, and *Intérieurs VI*. Chareau applied himself particularly to kitchens, bathrooms, and nurseries, the last-mentioned with wicker furniture.

Chauchet-Guilleré, Charlotte:

Born in Charleville (Ardennes) in 1878, Charlotte Chaucet was trained as an artist, exhibiting at the first Salon of the Société des Artistes Décorateurs, organized in 1904 by René Guilleré, whom she married shortly after. In 1913, her husband, an accomplished art administrator and entrepreneur, established the Primavera atelier and appointed his wife its artistic director.

It is difficult to determine the division between Chauchet-Guilleré's two roles, as decorator and administrator. Certainly the team of designers under her supervision was as talented as that of her foremost competitors, Le Studium Louvre, Pomone, and La Maîtrise. Sognot, alone, ensured that the Studio remain in the vanguard of modern taste and materials. As a decorator, Chauchet-Guilleré maintained a measure of artistic independence by exhibiting under her own name at the Salons. Her exhibits included a range of bedroom and dining-room ensembles, the pieces manufactured by Primavera. The Salon catalogues listed two addresses: 13 rue Eugénie-Girard, Vincennes, and 26 rue Norrins.

At the 1925 Exposition, Chauchet-Guilleré supervised the Primavera gallery exhibit, contributing a bedroom of her own on the second floor. The latter was unexceptional; only the bed's checkerboard coverlet drew attention to an otherwise plain room. Elsewhere at the Exposition she took stand 68 on the Esplanade des Invalides to display a dining room.

Most of her interiors appear undistinguished today, even a trifle cluttered. But a study exhibited at the 1922 Salon d'Automne proved particularly successful, its furniture designed *en série* with neatly fluted panelling. The critics were enthusiastic, praising the room's homogeneity and her choice of woods: palisander and stained sycamore. The following year at the exhibition of L'Art Urbain et le Mobilier, her ministerial office, purchased directly by the State, evoked an impression of gravity and comfort without intimacy. A year earlier Gaston Varenne provided the following comments in *Art et décoration* on the furniture in a young girl's bedroom at the Salon d'Automne: 'The shapes are perhaps a little fragile, a bit girlish, but I can picture clearly the young girl who would live in this setting: she would not be a Nietzschean.'

Chauchet-Guilleré continued as director of Primavera after her husband died in 1931 and was succeeded in 1939 by Colette Guéden. She lived in retirement until her death in 1964.

Cheuret, Albert:

Little biographical information exists on Cheuret beyond that he was trained in statuary by Jacques Perrin and Georges Lemaire, later establishing his atelier at 11 avenue Franco-Russe, where he both designed and executed commissions. He exhibited from 1907 at the Salon des Artistes Français; in 1924, for example, showing a 'Bird of Paradise' chandelier, a pair of 'Pearl' sconces, and a 'Pebbles' floor lamp. The mounts were in bronze, the shades in sliced alabaster with sharply contoured outlines.

Cheuret took boutique 33 on the Alexander III bridge at the 1925 Exposition, listing himself as a sculptor-decorator. He displayed a range of bronzeware, including animal and bird figures, furniture, clocks, and – his speciality – a wide range of light fixtures, ten examples of which were illustrated the following year in *Le Luminaire*.

Cheuret's pieces have an unmistakable freshness and charm. His furniture included a series of bronze mantel clocks, one of which – strikingly designed as the head of an Egyptian with flared coiffeuse, no doubt in celebration of Howard Carter's 1922 discovery of the Tutenkhamen tomb – is now firmly established as an Art Deco classic. Other garnitures provided variations on this theme. He also manufactured mirrors, radiator covers, and pedestals. A *guéridon*, designed as an aloe plant, was included in the 1975 dispersal of the Karl Lagerfeld collection at the Hôtel Drouot.

Coard, Marcel:

Born in Paris in 1889 into what he later described as a 'grande bourgeoisie' family, Coard studied architecture at the Ecole des Beaux-Arts. He emerged, however, as a decorator, establishing himself in 1914 on the boulevard Haussmann. At the outbreak of war he volunteered for action, but was demobilized through illness and spent the remainder of the war in a military hospital passing the time by sketching furniture designs. In 1919 he renewed his career as a decorator. As fashionable Parisian taste at the time favoured the past, Coard furnished most of his interiors with eighteenth-century antiques. This expediency explains, in part, his limited furniture production. But an additional reason was that he disliked duplicating his designs, as he explained in an interview in *L'Oeil* prior to his death in 1975: 'Such pieces of furniture, exquisitely wrought, were unique, because I have always avoided repeating the pieces I have made. I was never really concerned with large-scale production. These pieces were each made individually with the most beautiful materials I could find.' To maintain such integrity required wealthy clients; for Coard, most importantly, Jacques Doucet in Neuilly, and Pierre Cocteau in Touraine.

Coard's preferred woods were oak – often primitively cut – macassar ebony, and palisander. It was, however, his selection of veneers and encrusted materials that gave his pieces their stamp of individualism: parchment, mother-of-pearl, *galuchat*, rock crystal, tinted mirror, marbrite, and glass

with a silvered ground. Points of colour were added by the use of lapis lazuli and amethyst. Coard's ornamentation, however, was always subordinate to form; the contours of his furniture remained unbroken.

African and Oceanic tribal art and the Orient were everpresent influences on Coard's work. Only Legrain's furniture bore a pronounced similarity, to the point where certain pieces require provenance to determine authorship.

Coard was rigidly independent, avoiding both the annual Salons and the small groups, such as 'Les Cinq', which exhibited intermittently in Paris. Of his contemporaries, only Dupré-Lafon seemed as intent on privacy. A 1932 monograph in *Art et décoration* traced some of Coard's important commissions: in addition to Pierre Cocteau, private residences for M.S. near Boulogne and Mme D.S. in Paris. The illustrations show, in large part, a restrained Coard, many pieces of conventional, if not innocuous, design, reminding the reader that it was only in his work for a very narrow avant garde that Coard's creativity could be unbounded.

The pieces commissioned by Doucet are important today because they show this unbridled Coard. Many are now either in the Musée des Arts Décoratifs, Paris, or were offered in the 1972 auction of Doucet's collection at the Hôtel Drouot. Two pieces – a table and armchair – were made in collaboration with Josef Czaky and Gustave Miklos. Two others, a 'bird cage' table and a tabouret, are so similar to contemporary designs by Legrain that the issue of precedence becomes dominant. Elsewhere, an *armoire* in the collection of the Musée des Arts Décoratifs is stamped Roumy, providing a rare identification of one of Coard's cabinetmakers.

Compagnie des Arts Français (see Adnet)

Da Silva Bruhns, Ivan:

Parisian-born of Brazilian parents, da Silva Bruhns was working as an artist/decorator when in 1920 he was drawn to carpet design by a commission from Louis Majorelle. His early designs were conventional: garlanded fruit and flora, in a variation of the seventeenth-century Savonnerie style adopted by Coudyser (with whom da Silva Bruhns formed an early partnership), Benedictus, and Dufrène.

Da Silva Bruhns revolutionized both carpet manufacture and design. After dissecting an Oriental carpet, he developed his own variation of the 'point noué' (knotted stitch), described by Marcel Weber in a 1924 article on the artist in *Art et décoration*: 'Each of the spots of colour is made by tying a slip knot around the strands of the warp thread. After weaving, the juxtaposed knots are covered by rings which are then cut with scissors. This reveals the strands that will form the pile of the carpet.'

Da Silva Bruhns taught his technique to a worker, whom he then installed in a village in Aisne to set up a studio from local weavers. Da Silva Bruhns concerned himself mainly with two aspects of production: the colour selection of the wool and the preliminary watercolour maquette, the latter traced in microscopic detail onto squared paper. It was the first time twentieth-century design had been applied to carpets: overlapping rectangles, lozenges, and chevrons on muted grounds. His palette was sober: indigos, browns, pinks, greys, and apricots, to meet exactly the carpet's function within an ensemble, which the *Mobilier et décoration* critic described in 1928 as 'providing the harmony which is struck between the colours of the furniture and the tapestries – its fundamental bass note whose rich and warm resonance helps create a sum of varied and carefully wrought sensations like an orchestral chord.'

No further measure of the esteem in which da Silva Bruhns was held by his Salon colleagues is needed than a list of those who used his carpets in their exhibits: Leleu, Montagnac, Bouchet, Bagge, Fréchet, Printz, and Prou, to name only the most important. He also exhibited on his own until the late 1930s. Two addresses were given for him: 3 avenue du Château, Neuilly, and 9 rue de l'Odéon.

De Bardyère, Georges:

Born in Wassy (Haute-Marne), de Bardyère's date of birth is unrecorded. He participated regularly in the Salons from 1919 as a decorator/interior designer. Early ensembles were stiff and undistinguished. A dining room illustrated in *Mobilier et décoration* in 1923 today appears bland, the pieces unidentifiable either with their creator or the period. Nevertheless, other de Bardyère exhibits – at the 1921 and 1922 Salons – received favourable reviews from the critics. A psyche mirror in sycamore at the 1921 Salon des Artistes Décorateurs was described in *Art et décoration* as 'discreet and elegant'; a year later a dining room in Cuban mahogany and burl Burmese wood 'exactly caught the sentiment of contemporary modern life'. De Bardyère's understated classic forms, lightly decorated with carved bas-relief decoration and ivory veneer were fashionably safe.

At the 1925 Exposition, de Bardyère created several memorable interiors for his exhibit in stand 30 on the Esplanade des Invalides; in particular, a dining room with elegant scrolled furniture motifs, and an office described in *Mobilier et décoration* as containing 'dark furniture, enlivened by the whiteness of unobtrusive mosaics and the gold and silver work on display in the windows'.

By this time, de Bardyère's furniture was distinctly more interesting. A mahogany and burl Burmese wood cabinet at the 1926 Salon d'Automne generated further favourable comments in *Mobilier et décoration*: 'It is excellent cabinet-

making, worthy of its French past.' The piece incorporated carved volutes, the same Louis Philippe decorative theme that popularized the work of Süe et Mare at the time.

Numerous talents were drawn upon; in particular, Genet and Michon for lighting, and Pinguenet for paintings and carpets. Others included Dunand and da Silva Bruhns. No record appears to exist of de Bardyère's favourite cabinet-maker, though his choice of woods regularly drew praise. Gabriel Henriot, for example, wrote in *Mobilier et décoration* of a studio exhibited at the 1928 Salon d'Automne that 'M. de Bardyère displays beautiful furniture, elegant and well-finished, in burl walnut. Today's decorators revert more and more to this wood, so French and so richly grained.' De Bardyère also used palisander, mahogany, and amboyna.

He continued to exhibit at the Salons in the 1930s, placing increased emphasis on wallpaper and fabric designs. He died in 1942, his address still listed as 21 rue de Richelieu, where he had lived for nearly thirty years.

Desvallières, Richard:

Desvallières remains an anachronism among 1920s metal-workers. At a time when seemingly everyone else set aside the medium's traditional tools – the forge and anvil – for the modern industrial press and autogenous soldering techniques, Desvallières clung stubbornly to the past. As the critic for *Art et décoration* wrote in 1921, 'Our wrought-iron workers have a great diversity of temperaments. At the two extremes are Edgar Brandt and Richard Desvallières. The first plays on the difficulties of virtuosity. He transforms iron into a material so subtle and plastic that he can do with it as he will . . . the works of Desvallières, on the other hand, are filled with grace yet leave within the iron its innate qualities of strength and ruggedness.' Two years later the critic for *Les Arts de la maison* said of a wrought-iron grill by Desvallières, that it 'achieves the perfection of the "makers" of ornamental hinges in the twelfth century. The red hot metal, forged and beaten by this artist, acquires a rare malleability and a sombre beauty which recalls the delicate economy of the medieval metal works where the work of the smith still had an artistic value.' Naturally, an artist who placed such emphasis on handcrafting had a relatively small output. Shown at the Salon d'Automne were a selection of grills, screens, sconces, and firedogs. Larger commissions included a dining table for the architect Jean Patou in 1924 and a balcony and balustrade in Louis Süe's pavilion for La Compagnie des Arts Français. Ecclesiastical commissions, such as choir-stall grills and reliquaries, brought further work. Desvallières' designs were light and charming; grillwork designed as tasselled drapes or pierced bouquets, in a manner similar to that of Edouard Schenck, another traditionalist.

Desvallières was born in Paris in 1893, the son of the artist Georges Desvallières. His address in the 1920s is listed as rue Ernest-Legouvé, Saint-Port (Seine-et-Marne).

D.I.M. (see Joubert et Petit)

Djo-Bourgeois:

Djo-Bourgeois belonged to the new generation whose philosophy was that to decorate a space successfully, one should *unfurnish*, rather than furnish, it. Less was definitely more. His interiors, as M. T. and L. Bonney wrote in their 1929 pamphlet, *Buying Antique and Modern Furniture in Paris*, represented 'simplification carried to the nth degree, possibly further, you will say, when you see a bed of concrete, a unit in the wall! Harmony of spaces as well as of forms. A pleasing austerity, almost monastic, heightened by colour and design in rugs and textiles which challenge the emotions.' In bareness, geometry, and equilibrium lay the ingenious solutions to modern living. Djo-Bourgeois' furniture was comprised of rectangles, its interest provided by stepped shelves and supports.

Djo-Bourgeois was born in Bezons (Seine-et-Oise) in 1898. He graduated from the Ecole Spéciale d'Architecture in 1922, the following year joining Le Studium Louvre and making his début at the Salons. For the Studio's directors, Kohlmann and Matet, Djo-Bourgeois filled an embarrassing gap. With him as part of their design team they could match the modernist interiors of Sognot at Primavera and, independently, Lurçat, Perriand, and Mallet-Stevens.

At the 1925 Exposition, Djo-Bourgeois exhibited two ensembles in the Studium Louvre pavilion: a smoking room and office/library. Collaborators were listed as Léon Leyritz (sculpture), and Pierre Demaria (lacquered panels). The furniture and wall panels were in palisander. An item of special interest – apart from the sparseness of the furnishings – was a radio-telephone and phonograph built into the sides of a broad divan.

Modern design demanded modern furniture materials. Djo-Bourgeois' early preference was for a combination of wood, often lacquered, and glass; soon the former was replaced by tubular metal, aluminium, iron, and concrete. Conventional wooden wall panelling gave way to cork and a plastic composite.

At some point after 1926 Djo-Bourgeois left the Studium Louvre to establish his own business, his address by 1929 listed as 25 rue Vaneau. He developed a narrow group of avant-garde clients such as the Viscount Noailles, the Duke of Harcourt, M. Lahy, and M. Lange, designing both their houses and furnishings. Numerous magazines showed these interiors, in particular, *Intérieurs modernes* and *La Répertoire du goût moderne*. His major collaborator was his wife, Elise, who designed the geometric carpets and cushions which brought

colour, warmth, and comfort to the otherwise spartan interiors. Other frequent collaborators, through the years, were Paul Brandt and Louis Tétard.

A dining room shown by Djo-Bourgeois at the 1936 Salon pointed to future possibilities. The birch walls were made of movable partitions so that the room's dimensions could be altered if necessary.

Djo-Bourgeois continued to exhibit at the Salons until his premature death in 1937. His last interior, a yachtsman's apartment on the Cote d'Azur, was purchased posthumously by friends.

Domin, André (see Dominique)

Dominique:

The decorating firm of Dominique was founded in 1922 at 104 Faubourg Saint-Honoré, Paris, by André Domin, a self-taught artist born in Caen in 1883 and Marcel Genevrière, a trained architect, born in 1885. The partnership got off to a resounding and rapid start, within a year advertising in *Mobilier et décoration* a wide range of carpets, fabrics, furniture, and wrought-iron. Two important commissions came simultaneously: Jean Puiforcat's residence in central Paris and the offices of the Houbigant perfume works in Neuilly. In 1924, the critic Yvanhoë Rambosson could write in *Art et décoration* of their exhibit at the Salon des Artistes Décorateurs: 'The room and the bed which are reproduced here are in such harmony with life that a dumb but captivating eloquence is born out of them. These lovingly worked creations seem to say to us: Come live among us; here life is gentle, joyous, and measured, for here all is well-proportioned.'

In addition to the annual Salons, the firm participated in the Ambassade Française at the 1925 Exposition, presenting a lounge in collaboration with Charles Hairon (furniture carving), Hélène Lantier (silk upholstery), and La Maison Lunot (Aubusson tapestry). Elsewhere, the partners designed a boutique for Manteaux Salf. In the same year they were awarded first prize for their entry in a chair competition organized by the Union Centrale des Arts Décoratifs.

Around this time an agreement was formed between the five artists/designers whose inaugural exhibit was staged in 1926 at La Galerie Barbazanges. Known as 'Les Cinq', the union was especially valuable to Dominique, its furniture receiving a disproportionate amount of magazine coverage from year to year. Virtually all Chareau's exhibits – at the moment that he was pioneering the transition to metal furniture – were passed over for Dominique's ensembles. In 1927, for example, the critic G. Rémon set aside an entire article for Dominique's exhibit, singling out a bookcase and table-desk, the latter showing an arresting design of alter-nating concave and convex sides, the four pedestal feet enclosing shelves. Two years later at the Galerie de la Renaissance (the venue was changed every year; in 1928 it had been La Galerie Georges Bernheim), they showed numerous pieces of furniture, including a thuya *chiffonier* with silver mounts by Puiforcat and a walnut drop-front secretary veneered in blue-tinted sharkskin. The designs and selection of materials throughout showed exemplary taste.

Preferred woods in the early years were palisander, macassar ebony, and sycamore. Upholstery was in silk (on occasion by Raoul Dufy), velours, or leather. The 1930s witnessed a dramatic shift to synthetic fabrics: *duvetine*, artificial silk, Rodhia canvas, and silvered and ultramarine Tricotene. The search was for the new: crystal handles replaced Puiforcat's earlier models, black *dalles* of glass superseded walnut room panelling and doors. Modernity was *de rigueur*, as the *Mobilier et décoration* critic reminded his readers of Dominique's 1934 creations, 'A piece of furniture has worked when it successfully withstands the test of time and blends comfortably with earlier pieces.'

The firm reached maturity in the early 1930s, receiving an important commission to furnish a hotel in Havana. The entire interior was undertaken, and many of the rooms were illustrated in a *Mobilier et décoration* booklet by Gabriel Henriot. For the ocean liner *Normandie*, some years later, Dominique designed the de luxe apartment 'Rouen', its four rooms incorporating a selection of furniture against parchment walls hung with panels by Daragnès and Le Trividic. In 1935 came the Exposition de Bruxelles and two years later the Exposition des Arts et Téchniques. Domin died in 1962 and the firm was taken over by his son. It closed in 1970.

Dufet, Michel:

Michel Dufet enjoyed a long and distinguished career as a decorator and furniture designer. Born in Delville-les-Rouen in 1888, he graduated in architecture and painting at the Ecole Supérieure des Beaux-Arts, Paris, receiving instruction from Pascal and Raphael Collin. In 1913, he established the furniture retailing firm of M.A.M. (Meubles Artistiques Modernes) at 3 avenue de l'Opéra. Principal early commissions included a drawing room in grey maple and gold lacquer for M. Henri Duvernois, the room's interior in 'Poussin Bleu', and the interior for a villa at Arcachon for M. Edouard Moussie.

Dufet made his début at the Salon des Artistes Français in 1914, exhibiting again after the armistice, at which time he went into partnership with Louis Bureau, a painter and former student of Tony Robert-Fleury and Jules Lefèvre at the Académie Julian. The partnership parallels that of Süe et Mare: in both cases an architect and painter found that complementary skills exceeded individual talents. In both

cases, also, it was the architect who predominated, drawing experience from the union before branching out on his own.

Sometime between 1922 and 1924, Dufet and Bureau separated, the latter dropping from prominence, although continuing to exhibit sporadically at the Salons (a palisander desk with decorated parchment panels met with a critic's disapproval in 1927). The partnership had, however, produced several opulent and well-received ensembles. Preference was for rich furniture materials – exotic veneers such as palisander and linden – while minimizing the use of metal mounts and marquetry decoration, an early indication of Dufet's later predilection for functional furniture manufactured *en série*. The rest of the room, however, was lavish: royal blue or vermilion lacquered panelling, silver *lamé* fabrics, and black Pyrenees marble fireplaces provided the necessary warmth and sense of luxury. The *Art et décoration* critic, Emile Henriot, found a commode at the Salon des Artistes Décorateurs 'perfectly sober in colour and line, and well-constructed'. The next year a bedroom in lindenwood, with grey and violet linens and upholstery, was marketed by M.A.M.

In 1922 a variety of interiors and individual pieces were produced: a dining room, drawing room, and dressing table in mahogany and amaranth with lacquered and giltwood panels marketed by P. A. Dumas, to whom Dufet sold the M.A.M. firm. A small *salon*, exhibited in early 1924, appears to have been one of the pair's last combined creations. Modern, Ruhlmann-like furniture was placed in a high-ceiled room lined with tall black and white veined marble pilasters topped by fruit-carved capitals. A Louis XVI formality and elegance prevailed.

A 1920 article in *Art et décoration* indicates Dufet's resentment throughout this period of the limitations placed on the individual by the Salon's Jury, a body steeped in conservatism. He wrote: 'Tradition! What a lot of mistakes have been recommended to us in its name. As architects and painters at the Ecole des Beaux Arts we were drowning in a hotch-potch of unnecessary decors, coats of arms, excessive "mosiac" designs, all sorts of extravagances and badly assimilated Italian style which the masters brought back from the Villa Medici; and afterwards in life we suffered the influence of the limited and constricted theories of those who claim to judge, and even direct, our efforts. There are always men of letters or aesthetes ready to point the way to artists – dangerous sophists whose lack of knowledge of technique leads to the worst mistakes.'

Dufet's rebelliousness manifested itself in several quick career changes. He branched out into journalism, founding an art magazine *Les Feuilles d'art*, and then, around 1923, became director of a prominent firm of interior decorators, Red Star, in Rio de Janeiro. A two-year South American sojourn prevented participation in the 1925 Exposition, but Dufet participated the following year in the Salon des Artistes Décorateurs.

The general evolution toward metal furniture in the late 1920s matched exactly Dufet's resolve to manufacture furniture in editions rather than as single works of art, a crusade he had waged for a decade. In 1935, a critic recounted in *Mobilier et décoration* the significance of Dufet's 1927 decision to join 'Le Sylve', the art studio of the furniture retailer Le Bûcheron, a business dependent on mass-production. He wrote: 'Dufet thought – and the circumstances gave him good reason – that quality furniture should not remain the privilege of the wealthy. Times have changed since the days of lost wax casting, of the unique chest of drawers for the sole use of a rich patron, for the excellent reason that rich patrons have become, in a disquieting way, a rarity. And is it not better to please twenty Frenchmen with taste by selling a piece of furniture worthy of a lover of the arts at a realistic price, but reproduced several times, instead of keeping it for one more or less imaginary purchaser who would be forced to pay a good deal more for it?'

Dufet continued to participate in the Salons, now including in his exhibits a selection of prefabricated pieces of varying sizes for use in combination (*meubles juxtaposables*). Cubist influence was readily apparent, particularly in the dining room exhibited at the 1929 Salon. Starkly functional chairs incorporated pale Norwegian birch offset with dark macassar ebony mounts, the latter repeated on the buffets and table. An overlapping skyscraper wallpaper design completed the room's ultramodern look. In the same year, Dufet displayed a bar-restaurant at the Exposition de la Décoration Française.

Dufet's experimentation with new materials and design concepts invariably met with some criticism. The critic for *Mobilier et décoration* wrote in his review of the 1930 Salon d'Automne: 'Michel Dufet is continuing his interesting experiments, but the abundance of detail creates some confusion: too much reptile skin, too many different levels of shelves in the study, too many natural grains in the wood. . . . The materials he uses are beautiful (olive, palmwood, and polished metal), worthwhile discoveries; it is only the excessive use of them that is questionable.' Another ensemble was considered more successful. Likewise marketed by Le Bûcheron, it included sculpture by Bourdelle, zinc fixtures by the Compagnie Asturienne des Mines, carpets by Lainé, and lighting by Boris Lacroix.

The 1930s brought numerous and varied commissions in addition to Dufet's standard production for Le Bûcheron. In 1932 he furnished a waiting room for the Commissariat General of the Colonial Exposition, Marshal Lyautey; in the following year four cabins for Mme Armand Esder's yacht, *Aronia II* and, shortly after, commissions for the *Normandie*, *Foch*, and *Ile-de-France*.

New materials, interspersed with proven woods, paved Dufet's way to modernism. Chromed tubular steel, etched slabs of glass, and zinc were introduced in the late 1920s; synthetic fabrics, such as Duralumin, in the 1930s.

The 1935 Salon des Artistes Décorateurs generated new designs and further negative comments from the critics. A studio in white and royal blue included chairs in palisander upholstered in piebald animal skins, leading the viewer 'directly to places where we have no wish to go'. The table, consisting of a glass top supported by incurved sheet-metal trestle-ends with steel ball joints, brought further disquiet. Today the piece appears remarkably modern, a tribute to Dufet's pioneership in this medium. At the 1937 Exposition he participated with René Gabriel in a display in the wallpaper pavilion, following this with the commission to design the French pavilion at the 1939 New York Fair.

M. Dufet lives today in Paris, where he kindly consented to an interview for this book.

Dufrène, Maurice:

Nobody made the transition from 1900 to 1925 more gracefully or with more respect from his contemporaries than Dufrène. Born in Paris in 1876, he traced his early years in a 1921 article in *Art et décoration*. Exposed in childhood to a huge range of materials through his father's wholesale commodities business, he spent every free moment collecting scraps of fabric, wood, cardboard, and so on, to be fashioned into items of his own creation in a makeshift atelier. Even discarded railway engine wheels were transformed in the forge. In 1887 he decided to forgo his philosophy courses at the Ecole Communale and study instead at the Ecole des Arts Décoratifs. The experience proved frustrating; the theory was taught, but not its application. Escape came through employment in a modern print house, where, in the course of his new duties, Dufrène met Meier-Graefe, who persuaded him to join La Maison Moderne. There he entered the august ranks of van de Velde, Horta, Plumet, and T. Selmersheim on the eve of the 1900 Exposition.

The move established Dufrène. He surged to the forefront of modern design, in 1904 becoming a founder-member of the Salon des Artistes Décorateurs, through which he exhibited for thirty years. He taught Composition at the Ecole Boulle and other institutions from 1912 to 1922, in 1919 returning to the Salons as an independent decorator. Examples of his work during this period – for clients such as David Weill, Brissac, and Paul Watel – were illustrated in *Art et décoration*. The furniture, marketed by Ch. A. Geffroy, was neat and logical, much of it embellished with a recurring carved scroll motif today frequently misattributed to Süe et Mare. Further decoration was provided by marquetry floral medallions in boxwood, ebony, and ivory. The effect was a trifle feminine, even effete, a characteristic of Dufrène's furnishings in the 1920s.

In 1921 Dufrène was appointed artistic director of La Maîtrise, a studio with a marketing philosophy that dovetailed neatly with his own. Both advocated large machine-made editions of furniture at inexpensive prices. Dufrène was adamant in his belief that this goal need in no way diminish aesthetic standards: 'Anyway, in what way is a machine less whole than a tool? Where does the tool end and the machine begin? Isn't a planer a small machine? The important thing is to adapt the subject to the means, but also to bend the means to the subject, and not to expect the same result from different approaches.'

Dufrène's output matched his words. Nobody, in fact, was more prolific or versatile. The Salons displayed only a sampling of the furniture executed for him by La Maîtrise cabinetmakers. Many ensembles were given names ('Rusticana', 'Cantegril', 'Cordoue', etc.), as were individual pieces ('Claudine', 'Zola', 'Niagara'), their prices listed in a firm's catalogue published after the 1925 Exposition. Collaborators included Jacques Meistermann, R. Harang, and Gabriel Englinger (furniture design); Speich Frères, Olivier Desbordes, and Vasseur and Guilly (cabinetry); and Mme Lassudrie and Suzanne Guiguichon (fabrics and upholstery).

At the 1925 Exposition Dufrène was, simply, everywhere. Apart from his directorship of La Maîtrise pavilion, in which he displayed a dining room, and men's and women's bedrooms in collaboration with Englinger, Tcherniack and Brochard, he designed the *petit salon* in the Ambassade Française, a boutique for the furrier Jungman & Cie, and the entire row of shops on the Alexander III bridge.

The 1930s were no less frenetic. The earlier predilection for wood gave way gradually to metal and glass. Approaching sixty years of age, Dufrène could still adapt, as he had shown during the demise of Art Nouveau a quarter of a century earlier. He died in Nogent-sur-Marne in 1955.

Many of Dufrène's Art Deco pieces today pass unidentified, if not unnoticed, though his work was always of the finest design and execution.

Dunand, Jean:

Dunand's career spanned nearly half a century and can be divided into three relatively distinct phases: sculpture, metalware, and lacquerwork. He was born 20 May 1877 in Lancy, Switzerland, to French parents, his father a gold smelter in the clock-making business. Enrolment at the Ecole des Arts Industriels in Geneva was followed in 1896 by a scholarship for advanced study in Paris. On arrival he was reunited with some old Swiss friends, Bouet de Monvel and Carl Albert Angst.

continued on page 81

1 *Adnet:* cabinet in palisander and *galuchat* (shagreen) with gilt-bronze lock plate, *c.* 1928 (Photo: Christie's, NY)

2 *Adnet:* fall-front secretary, illustrated in *Petits Meubles du jour*, Paris, pl. 30

3 *Adnet:* ceiling lamp in chromed metal with frosted bulbs, marketed by La Compagnie des Arts Français. Illustrated in *Le Luminaire III*, Guillaume Janneau, Paris 1931, pl. 39

4 *Adnet:* chair in tubular chromed metal, marketed by La Compagnie des Arts Français. Illustrated in *Art et décoration*, Jan.–June 1930, p. 38; and *Sièges contemporains*, Paris, pl. 15

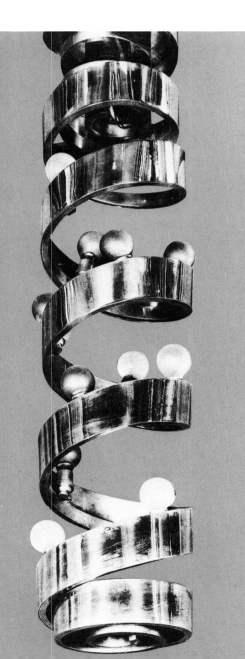

5, 6 *Aguesse:* two lady's desks, with chairs, exhibited at a desk competition at the Union Centrale des Arts Décoratifs, 1927. Illustrated in 'Bureaux secrétaires pays divers XXᵉ siècle', *Art et décoration*, Jan.–June 1928; and *Les Echos des industries d'art*, Feb. 1928

7 *Arbus:* dressing table and chair, in sycamore, lacquer, and vellum. Illustrated in *Meubles nouveaux*, Guillaume Janneau, Paris 1943

Below

8 *Arbus:* desk for a young girl in ebony and vellum, the chair in ebony upholstered in tufted grey satin. Exhibited at the Salon of the Société des Artistes Décorateurs, 1932. Illustrated in *Art et décoration*, Jan.–June 1935

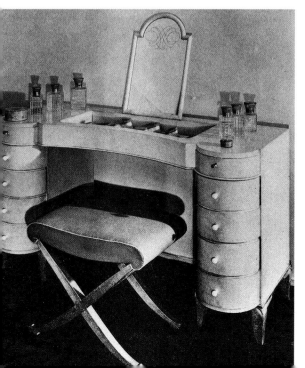

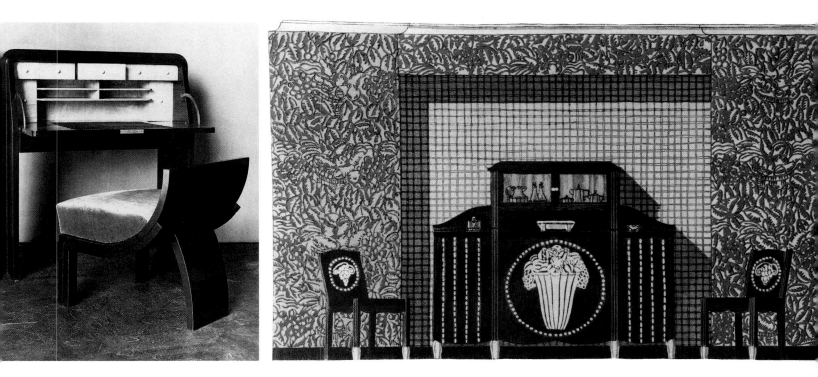

9 *Bagge:* desk and chair exhibited at the Union Centrale des Arts Décoratifs, 1927. Illustrated in *Bureaux secrétaires pays divers XXᵉ siècle*, 1928

10 *Bagge:* dining room in *bois de placage* with ivory veneer, exhibited at the 1925 Exposition and marketed by Saddier. Illustrated in *Intérieurs IV*, Léon Moussinac, Paris, pl. 4

11 *Barret:* desk and chair in chromed and painted metal, for the Marquis of Cholmondeley, *c.* 1935 (Photo: Sotheby Parke Bernet, Monaco)

12 *Beaumont:* two-panel screen with tapestry by Aubusson, the sketch illustrated in *Les Echos des industries d'art*, Jan. 1927

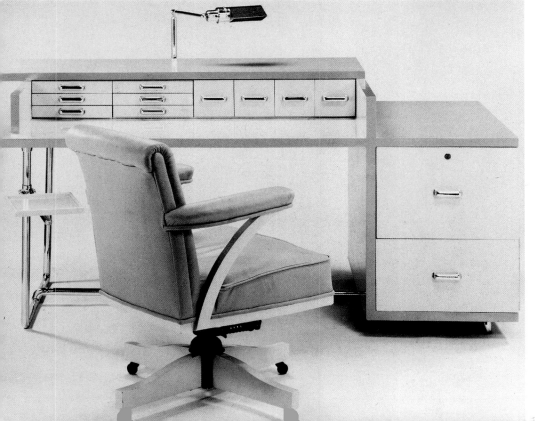

13   *Block:* lady's desk and chair, illustrated in *Petits Meubles du jour*, Paris

14   *Block:* child's desk and chair in painted wood, *c.* 1928, illustrated in *Petits Meubles du jour*, Paris

15   *Block:* dressing table and chair in wood and chromed tubular metal, *c.* 1927, illustrated in *Petits Meubles du jour*, Paris

16 *Bouchet:* furniture designs, *c.* 1920. Illustrated in *La Renaissance de l'art français et des industries de luxe*

17 *Bouchet:* armchair with fabric design by Raoul Dufy, exhibited at the Salon d'Automne, 1922, and marketed by Bianchini-Férier. Illustrated in *Art et décoration*, 1922, p. 12; and *L'Art décoratif français 1918–1925,* Léon Deshairs, Paris 1926, p. 76

18 *Bouchet:* furniture sketches, *c.* 1920. Illustrated in *La Renaissance de l'art français et des industries de luxe*

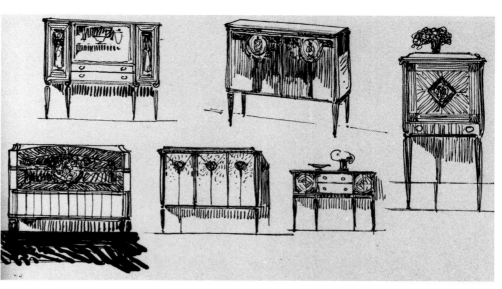

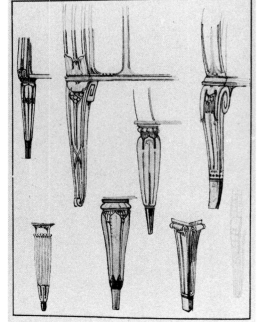

Opposite

19　*Brandt:* potiche in silvered-bronze, the model exhibited at the 1925 Exposition (Collection of de Lorenzo Gallery)

20　*Brandt:* console in wrought-iron with black marble top (Photo: Sotheby Parke Bernet, Monaco)

21　*Brandt:* 'L'Oasis', five-panel screen, in collaboration with Henri Favier, in wrought-iron enhanced with gilt-bronze. Illustrated in the firm's catalogue *Galerie Edgar Brandt* and *Art et décoration*, Dec. 1924, at a price of Fr84,000. Exhibited at the 1924 Salon d'Automne and the 1925 Exposition

This page

22　*Brandt:* table lamps in wrought-iron with frosted cylindrical shades, 1920s. Illustrated in *Le Luminaire III*, Guillaume Janneau, Paris 1931

23　*Brandt:* chandelier in wrought-iron with etched glass shades by Daum, exhibited at the 1925 Exposition and illustrated in *Le Luminaire I*, Guillaume Janneau, Paris 1926

24　*Brandt:* ensemble displayed at the Exhibition of French Decorative Arts at the Metropolitan Museum of Art, New York, 1926. Included are a pair of wrought-iron and alabaster 'Orient' floor lamps, a 'Noblesse' console table, and a 'Transition' mirror

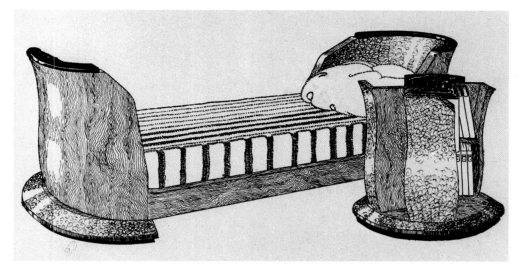

Opposite

25 *Burkhalter:* work-table in painted tubular steel and polished oak, illustrated in *Art et décoration*, March 1930, and *Bureaux secrétaires pays divers XXᵉ siècle*, 1928

26 *Burkhalter:* metal jardinière, exhibited at the 3rd Exposition de l'Union des Artistes Modernes. Illustrated in *Art et décoration*, 1932, and *Quand le meuble devient sculpture*, exhibition catalogue, 1930

27 *Champion:* cabinet in palisander and macassar ebony with silvered-metal lamps, exhibited at the Salon of the Société des Artistes Décorateurs, 1926, and marketed by G. & G. Guérin. Illustrated in *Les Echos des industries d'art*, June 1926

Above

28 *Chareau:* sketch for a day-bed and revolving bookcase in palisander and *amourette*, exhibited at the Salon d'Automne 1923. Illustrated in *Art et décoration*, Nov. 1923, p. 179; *L'Art décoratif français 1918–1925*, Léon Deshairs, Paris 1926, p. 63; and *Les Arts de la maison*, Winter 1923, p. 49

29 *Chareau:* leather and macassar ebony armchair. Illustrated in *Mobilier et décoration*, Nov. 1928, p. 219ff; *Nouveaux Intérieurs français*, Paris, pl. 15; and *Encyclopédie des métiers d'art I*, Paris, p. 64 (Collection of Barry Friedman, Ltd., NY)

Below

30 *Chareau:* table in metal and wood to house a phonograph and record compartments. Illustrated in *Pierre Chareau*, Paris 1954, p. 88; and *Bureaux secrétaires pays divers XXᵉ siècle*, 1928. The chair illustrated in *Pierre Chareau*, pp. 50, 94

31 *Chareau:* bedroom exhibited at the 1928 Lord & Taylor Exhibition, NY, including a palisander desk with wrought-iron frame, a palisander fan-shaped and hinged nest-of-tables, a palisander desk armchair with blue leather upholstery, a highbacked chair upholstered in hand-blocked linen and brown velours, an adjustable suspended hammock couch in palisander and wrought-iron with hand-woven drapes, sculpture by Jacques Lipchitz, chenille rug entitled 'Architecture' by Jean Burkhalter, and wall sconces in alabaster and wrought-iron

32 *Chauchet-Guilleré:* bedroom in grey sycamore with ivory and ebony veneer, executed by Primavera and exhibited at the Salon d'Automne, 1921. Illustrated in *Art et décoration*, Dec. 1921

33 *Cheuret:* patinated bronze and alabaster chandelier, *c.* 1928 (Collection of de Lorenzo Gallery)

Opposite

34 *Coard:* chest-of-drawers in palisander, ivory, and lapis lazuli. The model commissioned by Pierre Cocteau, near Tours. Illustrated in *Art et décoration*, July–Dec. 1932, p. 285 (Photo: Sully-Jaulmes)

35 *Coard:* table in palisander and vellum (Photo: Sotheby Parke Bernet, Monaco)

36 *Coard:* armchair in macassar ebony inlaid with mother-of-pearl. Commissioned by Jacques Doucet (Photo: Macklowe Gallery)

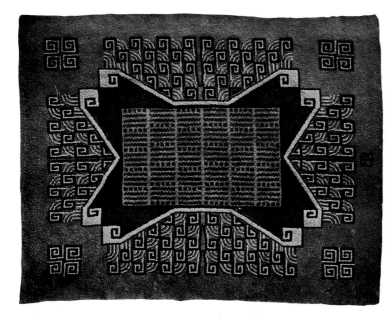

37 *Da Silva Bruhns:* carpet exhibited at the Salon of the Société des Artistes Décorateurs, 1924. Illustrated in *Art et décoration*, June 1924, p. 199

38 *De Bardyere:* boudoir exhibited at the Salon of the Société des Artistes Décorateurs, 1927. Illustrated in *Intérieurs français au Salon des Artistes Décorateurs*, P. Follot, Paris 1927, pl. 22

39 *De Bardyere:* cabinet in oak, illustrated in *Petits Meubles modernes*, Paris 1929, pl. 12

40 *Desvallières:* console table in wrought-iron with marble top, illustrated in *La Ferronerie moderne*, 3rd series, Henri Clouzot

41 *Djo-Bourgeois:* office-library, including sculpture by Léon Leyritz and lacquered panel, carpets, and drapes by P. Demaria. Exhibited at the 1925 Exposition and marketed by Le Studium Louvre. Illustrated in *Intérieurs en couleurs*, Léon Deshairs, Paris 1925, pl. 8; *Ensembles mobiliers*, 1st series, Paris 1925; and *Art et décoration*, 1925

42 *Djo-Bourgeois:* dining room exhibited at the Salon d'Automne, 1926. Illustrated in *Mobilier et décoration*, Dec. 1926

43 *Djo-Bourgeois:* lady's desk and chair, illustrated in *Art et décoration*, Jan.–June 1928

44 *Dominique:* living-room ensemble for Mme L. in Indian palisander, including a fall-front secretary in palisander and *galuchat*, a sofa in palisander and grey suede, and a vitrine in palisander and silvered-bronze. Illustrated in *Mobilier et décoration*, 1928

45 *Dominique:* sketch for a *salon*, illustrated in *Répertoire du goût moderne V*

46 *Dominique:* vitrine in *galuchat* with bronze feet (Collection of Félix Marcilhac)

47 *Dominique:* armchairs in macassar ebony inlaid with tin banding, the exterior upholstered in black Flemish silk, the interior in orange silk. Illustrated in *Art et décoration*, May 1924; and *L'Art décoratif français 1918–1925*, Léon Deshairs, Paris 1926

48 *Dominique:* cabinet in palisander and *galuchat* (Collection of Félix Marcilhac)

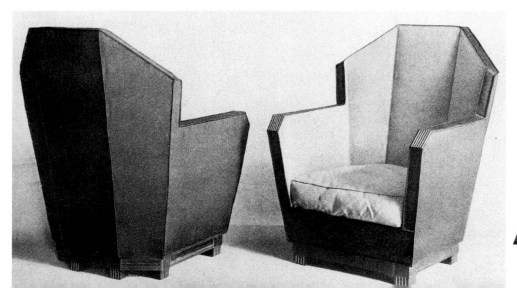

49 *Dufet:* desk, *c.* 1930 (Photo: Sully-Jaulmes)

50 *Dufet:* commode in collaboration with Louis Bureau, in sycamore, aluminium, and ebonized wood, with marble top. Exhibited at the Salon of the Société des Artistes Décorateurs, 1922, and marketed by M.A.M. Illustrated in *Art et décoration*, May 1922, p. 189; *Art et décoration*, Dec. 1921, p. 189; and *Les Arts de la maison*, Autumn and Summer, 1923, p. 52

51 *Dufet:* bedroom in collaboration with Louis Bureau, *c.* 1922, marketed by P. A. Dumas. Illustrated in *Décors et ameublements au goût du jour*, Gaston Fleury, Paris 1926, pl. 5; and *Art et décoration*, Nov. 1922, p. 174

52 *Dufet:* living room in collaboration with Louis Bureau, in lacquered and gilt-wood, marketed by M.A.M. A similar ensemble illustrated in *L'Art décoratif français 1918–1925*, Léon Deshairs, Paris 1926, p. 5

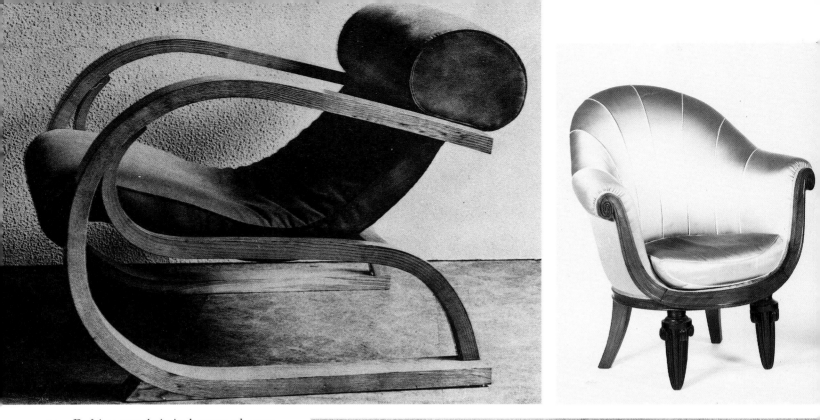

53 *Dufrêne:* armchair in bentwood, marketed by La Maîtrise. Illustrated in *Sièges contemporaines*, Paris

54 *Dufrêne:* pair of upholstered mahogany *bergères gondoles* exhibited at the Salon d'Automne, 1913. Illustrated in *Art et décoration*, May 1921; *La Renaissance de l'art français et des industries de luxe*, 1925; *Le Style moderne*, Henri Clouzot, Paris; and *Le Style 1925*, Yvonne Brunhammer, Paris, p. 43 (Collection of Primavara Gallery)

55 *Dufrêne:* sketch for a dining table and chairs in palisander and amboyna, marketed by La Maîtrise, *c.* 1924

56 *Dufrêne:* lady's desk and chair, marketed by La Maîtrise. Illustrated in *Art et décoration*, Jan.–June 1928; and *Petits Meubles modernes*, Paris 1929

57 *Dufrêne:* end-table, marketed by La Maîtrise. Illustrated in *Petits Meubles modernes*, Paris 1929, pl. 8

58 *Dufrêne:* smoker's table illustrated in *Petits Meubles modernes*, Paris 1929, pl. 8

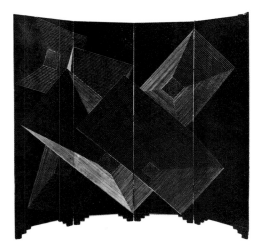

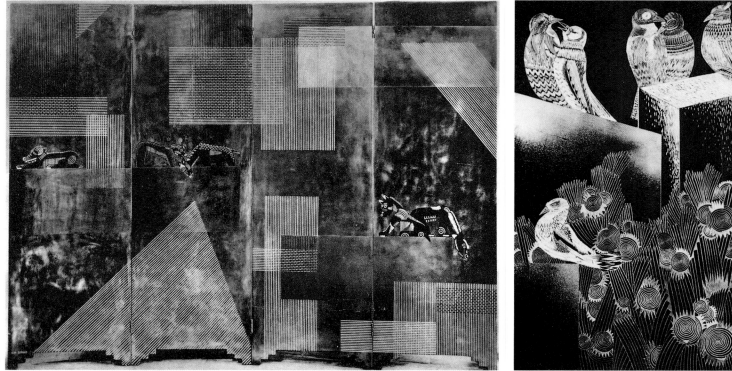

Opposite

59 *Dunand:* chair in lacquer commissioned by Mme Labourdette, *c.* 1928. Illustrated in *Jean Dunand, Jean Goulden,* exhibition catalogue, Galerie du Luxembourg, 1973, p. 5 (Photo: Sully-Jaulmes)

60 *Dunand:* four-panel screen in lacquer (Photo: Sully-Jaulmes)

61 *Dunand:* ensemble exhibited at the 1928 Lord & Taylor exhibition, including a gilt-oak two-tier table, two lacquered armchairs, a four-panel black lacquered small screen decorated with gold fish, a four-panel lacquered and gold-leaf screen, and a lacquer and eggshell portrait of Mme Agnès

bottom

62 *Dunand:* Four-panel screen in lacquer and ivory with decoration by Lambert-Rucki, *c.* 1925

63 *Dunand:* panel in lacquer depicting birds on a black background, *c.* 1929 (Collection of Jean-Jacques Beaumé)

This page

64 *Dupas:* pair of panels in *verre églomisé,* executed by Charles Champigneulle, 1935. Duplicates of the two central panels in the mural depicting the History of Navigation designed by Dupas for the *grand salon* on the ocean liner *Normandie* (Photo: Christie's, NY)

65 *Dupas:* 'Sylvie', mural in the *salon de thé* on the ocean liner *Ile-de-France.* The furniture is by Ruhlmann, the porcelain *vases réflecteurs* by Sèvres

66 *Dupré-Lafon:* desk in oak and chromed metal, early 1930s (Photo: Sully-Jaulmes)

67 *Dupré-Lafon:* table in oyster-veneered wood, *c.* 1930 (Photo: Sully-Jaulmes)

68 *Englinger:* boudoir, marketed by Le Studio Abran. Illustrated in *Intérieurs d'aujourd'hui*, Paris, pl. 15; and *Mobilier et décoration*, July–Dec. 1928

69 *Fabre:* dining room in grey maple executed and marketed by Les Artistes Décorateurs Français Modernes, in collaboration with Cardeilhac (silverware), Lachenal (faience vases), and Pompon (sculpture). Illustrated in *Ensembles choisis*, Paris, pl. 20; and *Mobilier et décoration*, July 1923, p. 9

Opposite top

70 *Follot:* dressing-table in giltwood and marble, illustrated in *Art et décoration*, April 1920, p. 114

71 *Follot: grand salon*, marketed by Pomone and exhibited at the 1925 Exposition. Illustrated in *Mobilier et décoration*, June 1925; and *Ensembles mobiliers*, Paris, pl. 7

Centre

72 *Follot:* private office, exhibited at the Salon of the Sociéte des Artistes Dé-

corateurs, 1931. Illustrated in *Intérieurs au Salon des Artistes Décorateurs 1931*, J. Hiriart, Paris 1931, pl. 17

73 *Follot: salon*, marketed by Pomone. Illustrated in *Intérieurs modernes*, Albert Novi, pl. 2

Right

74 *Follot:* desk, marketed by Pomone, *c.* 1923. Illustrated in *Intérieurs IV*, Léon Moussinac, Paris; and *Intérieurs modernes*, Albert Novi, pl. 4

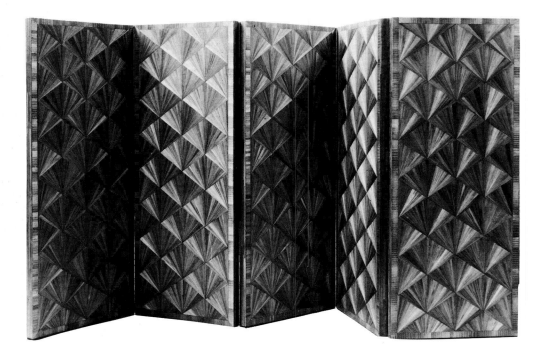

Top, left to right

75 *Frank:* pair of hinged nests of tables with straw veneer (Collection of Gallery Modernism)

76 *Frank:* cabinet in lacquer and *galuchat*

77 *Frank:* grand piano with central panel in *galuchat*

78 *Frank:* armchair veneered in *galuchat* (Collection of Barry Friedman, Ltd., NY)

Bottom

79 *Frank:* five-panel screen with repeating fan-shaped pattern in straw veneer (Collection of Gallery Modernism)

80 *Frank:* end-table in *galuchat* with ivory pull (Collection of Galerie Vallois)

81 *Frank:* tabouret in carved oak

82 *Frank: salon* for Templeton Crocker's house in San Francisco, *c.* 1928, showing a selection of furniture in straw veneer, vellum, and *galuchat*

83 *Fréchet:* cabinet in macassar ebony, gilt-bronze, and *galuchat, c.* 1935. Illustrated in *Mobilier et décoration*, Aug. 1937, p. 249 (Photo: Christie's, NY)

84 *Fréchet:* end-table in macassar ebony, marketed by E. Jacquemin. Illustrated in *Art et décoration*, July–Dec. 1931, p. 9. Part of the Karl Lagerfeld collection sold at the Hôtel Drouot, 21 Nov. 1975 (Photo: Lillian Nassau, Ltd.)

85 *Fréchet:* sketch of the drawing room exhibited in Le Pavillon de la Ville de Paris at the 1925 Exposition, the furniture executed by students at L'Ecole Boulle

86 *Gabriel:* corner of a studio, exhibited at the Salon of the Société des Artistes Décorateurs, 1927. Illustrated in *Intérieurs français au Salon des Artistes Décorateurs*, P. Follot, Paris 1927, pl. 18

87 *Gray:* desk in black lacquer with ivory handles, 1924. Illustrated in *Les Arts de la maison*, Summer 1924 (Photo: Sully-Jaulmes)

88 *Gray:* interior for Suzanne Talbot, illustrated in *L'Illustration*, 1933 (Photo: Sully-Jaulmes)

89 *Gray: salon* designed for Suzanne Talbot, the screen in the background in silvered glass by Paul Ruard. Illustrated in *L'Illustration*, 1933

90 *Gray:* 'The Night', four-panel screen in dark blue lacquer with applied silver decoration. Illustrated in *Wendingen*, No. 6, 6th series, Amsterdam 1924

91 *Gray:* day-bed in black lacquer with white feet, illustrated in *Wendingen*, No. 6, 6th series, Amsterdam 1924

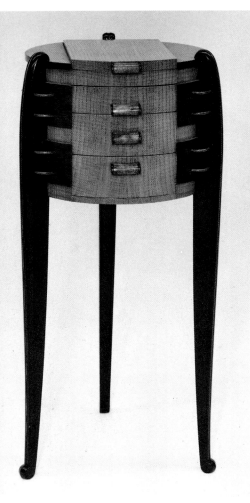

92 *Groult: poudreuse* in light and dark woods with *galuchat* handles (Collection of Barry Friedman, Ltd., NY)

93 *Groult:* armchair in *galuchat* (Collection of Barry Friedman, Ltd., NY)

94 *Groult:* side-chair in burl maple and ebonized wood, illustrated in *L'Art décoratif français 1918–1925*, Léon Deshairs, Paris 1926, p. 57 (Collection of Barry Friedman, Ltd., NY)

95 *Groult:* cabinet in *galuchat, c.* 1925. Illustrated in *Les Arts de la maison*, Autumn 1925

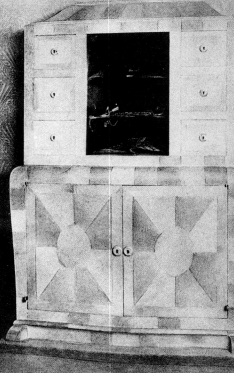

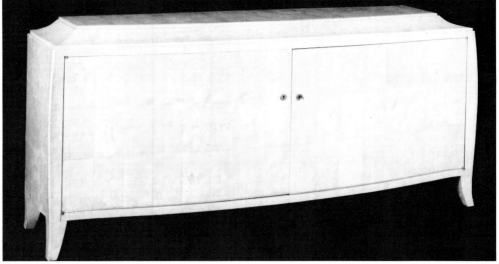

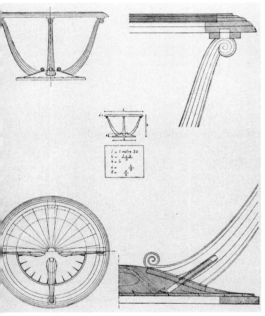

96 *Groult:* table in ebony with *galuchat* top executed by Adolphe Chanaux, the model exhibited by Groult in his bedroom at the 1925 Exposition (Collection of Barry Friedman, Ltd., NY)

97 *Groult:* commode veneered in *galuchat, c.* 1928, commissioned by Templeton Crocker for his San Francisco home (Collection of Peter and Sandra Brant)

98 *Groult:* design for a circular table, 1923

99 *Groult:* sketch of a bedroom, *c.* 1924, the bed housed in an alcove and flanked by built-in *armoires.* The chairs and bed in green *galuchat,* the tables and console in ebony with green amazonite tops. Illustrated in *Les Arts de la maison,* Spring 1925

100 *Groult:* salon, the furniture in ebony inlaid with ivory and *galuchat.* Illustrated in *Les Arts de la maison,* Spring 1925

101 *Guillemard:* desk with chair by Sognot, marketed by Primavera, *c.* 1927. Illustrated in *Petits Meubles modernes*, Paris 1929

102 *Guillemard:* desk with chair by Sognot, marketed by Primavera. Illustrated in *Petits Meubles modernes*, Paris 1929

103 *Hamanaka:* six-panel lacquered screen depicting a Bacchanal (Collection of Robert Vallois)

104 *Hamanaka:* six-panel screen in gold and maroon lacquer (Photo: Alain Lesieutre)

Opposite

105 *Herbst:* metal chair executed for Maurice Ravel, *c.* 1929 (Photo: Sully-Jaulmes)

106 *Herbst: torchère* in wrought-iron, exhibited at the 1925 Exposition and marketed by Cottin & fils. Illustrated in *Le Luminaire I*, Guillaume Janneau, Paris 1926

107 *Herbst:* pair of chairs in tubular aluminium with perforated metal seating, *c.* 1930 (Photo: Sotheby Parke Bernet, Monaco)

108 *Herbst:* living room in Herbst's house, 4 rue de Chateaubriand, Paris (Photo: Maria de Beyrie)

109 *Herbst:* smoking room in nickelled tubular steel and velours, exhibited at the Salon of the Société des Artistes Décorateurs, 1928. Illustrated in *Mobilier et décoration*, 1928; *L'Art vivant*, May 1928; and *Art et décoration*, 1928

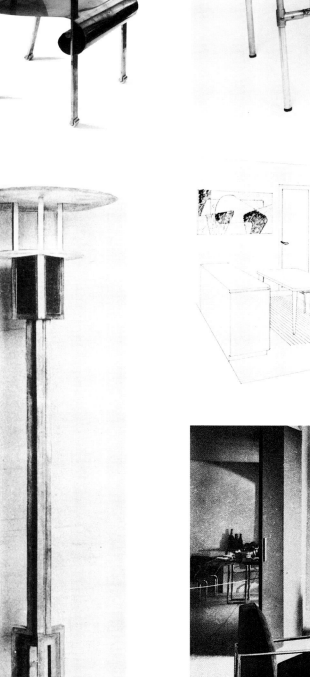

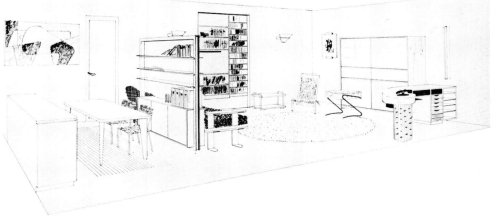

110 *Iribe:* commode in ebonized wood with gilt-bronze mounts (Photo: Sully-Jaulmes)

111 *Jallot (L):* writing table and chair for a girl's room, in sycamore and amaranth, with metalware by René Pacquel. Exhibited at the 1925 Exposition. Illustrated in *Mobilier et décoration*, Dec. 1925

112 *Jallot (L):* boudoir, *c.* 1927. Illustrated in *Intérieurs III*, Léon Moussinac, Paris, pl. 14

113 *Jallot (L):* secretary in macassar ebony with ivory veneer. Illustrated in *Art et décoration*, Sept. 1924; and *L'Art décoratif français 1918–1925*, Léon Deshairs, Paris 1926, p. 19

114 *Jallot (M):* reception hall, exhibited at the Salon of the Société des Artistes Décorateurs, 1930, in collaboration with Raymond Subes (wrought-iron), Despiau (sculpture), Paul Jouve (engravings), Perzel (desk lamp), Rodier (drapes and window shades), La Maison Besnard (Stic-B painting), and Mazda (general lighting). Illustrated in *Intérieurs V*, Léon Moussinac, Paris, pl. 42

115 *Jaulmes:* tapestry design for a couch designed by Louis Süe and comissioned by Mme de Ganay. Illustrated in *Art et décoration*, Jan. 1920, p. 20

116 *Joubert et Petit:* armoire in palisander and burl fernwood with oyster-patterned veneer, the model exhibited in a bedroom for Mme de G. Illustrated in *Art et décoration*, July 1924; *L'Art décoratif français 1918–1925*, Léon Deshairs, Paris 1926, p. 68; and *Intérieurs II*, Léon Moussinac, Paris pl. 34

117 *Joubert et Petit:* sketches for the secretary in pl. 118. Illustrated in *Intérieurs I*, Léon Moussinac, Paris, pl. 33

118 *Joubert et Petit:* secretary in palisander with ivory veneer, exhibited in a bedroom ensemble for Mme de G., 1924. Illustrated in *Art et décoration*, July 1924; *Mobilier et décoration*, May 1928; *Intérieurs d'aujourd'hui*, Waldemar George, Paris 1928, p. 6; *L'Art décoratif français 1918–1925*, Léon Deshairs, Paris 1926, pls. 17, 50; and *Le Mobilier français d'aujourd'hui (1920–1925)*, Pierre Olmer, Paris 1926, pl. 29 (Collection of Sydney and Frances Lewis)

119 *Joubert et Petit:* commode in stained oak, illustrated in *Petits Meubles du jour*, pl. 24

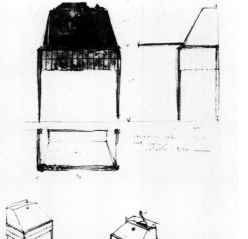

120 *Jourdain:* office in waxed oak, exhibited at the Salon d'Automne, 1922. Illustrated in *L'Art décoratif français 1918–1925*, Léon Deshairs, Paris 1926, p. 16; and *Art et décoration*, Nov. 1922

121 *Jourdain:* man's bedroom including a bed in polished walnut with portable metal lamp on a sliding table with shelf attachment, an armchair with adjustable back, and an oval bookcase table. Exhibited at the Lord & Taylor exhibition, New York, 1928

122 *Kinsbourg:* desk in macassar ebony, illustrated in 'Modern Interiors in Europe and America,' Herbert Hoffman, *The Studio*, 1930, p. 42 (Collection of Gallery Modernism)

123 *Kiss:* desk in wrought-iron, the lamp with alabaster shade. Illustrated in *La Ferronnerie moderne*, 3rd series, Henri Clouzot, pl. 28

124 *Kiss:* torchère in wrought-iron, illustrated in *La Ferronnerie Moderne*, 3rd series, Henri Clouzot, pl. 26

Angst introduced Dunand to his employer, the noted sculptor Jean Dampt, who took him on as an apprentice. Up to 1902 he studied sculpture and mastered its materials: bronze, plaster, stone, and ivory.

Dunand appears to have established himself in a small studio near the Orléans gate in 1903, making his début at the Société Nationale des Beaux-Arts the same year. Two years later he introduced a selection of Art Nouveau metal vases with designs in *repoussé* copper, followed by vases, bookcovers, jewelry, and even fabric designs in copper, tin nickel, lead, pewter, steel, and bronze. Decoration was applied to the hammered metal objects by engraving, chasing, and encrustations of gold, silver, and nickel.

The transition to lacquer came in 1909 when Dunand first saw the lacquered creations of Paris-based Japanese artisans. He was immediately drawn to the medium, recognizing its lavish gloss and vibrant colours as the ideal embellishment for his metalware. An exchange followed, Dunand trading his hammering technique for the secret formulas of lacquer application. In 1912 he became associated with the Japanese master, Sougawara, with whom Eileen Gray had worked since 1907.

Lacquer is the most onerous of materials, requiring time and energy to achieve its dramatic and sparkling effects. Dunand refused any compromise, applying it in the traditional Eastern manner (see Introduction, p. 12). Some lacquered furniture was applied with a rough, chipped surface finish known as *laque arrachée*. This technique, often used in landscape panels, was described by Jean Guiffrey in a 1927 article in *La Renaissance de l'art français et des industries de luxe*: 'Over the well abraded and polished layers a mixture of lacquer and the appropriate clay is applied, from which certain parts are scraped with a spatula; thus an uneven surface, with roughness and holes, is obtained, which is then gilded ... Treated in this way, mere panels are pleasing to the touch, harmonious to the eye, and pick up the light in the most attractive way.'

Dunand served as a Red Cross volunteer in the First World War, moving after the armistice to larger quarters at 70 rue Hallé which included metal, cabinetry, and lacquer workshops. The latter employed mainly Indochinese artisans, preferred not only for their mastery of lacquerwork, but also because they appeared to have developed an immunity to the health hazards involved in working with lacquer.

Dunand had been credited with the invention of crushed eggshell as a decorative motif. The technique was developed as a dramatic substitute for the colour white which could not be obtained through vegetable dyes. He described its application in a 1936 interview with M.-A. Dayot published in *Art et téchnique*: 'With nothing but this eggshell, you can obtain very varied effects if you apply it on to fresh lacquer in large crushed pieces, either the inside of the egg upwards, or

the outside, or even in small juxtaposed pieces or perhaps sprinkled in fine particles.' The impact of eggshell was most pronounced on a red or black lacquered ground.

Although Dunand tried personally to execute as many commissions as possible, he drew freely on the talents of his associates to decorate his work, in particular, Lambert-Rucki, Goulden, Schmied, and Jouve. Infrequent collaborators were Bieler, Henry de Waroquier, Georges Dorinac, and Sergé Rovinski. Completed items were displayed both independently and through others, Dunand providing lacquered screens for the ensembles of Salon coexhibitors such as Michel Roux-Spitz, Léon Bouchet, Théodore Lambert, and Mallet-Stevens. He also provided a wide range of lacquered finishes for other cabinetmakers, notably Ruhlmann, Printz, and Legrain.

Dunand's most important client was the milliner Mme Agnès, for whom he designed a complete interior, jewelry, and scarves. Other clients included Jeanne Lanvin, Madeleine Vionnet, Ambassador Philippe Bertholet, Mme Yakoupovitch, and Mme Labourdette. Further commissions were afforded by the ocean liners: a games room for the *Ile-de-France* (1928); a dining room for the *Atlantique* (1931); and, for the *Normandie*, a series of panels entitled 'Pastures and Joys of Mankind' in incised gold lacquer.

Dunand grasped every opportunity to exhibit, not only at the two annual Salons but, throughout the 1920s and early 1930s, at the Galeries Georges Petit and Galerie Jean Charpentier with Goulden, Schmied, and Jouve. Other exhibitions included the Société Nationale des Beaux-Arts, Galerie des Arts Modernes, Galerie George Rouard, and the Salon des Tuileries. At the 1925 Exposition he designed the smoking room in the Ambassade Française, in collaboration with Charles Hairon and Léon Jallot. Included was a large pentagonal cabinet in black lacquer with incised silver animals by the Polish-born cubist painter and sculptor, Jean Lambert-Rucki, which is recognized today as one of the period's most sensational objects. For the Hôtel du Collectionneur he provided lacquered panels and *dinanderie*. In 1928 he participated in the Lord and Taylor exhibition, returning to New York the following year for a two-man show (with Jean Pellenc) at the Rosenbach gallery. He also exhibited in Tokyo, Madrid, Athens, Bucharest, and Barcelona.

Dunand's evolution from small metalware objects to large lacquered wood furniture can be traced in his changing choice of decoration. By 1913 the earlier *repoussé* flora on copper vases had given way to painted overlapping triangles and chevrons, and by 1921, when he exhibited his first postwar models of lacquered wood furniture at the Galerie Georges Petit, the earlier geometric decoration had been expanded to meet the demands of a broadening clientele. Every style was now embraced. Panels were painted with African and Oriental figures, abstractions, realistic land-

scapes, stylized flowers, exotic fish and birds, and Lambert-Rucki's fantastic animals. Dunand's only apparent failure was a range of mosaic panels, two of which, 'Leda' and 'Two Figures', are illustrated in a 1932 article in *Art et décoration*.

In 1925 Dunand was joined by his elder son, Bernard (b. 1908). The outbreak of the Second World War terminated the flourishing business and brought family tragedy. Bernard was mobilized and captured. The second son was killed in 1940. Raw materials became increasingly scarce, forcing Dunand to close his workshops. He died 7 June 1942.

Dupas, Jean:

Although a painter by profession, Dupas warrants inclusion here because his work was commissioned to complement the furnishings of many of the most important interiors of the 1920s and 1930s. No other contemporary artist caught so exactly the stylistic mood of the period's interior decorators; no other paintings and panels are so eagerly sought after by today's Art Deco collector.

Dupas was born in 1882 in Bordeaux, the home of the ceramicist René Buthaud, later a close friend and collaborator. He was educated in the city's School of Fine Arts, transferring later to Paris to complete his education under Carolus Duran and Albert Besnard. Listed at the Salons from 1909, Dupas was awarded the celebrated Prix de Rome the following year for his 'Eros vainqueur de Dieu Pan'. His distinctive 1920s style, in stark defiance of his training and the spirit of the Jury's award, evolved during a sabbatical in Italy.

The early 1920s brought two important works, 'Jugement de Paris' and 'Les Antilopes'. The elongated figures in both brought quick censure. Dupas defended himself in a 1928 article in *creative art*: 'I do not aim at a systematic deformation . . . but one must realize that a painted decoration is part of an architectural scheme, and hence it demands scale and strong vertical lines. . . . Here, in the art of the South, the figures are tall, slim, and distinguished. For me elongation is not even a stylization, but rather a means of expression. . .' Dupas explained further the deliberation behind his style: 'Why are there so many voluminous robes in my pictures? Not because I have a special predilection for them, but merely because they are useful to me. The same holds good of the very tall hats worn by certain of my figures. Of course I find this very expressive, but it is a purely subjective impression; while I consider that they occupy indispensable surfaces on my canvas. My frequent use of birds in my compositions is because they give me the opportunity of putting in patches of light where it seems to me fitting. The ancients, who carefully arranged their compositions with figures lying down, seated, standing or on horseback, often had recourse to angels in order to provide patches of light at the top. I have substituted

birds, which for us moderns are the best available expedient.'

The 1925 Exposition generated an important commission, 'Les Perruches', for the *grand salon* in Ruhlmann's Hôtel du Collectionneur. Dupas also exhibited a portrait in the *salon* of the Ambassade Française, and a large mural, 'Les Vins de France', in the Bordeaux pavilion. Later works included Ruhlmann commissions for La Chambre de Commerce de la Seine and the *Ile-de-France*; posters and catalogue covers for the Salon des Artistes Décorateurs; a brochure for the furrier Max; and decoration for Sèvres vases executed by Gensoli.

Dupas' mural for the *grand salon* on the *Normandie* has proved his most celebrated commission. Executed by Charles Champigneulle in *verre églomisé* panels, the work depicts the History of Navigation, extending across two full sides of the sumptuously furnished room. Numerous individual panels survived the fire which destroyed the ocean liner at its berth in New York harbour during the Second World War, and a complete section has recently been installed in the Metropolitan Museum of Art. Other works, such as the panel 'Le Ciel et l'eau' which separated the *grand salon* from the smoking room, were commissioned throughout the de luxe areas on the *Normandie*.

Dupré-Lafon, Paul:

Dupré-Lafon remains an elusive talent. His furniture either seldom reaches today's market or, more probably, is seldom identified as his. That it is invariably unsigned is only part of the problem; virtually no biographical information or illustrations have survived on its author or his work.

Born in Marseilles in 1900, Dupré-Lafon studied at the city's Academy of Art before moving to Paris in 1923. A career in interior decoration followed, from which he emerged in the late 1920s with a wealthy private clientele which included the bankers Dreyfus and Rothschild. He designed complete interiors for private homes and villas and from this it can be assumed that a large number, if not all, of his furniture were *pièces uniques*. He avoided both the annual Salons and the 1925 Exposition, so reducing his exposure to a minimum. Only one contemporary magazine, *Ensembles mobiliers V*, appears to have shown examples of his work – a dining room/bar and a bedroom, *c.* 1935. Both are clean, functional, and completely anonymous, indistinguishable from those of Jean Royère, Saddier, Maurice Champion, and Pascaud in the same pages. Earlier pieces bear a close resemblance to Dufet's designs at the time. A pair of chairs in mahogany and burl amboyna auctioned recently in Paris shows his forceful linear style to better advantage. His treatment of the front and back feet, in particular, is innovative and exciting. The cushioned leather seat, upholstered by Hermès, reminds the viewer of Dupré-Lafon's emphasis on sumptuousness.

No other biographical information is available on Dupré-Lafon beyond that he died in Boulogne-Billancourt in 1971.

Ecole Boulle:

A 1923 article in *Mobilier et décoration* traced the history of Ecole Boulle. Founded in 1886 by the City of Paris in the 12th *arrondissement* as l'Ecole Supérieure des Arts Appliqués aux Industries de l'Ameublement, this cumbersome title was shortened in 1891 to l'Ecole Boulle, after Louis XIV's celebrated cabinetmaker, André-Charles Boulle. André Fréchet, the school's director from 1919 to 1934, formulated its 1920s charter: 'We are training young people so that they will be able to work in an adaptable and knowledgeable way with artists or in industry. We would also hope that they could become skilful executants for those talented designers through whom modern French furniture is about to make its mark.' Today, its function remains fundamentally unchanged: to provide the finest possible instruction for the nation's next generation of cabinetmakers.

Students were provided with tuition (a four-year apprenticeship) in three broad categories: furniture, bronze-work, and precious metals. By the early 1920s the school could boast of close to three thousand graduates, many of whom had achieved recognition far beyond the Faubourg Saint-Antoine, Paris's furniture manufacturing district. In an Art Deco context, such graduates included Genet and Michon, Raymond Subes, Louis Gigou, Armand Rateau, Gabriel Englinger, Etienne Kohlmann, and G. Boisselier, all of whom participated in a student retrospective exhibition at the Musée Galliera in 1923.

Frequent competitions were arranged among the students. A typical contest, in 1927, provided for the design and execution of a commode which measured one metre in length, 90cm in height, and 45cm in depth, with one or more doors and drawers, the front partially or totally *bombé*.

Whenever appropriate, Fréchet exhibited the school's workmanship at the Paris Salons, often using his own furniture designs to ensure their entry. In 1922, for example, furniture executed by the students to his designs was shown at the Salon d'Automne. Outstanding individual cabinetry works were also occasionally displayed. A 1924 article in *Art et décoration* illustrates an extremely handsome Art Deco-style commode in amaranth with marquetry cross-banding, designed by the student J. Rothschild and executed by three others, J. Poussin, R. Bourdon, and J. Faure. Two years later, a fourth-year student, P. Prabon, designed and executed a palisander and violetwood cabinet displayed at the Salon des Artistes Décorateurs. The critics were invariably enthusiastic: such examples were found to incorporate a blend of harmony, logic, and rigorous construction!

Professors at the school exhibited independently of the students, Letessier, for example, displaying a living-room ensemble in palisander and thuya at the exhibition L'Art Urbain et le Mobilier at the 1923 Salon d'Automne.

At the 1925 Exposition, under Fréchet's general supervision and in collaboration with Pierre Lardin and Henri Martin, the school provided the furnishings for the Salon of Honour in the Pavillon de la Ville de Paris. The pavilion was by tradition a group project for all the city's technical schools, each being assigned a room or gallery in which to display its talents. Ecole Boulle participated in a similar event ten years later at the 1935 Exposition de Bruxelles, the furniture designed by M. Charlot, Fréchet's successor.

Englinger, Gabriel:

Born in Paris in 1898, Englinger attended the Ecole Boulle before joining La Maîtrise in 1922. He established himself quickly as one of the Studio's foremost decorators, participating in various projects in its pavilion at the 1925 Exposition: a dining room, library, and man's bedroom, in collaboration with Dufrène; a small *salon* with Guiguichon; and a carpet for the pavilion's ground floor reception area. The dining room, in particular, proclaimed Galeries Lafayette's message of 1920s opulence to the visiting bourgeoisie: plush silk-upholstered chairs and floral wallpapers announced the new prosperity.

Englinger remained at La Maîtrise for three more years, collaborating on the Studio's projects and also exhibiting independently at the Salons. A 1926 dining room, with tableware by Georges Chevalier and drapes by Mme Chabert-Dupont, was marketed by La Renaissance de Meuble. A year later a bedroom in violetwood and amaranth at the Salon des Artistes Décorateurs was offered by La Maîtrise. At some point in 1928 Englinger moved to Le Studio Abran, a change that may be judged propitious in the light of his most successful interior to date, which he displayed at the 1929 Salon des Artistes Décorateurs: a living room containing furniture designed on the semicircle, with silk upholstery, beneath illuminated frosted-glass ceiling panelling. Other interiors at the Salons that same year included a smoking room and an exhibition hall.

Englinger's furniture for La Maîtrise was manufactured by the Studio's cabinet shop. From 1928 his designs were executed, among others, by Véroni and Larchevêque. Some designs are too stiff; others, such as tubular steel armchairs in 1931, are at first glance indistinguishable from contemporary examples by Mies van der Rohe.

Englinger continued to exhibit in the 1930s, joined now by Marguerite Englinger for draperies and embroidered panels. In 1934 he moved to L'Isère, accepting a lectureship in the decorative arts in Grenoble and another in applied design at

Voiron. After the Second World War he returned to the Paris Salons, moving again in 1949 to accept an appointment at the Ecole Régionale des Beaux-Arts in Rennes.

Fabre, Auguste-Victor:

Virtually nothing is known of Fabre beyond that he was born in Montpellier (Hérault). A decorator by profession, he exhibited at both annual Salons from 1919, showing a selection of single pieces of furniture and complete ensembles manufactured at his studio at 20 rue de Miromesnil.

Fabre's furniture was ultraconservative, and its neat, unpretentious lines are today impossible to identify. The warmth and comfort within his rooms was created by his selection of bright floral wallpaper. Surprisingly, most critics approved unreservedly of his work; in *Mobilier et décoration*, an *armoire* shown at the exhibition of L'Art Urbain et le Mobilier at the 1923 Salon d'Automne was deemed to have a 'beautiful simplicity' which 'defies all criticism'. Yvanhoë Rambosson, in his review of the 1922 Salon des Artistes Décorateurs, wrote of 'a *bergère* by Fabre and Steeg which seems to me the best piece in the Exposition at a cost of only Fr1,300'. Fabre's furniture seems to have evoked only one unfavourable criticism, that of Gaston Varenne in a 1921 *Art et décoration* article: '. . . an enormous divan-bookcase, where the books are banished behind piles of cushions and which also has, heaven knows why, a mirror that assumes an excessive importance. This piece of furniture, designed for many ends (always a dangerous idea), fits in poorly with the serious side of this place which is neither a real study nor a traditional bourgeois drawing room.'

Fabre's preferred woods were maple, macassar ebony, and walnut. His furniture was marketed through either his own studio or La Maison Decaux et Maous.

Follot, Paul:

Follot was born in Paris in 1877, the son of Félix Follot, a noted wallpaper manufacturer. Trained as a sculptor, he had the good fortune to be taught by Eugène Grasset, whom he succeeded in 1904 at the Ecole Supérieure des Arts Décoratifs on the rue Vavin. The years 1901–03 were spent at La Maison Moderne, where he worked alongside Abel Landry and Maurice Dufrène. The experience was beneficial, Follot managing to extricate himself afterwards from these heady *fin-de-siècle* days with a reinforced sense of the true French tradition and the road to its resurgence. By 1904 he had branched out on his own, his versatility and aristocratic taste documented in a 1909 *Art et décoration* article by Charles Saunier. His jewelry, clocks, furniture, light fixtures, and carpets show a neoclassical discipline allied to rich decoration, characteristics which he maintained throughout a lengthy career in the decorative arts.

Follot's furniture in the transitional prewar years is today classified as 'pure' Art Deco, a tribute to his pioneership. The Musée des Arts Décoratifs correctly anticipated the importance of his work, purchasing several pieces directly from the 1912 Salon. One chair in particular – its pierced back carved with a basket of fruit and summer blooms – is today seen as an Art Deco classic.

By the outbreak of the First World War, Follot was installed in the grand home and office built for him by Pierre Selmersheim at 5 rue Schoelcher, Montparnasse. In 1919 he returned to the Salons, his furniture executed by Lucien Rigateau, among others, and marketed by Coupé. His designs were, as ever, neoclassical and aristocratic, their richness imparted by brightly coloured and tufted damask upholstery on giltwood frames carved by Laurent Malclès. Added opulence came from floral carpets and wallpapers executed to his designs by Savonnerie and Cornille Frères. Follot gave full vent to his design skills in the 1921 commission of a first-class drawing room on the ocean liner *Paris*.

In 1923 Follot accepted the directorship of the design studio Pomone, opened by Au Bon Marché on the rue de Sèvres. He remained with the firm until 1928, when he joined Serge Chermayeff at the newly established Paris branch of Waring and Gillow at 130 rue la Boétie. The Paris critic for London's *Morning Post* caught exactly Follot's style and panache in his review on 22 July 1929 of the exhibits at the Salon des Artistes Décorateurs: 'Undoubtedly the finest was a dining room by M. Paul Follot, executed by Messrs Waring and Gillow. Coral wood and sycamore were here used for table and chairs, the latter being upholstered in rich orange, and the former laid for dinner without a cloth. This combination set in walls covered with lacquered wood panels, with scenes of exotic plants, birds and beasts gave an indescribably rich effect. Such a dining room, indeed, could only be used by princely persons.' If not all Follot's clients were royal, they could be forgiven in such an ambience for thinking themselves momentarily to be so.

Waring and Gillow disbanded its Paris office at the end of 1931 and Follot reverted to his immediate postwar role as an independent decorator. He continued to exhibit his ensembles at the Salons, and some of these were marketed by his brother, Charles. In 1935 came a commission on the *Normandie* and participation in the Exposition de Bruxelles. Follot died during the German occupation in 1941 at Sainte-Maxime.

Follot saw himself as traditionalism's protector, fighting on both flanks. André Salomon described his philosophy in a 1925 article in *L'Art vivant*: 'Paul Follot, more than anyone else among the best, manifests a highly logical mind and a rigorous feeling for French continuity. As in politics, it is

often the most daring who remain within the tradition, who are the tradition and its real keepers.' On the one flank was an old adversary: the advocates of mass-production, headed by his former colleague, Maurice Dufrène. On the other, somewhat allied but incalculably more insidious in that they claimed the future for themselves, were the rationalists. Follot totally rejected such 'extremism', expounding on his beliefs at every opportunity. His words went unheeded, however, and in 1929 Pomone appointed René Prou, a confessed modernist, to lead it into the new decade.

Follot's participation in the 1925 Exposition was greater than that of any other designer. With the assistance of Th. Leveau and Albert Guénot, he designed *all* the rooms in the Pomone pavilion. The furniture was mostly in macassar ebony, the *salon*, in particular, proving a great success with the critics, as were the pavilion's two Pleyel pianos. He also designed the antechamber in the Ambassade Française and collaborated with René Crevel on the Art et Industrie des Textiles exhibit.

Frank, Jean-Michel:

Frank was born in Paris in 1895, the third son of Léon Frank, a German Jew who had settled in Paris to establish a stockbrokerage in partnership with a M. Wolfsohn. He grew up on the avenue Kléber and attended the Lycée Janson de Sailly from 1904. The outbreak of the First World War brought the emigrant family into conflict with its German relatives. Jean-Michel's brothers, Oscar and George, were mobilized, as were their northern cousins. In 1915 tragedy struck. The brothers were killed within one week of each other on the Western front. The father, overwhelmed by grief and the conviction that the deaths had been desired by the cousins in the opposing trenches, committed suicide by throwing himself out of a window. The mother, likewise inconsolable, withdrew totally from the world and was placed in an insane asylum, where she died in 1919. (Family tragedy repeated itself in the Second World War when Jean-Michel's paternal niece, Anne Frank, author of *The Diary of Anne Frank*, died in a German concentration camp.)

At the beginning of 1920 Frank found himself alone, supported, fortunately, by a substantial inheritance from his mother. He appears to have spent the next five years eradicating the past, travelling extensively and establishing himself in Paris's fashionable inner circle, a milieu which would later serve him well in his decorating business. In 1927 he commissioned Chanaux to decorate his apartment at 7 rue de Verneuil. Thus begun a partnership which was to survive until the Second World War. Chanaux's workshop and warehouse in the Ruche section of the rue Montauban continued to operate, its floors now used by an expanded team of carpenters (under M. Martin), cabinetmakers (under M. Verneau), varnishers (M. and Mme Greff), and draughtsmen (under M. Saladin). Also included were a straw marquetry workshop, showroom, upholsterer, and leatherworker (Mlle Classen-Smith). Finished works were displayed from 1930 at the firm's showroom at 140 Faubourg Saint-Honoré.

But beyond the rue Montauban were other well-established collaborators whose assistance greatly enhanced Frank's own reputation. Included were a stellar group: the brothers Alberto and Diego Giacometti, who from 1934 were commissioned to provide a wide range of furnishings, such as light fixtures, vases, andirons, and chimneys, in plaster and bronze, the latter cast by Alexis Rudier; Christian Bérard (carpet designs); Paul Rodocanachi (furniture); Emilio Terry (furniture and interior designs); Ernest Boiceau (carpets and objects); Salvador Dali (furniture and screens); and even Picasso (screens and fabrics). Frequent visitors to the Faubourg Saint-Honoré shop, these artists put the stamp of fashion on Frank's work.

In the light of his association with the virtuoso Chanaux and the host of talented artists and craftsmen with whom he collaborated, the following questions need asking: How much did Frank himself actually design? Was he, in fact, the creative force behind his interiors or was he rather a catalyst whose energies and enthusiasm inspired others? The answers lie somewhere in the middle ground. Frank apparently concerned himself primarily with an object's form and historical influences. The exact design and its execution he left to the artist.

Frank's style evolved from his respect for French traditionalism. The late-eighteenth-century's rigid forms were stripped of their relief ormolu ornamentation and applied with sumptuous veneers. The result, soon known as 'the Frank line', was highly distinctive: furniture with stiff, functional proportions, its decoration limited to flat surface areas. Like other modernists – Djo-Bourgeois, Lurçat, and Barret – Frank reduced furniture to its simplest expression, but, unlike them, remained faithful to the principles of refinement and luxury, believing that people need an environment of warmth and elegance for their psychological well-being. Beyond this, Frank's conception of interior decoration was architectural. There is a finely tuned relationship between the length of a sofa and that of a mantelpiece which, in turn, relates to the dimensions of the windows, the height of the ceilings, or the space of the doors. And, like Djo-Bourgeois, less furniture was more. A story survives of Jean Cocteau's comments on leaving Frank's sparsely furnished apartment on the rue de Verneuil, 'A nice young man. Very nice, in fact. Pity the burglars got everything.'

An early and valued client was Elsa Schiaparelli who in 1927 was, like Frank, trying to establish herself. His furnishings for her apartment on the rue Barbet-de-Jouy matched her purse: bare, white interiors with inexpensive

upholstery and drapes. Later, as her acclaim as a dress designer grew, he designed both her shop in the place Vendôme and her townhouse in the rue de Berri. Other commissions followed in quick order, most importantly for the Viscount Charles de Noailles, for whom Frank furnished two rooms in his townhouse on the place des Etats-Unis. By 1930 Frank was known widely by the Paris plutocracy as the arbiter of taste in interior design. Clients sought him out, among them M. and Mme Robert Gérard (the château de Villette), Ambassador Bertholet (a residence on the boulevard des Invalides) Mme Esterez, Mme Cerf, Mme Artaud, and Jean-Pierre Guérlain. His overseas clients included, in the United States, Templeton Crocker in San Francisco (c. 1928) and Nelson Rockefeller in New York (1930s).

Today it is Frank's veneers which distinguish his works from those of his contemporaries. All were in earth tones and lavish in appearance: straw marquetry, vellum, parchment, snake- and sharkskin, suede, cane and gypsum. These were applied to walls, furniture, doors, and chimney surrounds. Lamp bases, if not in bronze or plaster by the Giacometti brothers, were made of curved strips of ivory or hewn from rock crystal, quartz, or alabaster. Curtains and fabrics were provided by Broenne or Mme Cronen-Fels; lace by Selloes, and leather by Hermès. Béraud's carpet designs were executed by Lauer. Frank's choice of furniture woods, initially hidden by the feast of straw and sharkskin, included ebony, sycamore, and maple.

In early 1939, faced with the imminent German invasion of Paris, Frank set sail for South America, where he settled momentarily in Buenos Aires, finding patronage and friendship in Mme Eugenia Errazuriz and other South American clients. The Paris workshop and gallery were closed while he awaited events. The fall of the capital was followed by the Nazi requisition of part of his inventory on the rue de Montauban. The balance was ransacked. Frank's hopes of returning were dashed and, encouraged in part by a lectureship offer from the New York School of Fine and Applied Arts and sponsorship by Mrs Archibald Manning Brown, he decided to move to the United States. In March 1941, in one of the deep bouts of depression which had punctuated his life, he jumped from a New York building to his death.

Fréchet, André:

Born in Châlons-sur-Marne, Fréchet was a professor of Art History at the Ecole des Beaux-Arts in Nantes from 1905 to 1911 before moving to Paris to join the faculty at the Ecole Boulle. In 1919 he assumed the directorship of the school, a position he held until 1934. The following year, aged sixty, he stepped down, accepting a part-time lectureship to teach Design and Art History at the Académie Julian.

As a furniture designer, Fréchet is best known for his association with the Ecole Boulle, for which he proved a most inspired and effective administrator and instructor. He retained a dual identity, however, displaying objects at the Salons in his own name, in addition to those which he designed for manufacture by the Boulle students.

Fréchet exhibited at the Salons from 1919 until the late 1930s. A suite of furniture in macassar ebony inlaid with copper and amaranth commissioned in 1919 by M. Levasseur, is now in the collection of the Musée des Arts Décoratifs, Paris. Three years later, at the Salon des Industries d'Art, Fréchet showed an armoire/psyche in maple with bronze mounts by the sculptor L. Malclès. A dining room at the 1924 Salon des Artistes Décorateurs was perhaps his finest creation. In walnut and palisander with carved floral panelling by Malclès, the overall effect was one of restrained opulence. Warm colours and expensive woods generated an ambience that disguised the furniture's austere Louis XVI influence.

At the 1925 Exposition, Fréchet's work was omnipresent. In addition to his participation in the Ecole Boulle's exhibit in the Pavillon de la Ville de Paris, he displayed four other ensembles: a dining room, marketed by the Strasbourg firm of Jacquemin; a bedroom offered by E. Vérot; and, in collaboration with Lahalle et Lévard, a reception *salon* and boudoir for the Studium Louvre. The critics found the boudoir, in particular, most refined; lemonwood furniture upholstered in silk damask was set off against mural fabrics by A. Marty.

Fréchet marketed his furniture at the Salons in the late 1920s through Vérot and Jacquemin; later also through Jeanselme. Several pieces bear a close resemblance to models created by others at the time, particularly Dominique and D.I.M. There is no way to determine now who influenced whom. A Fréchet dressing-table in 1929 shows the dilemma facing today's art historian: its design is nearly identical to a model offered by Dominique in the same year; in both, the sides curve inward at the foot to form a broad stretcher centring as a padded footrest. To complicate matters further, the matching chair was virtually identical to a host of others at the same Salon. Successful Art Deco designs, as in all periods, provided immediate inspiration to others. Fréchet managed to retain his individuality, however, by juxtaposing pale woods, especially maple and Canadian birch, with feminine fabrics and wallpapers.

In the 1930s Fréchet was frequently in partnership with Paul Fréchet. Their study, displayed at the 1930 Salon des Artistes Décorateurs, listed a score of collaborators, including Max Vibert (carpets), Genet and Michon (lighting), and Brunet-Meunié (fabrics). Walnut and palisander became preferred woods. New collaborators emerged; for example, the muralist Pico and the lighting firm of Véronèse. In 1931, Fréchet showed a bedroom which included a striking two-

tier end-table, an example of which was offered in the celebrated 1975 auction of Karl Lagerfeld's Art Deco collection at the Hôtel Drouot, Paris. Fréchet was still productive at the advent of the Second World War.

Gabriel, René:

Gabriel was born in 1890 at Maison Affort (Seine). A wallpaper designer by profession, he soon branched out into the related fields of fabrics and carpets and from there to porcelain decoration, theatre design, and furniture ensembles. Three Paris addresses are listed from 1920 to 1939: a wallpaper shop, Sansonnet, in the rue de Solferino; another at 20 avenue de l'Opéra; and a third at 24 rue Victor-Noir, Neuilly, where Gabriel opened his Ateliers d'Art in 1934.

He exhibited furniture from 1919 at both the annual Salons, often in combination with fabrics and wallpapers, the last-mentioned marketed by Les Papiers Peints de France or Nobilis. In 1921, at the Salon des Artistes Décorateurs, he displayed a boudoir which included an ebony chair upholstered in cream silk and a small table-desk. The critics felt that the chair was 'inspired' by an earlier example by Louis Süe. The following year came two further room settings: first, a bedroom in which the furniture was veneered in broad bands of pylma and grey sycamore set off against bright yellow and lemon floral wallpaper and upholstery. The critics approved, in most part. Yvanhoë Rambasson, for example, wrote in *Art et décoration* that it was 'pleasing and comfortable. I object only to the narrow opening of the chairs, which is quite illogical. The *armoire*, however, which has a simple form, is enriched by the choice of juxtaposed woods. The idea of the four uprights rising from the floor up to the top is excellent. I regret only that they were truncated at the ends like gate posts. A way should have been found to link them more successfully to the cornice on the piece.'

Also exhibited was a dining room in cherry and burl elm. Another dining room, in 1923, was less successful. The critic for *Mobilier et décoration* found it of ill-considered proportions – the buffet too massive for the lightly proportioned chairs and tables. To compound the problem, the carpets and curtains showed 'an audacious selection of colours'.

The 1925 Exposition brought measured success: Gabriel showed a vestibule for Primavera in which crisp, modern furniture was given optimum effect by high, vaulted ceilings. A kitchen, however, marketed by Les Etablissements Harmand, with a chevron parquetry floor, appears today to be outmoded: a provincial simplicity pervades, in stark contrast to neighbouring exhibits which boldly proclaimed the new modernism. Gabriel participated also in the pavilion of the Ambassade Française, coordinating the decoration for a young woman's bedroom with, among others, Jean Perzel for the lighting, Schenck for the metal-work, Jean Luce for the ceramics and glassware, Georges Gimel for the fabrics, and Jan and Joel Martel for the sculpture. By 1925 Gabriel's belief in large edition furniture – inexpensive and for the bourgeoisie – was becoming more pronounced. A room corner shown at the 1927 Salon des Artistes Décorateurs included oak furniture designed for mass production, as did a study and dining room two years later retailed by Viacroze-Décoration. Soon to come was a study with built-in desk and couch beneath adjustable shelving screwed directly into the walls.

Gabriel continued to exhibit at the Salons, in 1931 showing a *coin de repos* for the ocean liner *Ile-de-France* and, four years later, a suite of colonial furniture in oak with tubular chromed mounts, entitled 'L'Equipment d'une salle à manger et d'une chambre.' The dining room reinforced Gabriel's message on mass-production: furniture should consist of multiple, interchangeable parts, the theme of a 1934 article by Léon Chancerel in *Art et décoration* entitled 'Eléments... combinaisons... ensembles, de René Gabriel'. Illustrated were three pages of designs for modular furniture – called 'Eléments R.G.' – to be assembled as required for bedroom, kitchen, or bathroom. Gabriel 'wished to put his art not at the service of the rich collector or snob, but of the average Frenchman'. His intended market, M. Chancerel explained, was not for the financially rich, but for the rich in spirit.

Gabriel's furniture is today virtually impossible to identify without a corroborating illustration from a contemporary magazine. A minor force in Paris's Art Deco furniture movement, his designs were frequently fresh and inspired though the impact of his interiors depended in large part on his wallpapers. His furniture, seen on its own, often appears bland and anonymous.

Genevrière, Marcel (see Dominique)

Goulden, Jean:

Goulden's inclusion in this book is based on his role as a designer of small household furnishings – clocks, lamps, and panels – and as an occasional collaborator on Dunand's furniture. He was born 14 June 1878 in Charpentry (Meuse), the son of a prosperous Alsatian farmer. A gifted student, Goulden graduated in medicine from the Ecole Alsacienne, moving to Paris in the late 1890s to set up his practice. A picture of an aesthete, if not a dilettante, emerges, the wealthy young physician dabbling in the arts and revelling in Montmartre's night-time activities. In 1908, following the publication of his thesis on the physiology of a detached heart, Goulden was appointed a consultant to Paris's hospitals.

continued on page 97

30 *Groult:* side-chairs in ebony and stained tortoise shell painted by Marie Laurencin and executed by Adolphe Chanaux. The model was awarded third prize in a competition of chair design organized by David Weill in 1924. Illustrated in *Art et décoration*, 1925 (Photo: Sotheby Parke Bernet, NY)

31 *Groult:* sideboard in ebony with *galuchat* panels and openwork frieze in palisander inlaid with ivory (Collection of Sydney and Frances Lewis)

32 *Groult:* table and *bombé* chest-of-drawers in *galuchat*, the painting by Marie Laurencin. The chest-of-drawers was exhibited in Groult's bedroom in the pavilion of the Ambassade Française at the 1925 Exposition (Photo: Sully-Jaulmes)

33 *Herbst:* lady's desk with detachable lamp, exhibited at the Exposition de Bureaux des Dames organized by the Union Centrale des Arts Décoratifs at the Pavillon de Marsan, Feb. 1928. Illustrated in *Art et décoration*, Jan.–June 1928; *Meubles et objets d'architecture dans les années 1925*; exhibition catalogue, Galerie Maria de Beyrie, 19 Nov.–31 Dec. 1976; *Les Echos des industries d'art*, Feb. 1928; and *25 années U.A.M.*, René Herbst, Paris 1956, p. 99 (Collection of Maria de Beyrie)

34 *Herbst:* dressing-table in chromed steel and mirror, commissioned by the Princess Aga Khan, 1930. Illustrated in *25 années U.A.M.*, René Herbst, Paris 1956, p. 99; *Mobilier et décoration*, 1933; *Meubles et objets d'architecture dans les années 1925*, exhibition catalogue, Galerie Maria de Beyrie, 19 Nov.–31 Dec. 1976; and *Art et décoration*, Jan.–June 1932, p. 99 (Collection of Maria de Beyrie)

35 *Iribe: bergère gondole*, in sculpted wood. A similar pair is illustrated in *Femina*, Jan. 1925, p. 30; and *Maison et jardin*, Dec. 1961, p. 110 (Photo: Sotheby Parke Bernet, Monaco)

36 *Jallot (L and M):* ensemble with lacquered cabinet, screen, and table, exhibited at the Salon of the Société des Artistes Décorateurs, 1929. Illustrated in *Art et industrie*, June 1929, p. 32; and *L'Amour de l'art*, July 1929, p. 241. The painting by Tamara de Lempicka, clock by Baccarat, and carpet by Francis Bacon (Photo: Sully-Jaulmes)

37 *Joubert et Petit:* jewelry cabinet in eggshell and Chinese red lacquer. Illustrated in *DIM, exposition générale de ses oeuvres*, firm's catalogue, 1926; and *Mobilier et décoration*, 1926 (Collection of Jacques Mostini)

38 *Legrain:* filing cabinet in red lacquer with silver mounts, the drawer pulls numbered alphabetically, for Jacques Doucet. Exhibited in Paris in September 1929 (Collection of Sydney and Frances Lewis)

39 *Legrain:* (left and centre) table and stool in silvered and black lacquered wood and chromed metal, *c.* 1924. Designed for the veranda of Mme Tachard's house at Celle-Saint-Cloud. (Right) birdcage for Doucet, *c.* 1923, in ebony, lacquer, and vellum. Illustrated in 'Quelques ensembles de Pierre Legrain', *L'Amour de l'art*, 1924 (Photo: Sully-Jaulmes)

40 *Legrain:* cabinet in stained oak and metal, for Jacques Doucet, *c.* 1924. The gilt-bronze and enamelled andirons by Gustave Miklos, 1925; a similar pair is illustrated in *La Renaissance*, 1928, p. 200 (Photo: Sully-Jaulmes)

41 *Legrain:* fall-front desk in sycamore and chromed metal, *c.* 1929. Exhibited at the 1930 Salon des Artistes Décorateurs, and illustrated in *Art et décoration*, July–Dec. 1930, p. 47 (Collection of de Lorenzo Gallery)

42 *Mallet-Stevens:* desk with inset leather writing surface and recessed nickelled metal pentrays, *c.* 1928, the chair in lacquer and tubular steel by Labormétal, *c.* 1929. The desk lamp by Le Chevalier; the lacquered screen by Jean Dunand; the floor lamp by Damon. The desk, from Mallet-Stevens' house in Auteuil, was donated by his widow to the Musée des Arts Décoratifs, Paris, in 1958. Illustrated in *Répertoire du goût moderne III*, Paris; and *Meubles modernes en métal*, Pierre Pinsard, pl. 15 (Photo: Sully-Jaulmes)

43 *Mère:* sideboard in macassar ebony, lacquered *repoussé* leather, and ivory (Collection of Félix Marcilhac)

44 *Mère:* cabinet in macassar ebony, lacquered *repoussé* leather, and ivory (Collection of Félix Marcilhac)

45 *Mergier:* three-panel screen in *repoussé* copper and wrought-iron depicting Diana the Huntress, the wrought-iron frame by Edgar Brandt (Photo: Christie's, NY)

46 *Printz:* cabinet with seven copper doors inlaid with silvered geometric decoration, on copper *toupie* feet (Photo: Sully-Jaulmes)

47 *Printz:* dressing-table with crosshatched Gabonese ebony veneer, on oxidized metal feet (Collection of J.-J. Dutko)

48 *Printz:* desk in kekwood with gilt-metal mounts and legs, the model illustrated in 'Eugène Printz et son atelier', *Mobilier et décoration*, 1938, p. 4; and *Art et décoration*, Oct. 1982, p. 42 (Collection of J.-J. Dutko)

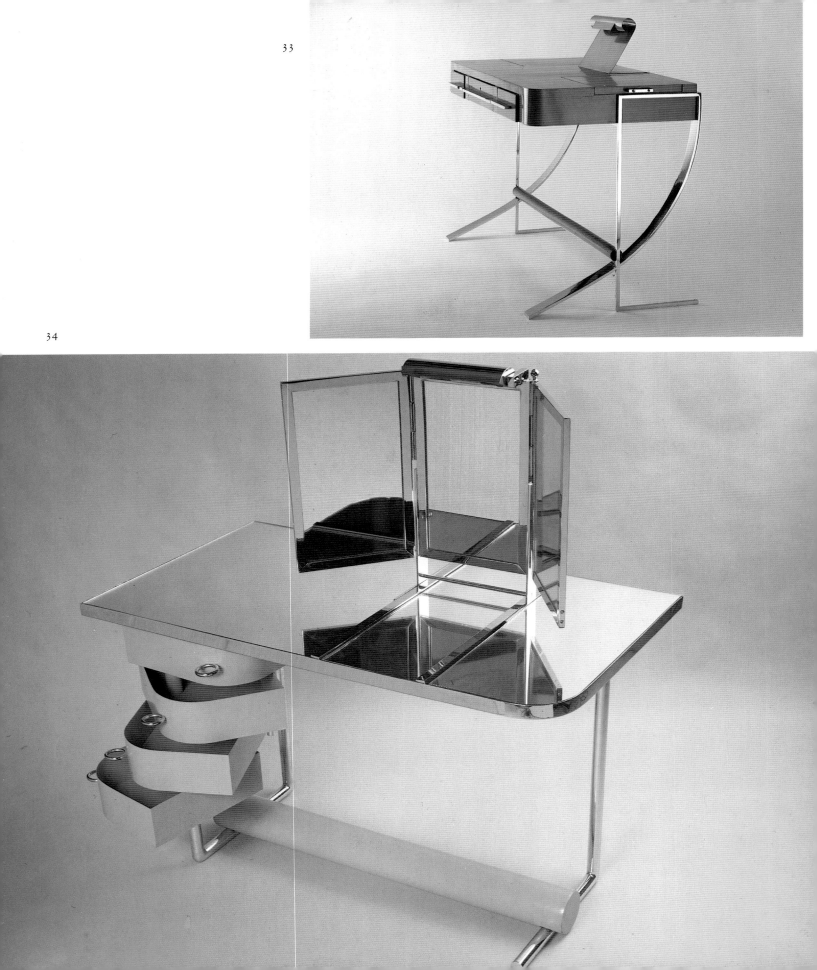

33

34

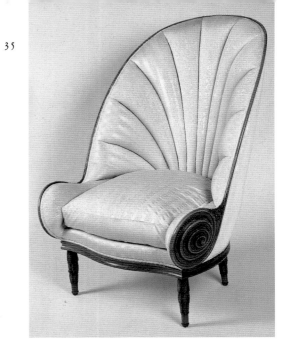

147

Goulden volunteered during the First World War and was assigned to the Macedonian front. Demobilized, he was invited by the monks at nearby Mont Athos to stay on. The sojourn exposed Goulden to Byzantine enamelware. On returning to Paris, he sought out Jean Dunand for instruction in the technique of *champlevé* enamelling. Teacher and student became collaborators, Goulden soon working on several Dunand projects.

Accepted into Dunand's circle, whose members included Paul Jouve and François Louis Schmidt, Goulden participated in the group's exhibitions at Les Galeries Georges Petit and La Galerie Charpentier. He also exhibited independently at the Salon des Artistes Décorateurs, especially from 1929, after he had transferred to Rheims to continue his medical career. He died in 1947.

Goulden rejuvenated the technique of *champlevé* enamel, bringing to it a modern interpretation. A range of boxes, *coffrets*, lamps, panels, book plates, and clocks were decorated with strikingly abstract designs. The cubism of Braque and Picasso was transformed sharply into three dimensions. The enamelled 'fields' were housed in silvered or gilt copper mounts, the object's curved or angular contours often enhanced further with lacquer.

Goulden's works are highly prized by today's collectors. Fortunately, he signed most of his creations, so eliminating the confusion that could have arisen between his abstractions in metal and those of Gustave Miklos.

Gray, Eileen:

Gray was born 9 August 1879 in Enniscorthy, County Wexford, Ireland. Her mother, the granddaughter of the tenth Earl of Moray, inherited the title Baroness Gray, a name taken later by the children. Eileen's father, James Maclaren Smith, was a minor Victorian painter and it was in this tradition that his daughter entered London's Slade School of Art in 1898. In her free time she learned the technique of Oriental lacquer in the shop of D. Charles at 92 Dean Street, in Soho.

Gray arrived in Paris in 1902, installing herself five years later in a flat at 21 rue Bonaparte, which she retained for the rest of her life. Lacquer remained her prime interest, and she sought out the Japanese lacquer master, Sougawara, to perfect her rudimentary training. A close friendship and working relationship developed, from which, around 1910, came her first pieces of lacquered furniture.

She remained a brilliant individualist and pioneering spirit, her prewar furniture anticipating the international modern style fifteen years later. She recalled her philosophy at the time in a 1973 interview with Eveline Schlumberger in *Connaissance des arts*: 'My idea was to make things for our time; something which was possible but which no-one was doing. We lived in an incredibly outdated environment.' Her style, original and therefore difficult to categorize, was a pastiche of Far Eastern and French influences well in advance of her contemporaries. She rejected the past, and later vehemently denied any kinship with the Art Deco movement, which she saw as based on retrospective tendencies.

In 1913 Gray's exhibit at the Salon des Artistes Décorateurs came to the attention of the discerning Jacques Doucet, who the next year commissioned three important *pièces uniques*: the celebrated 'Le Destin' screen and two tables, one an exotic creation with leg capitals carved as lotus blooms, the other a two-tiered circular model with four pairs of twin block-carved feet. The screen marked the transition in style soon to emerge in Gray's work. On its front were depicted classical figures; on the reverse a starkly abstract design on the same red-lacquered ground – a bold proclamation by the artist that she could move easily in either direction.

Nearly all Gray's early pieces were unique, despite her intention to market her work in small editions. She made most of her furniture herself, assisted for many years by a Japanese artisan, Inagaki, who specialized in ivory carving and lacquer application.

Gray's career was interrupted by the war years, part of which she and Sougawara spent in London. She returned to Paris after the armistice to reopen her workshops and immediately received a major commission: decoration in 1919 of the apartment of the milliner Suzanne Talbot (Mme Mathieu Lévy) on the rue de Lota. The result included some of Gray's most luxurious and theatrical creations, two of which were particularly eye-catching. The first was an African-inspired boat-shaped chaise longue on twelve arched feet, and the second an armchair upholstered in salmon pink, its front legs carved as rearing serpents. Draped animal skins added to the air of luxury. It was immediately evident, however, that Gray had taken a step away from her earlier style and toward a more architectural approach, especially in the gallery leading to Mme Lévy's bedroom, which was panelled with a black lacquered block screen.

In the late spring of 1922 Gray opened the Jean Désert gallery at 217 Faubourg Saint-Honoré opposite a Pleyel showroom. The significance of its name is not known. She displayed a range of *pièces uniques* – lacquered screens, furniture, carpets, wall hangings, lamps, and mirrors – in addition to sculpture by Ossip Zadkine and engravings by Chana Orloff. She also offered a personal decorating service. Her furnishings were manufactured in three studios; one in the rue Bonaparte (furniture); another in the rue Visconti (rugs and carpets), and a third at 11 rue Guènégaud (lacquerware). The venture was never a great success; only the carpets managed to find regular buyers. Gray abandoned the gallery in early 1930, the same year in which she was

commissioned to design some pieces of furniture for the Maharajah of Indore.

In the 1920–25 period Gray exhibited only intermittently at the Salons. The severe criticism awaiting her 'bedroom/boudoir for Monte Carlo' at the 1923 Salon des Artistes Décorateurs no doubt finally convinced her that recognition lay only in private patronage. The exhibit drew praise only from J. J. Oud, leader of the de stijl movement, whose enthusiasm was responsible for an entire 1924 issue of the Dutch journal *Wendingen* being set aside for a survey of Gray's interior decoration. Two further publications illustrate a range of Gray's furniture during this period: *Les Arts de la maison* (Summer 1924), and *1925* (exhibition catalogue, Musée des Arts Décoratifs, Paris, 15 October 1976–2 February 1977). Lacquer continued to dominate in her bookcases, desks, floor lamps and panels. From 1925, however, Gray introduced chromed tubular steel and aluminium increasingly into her furniture. Some of these pieces were marketed in London by Aram Designs. Here again, Gray was in the avant-garde: her articulated chaise longue in sycamore, leather, and steel preceded that of Le Corbusier, and her tubular chairs those of van der Rohe and Breuer.

The third phase in Gray's creative development came in the mid-1920s. Between 1927 and 1929, encouraged and assisted by the Rumanian architect Jean Badovici, she built a villa for herself, called 'E-1027', at Roquebrune on the Mediterranean coast. She explained her philosophy on architecture as follows: 'The interior design must not be an accidental consequence of the façade; it must have a complete, harmonious, and logical life. Far from being subordinated to the exterior structure, it must on the contrary govern it.' The house's interior was comprised of an 'organization of space', and contained several well-known models, such as the 'Transat' chair and a circular bedside table. In 1930–31 she undertook a second architectural project, that of a studio/apartment for Badovici in the rue Chateaubriand. Her third and final project, in 1934, was a second villa for herself called 'Tempe a Pailla', at Castellar, four kilometres from Menton. As in the two earlier ventures, the furniture was ultramodern and gadgety: cantilevered tables, cabinets with pivoting drawers, tubular chairs, and sliding cupboards and windows.

Gray lived at Castellar until 1939, when she moved into a small flat in Saint-Tropez. The next year, as an enemy alien, she was exiled by the occupying German army to Lourmarin. She came back after the war to find her home ransacked. By the mid-1950s her eyesight had deteriorated to the point where she was no longer able to drive, so she returned to her apartment in the rue Bonaparte. Here she continued to experiment with new materials and design concepts. In 1974 Mary Blume, a journalist from *Réalités*, found her busily at work with new forms of plastic, as diffident and energetic at

the age of ninety-five as she had always been. She died in 1976.

Groult, André:

No record appears to exist of Groult's upbringing and education. Born in Paris in 1884, he made his début at the Salons around 1910 as a decorator, exhibiting intermittently into the 1930s.

By 1904 Groult had rejected Art Nouveau as specious, its philosophies a cruel hoax foisted on a credulous public by loud but misguided publicists. The search for a logical style lay elsewhere. Groult believed that the most important variable in the road ahead was the client. Although every epoch had its share of skilled artisans, these could do nothing without an elite clientele which approved or disapproved of their attempts. The customer was, as always, right. The future lay in the past, but only insofar as there is a permanent order and harmony essential to good taste. If one detected Louis XVI and Restauration in Groult's furniture designs, it was only because they, too, drew on this timeless order.

Groult's designs were executed by a small group of craftsmen at his atelier at 29–31 rue d'Anjou. The most noted of these was Adolphe Chanaux, whose brief collaboration after the Second World War influenced Groult's choice of materials immeasurably. A range of artists were commissioned to provide the paintings and murals which brought colour into his interiors: most particularly, Marie Laurencin, but also Charles Martin, Espagnat, Laprade, Drésa, and Iribe (before 1914).

To a considerable extent, Groult's reputation rests today on the woman's bedroom which he exhibited in the Ambassade Française at the 1925 Exposition. The furniture was at once restrained and provocative. The marvellous *bombé* chest-of-drawers, veneered in *galuchat* with ivory banding, became the pavilion's 'conversation piece', its anthropomorphic shape an endless source of conjecture among the critics. The remaining furniture, in a mixture of *galuchat*, ebony, and upholstery velours by La Maison Delaroière et Leclercq, imparted the intended feeling of elegance and femininity. Other collaborators were listed as Paul Brandt, Georges Fouquet, and Raymond Templier. Elsewhere in the Exposition Groult participated in exhibits for Fontaine & Cie, Christofle-Baccarat, Les Arts du Jardin, La Société de l'Art Appliqué aux Métiers, and Instruments de Musique.

Articles in *Art et décoration* (June 1920) and *Les Arts de la Maison* (1924) analysed the absence of curves and relief decoration on Groult's furniture. Sumptuous materials – especially *galuchat* and horn – provided the desired effect. By 1930 some of his interiors looked distinctly like those of Frank, the walls and chairs in straw paper. He was not,

however, above occasional censure; his living room at the 1920 Salon des Artistes Décorateurs was judged by the *Art et décoration* critic to be too theatrical: the vermilion and gold band of Austrian feathers an unfortunate contradiction of modern dictates. Groult died in 1967, at the moment that his works again became fashionable.

Guiguichon, Suzanne:

Guiguichon was born in Paris in 1900; her address in the 1920/30s is listed as 11 rue Constance. She joined La Maîtrise in 1921, making her début at the Salon d'Automne the following year. Much of her work remained anonymous, for though the firm encouraged its designers to exhibit independently on occasion, their primary function was to design modern interiors offered through Galeries Lafayette. This clearly inhibited personal ambitions, and may have influenced Guiguichon's decision to become independent in 1929.

Her furnishings were marketed by various firms, La Compagnie des Arts Français, La Pépinière, and the cabinet-makers Speich Frères in the Faubourg Saint-Antoine. Collaborators included Henri Brochard.

At the 1925 Exposition Guiguichon exhibited two ensembles, the first an artist's studio in the stand on the Esplanade des Invalides which she shared with Paul Pouchol. The room, entitled charmingly a *coin pour causer* (corner for 'chat'), attempted 'an informal formality'. Guiguichon participated also in La Maîtrise pavilion, sharing the credit with Gabriel Englinger for a living room. The furniture, executed by La Maison Morand et Angst and La Maison Debusscher, was strikingly Art Deco. The couch, in particular, was lavishly *à la mode*, with plush deep damask cushions within a gondola-shaped frame. Guiguichon also participated in the Ambassade Française.

Her style was sober and less feminine than that of contemporary women designers. By 1930, a dull functionalism predominated. A dining room and studio displayed at the 1931 Salon des Artistes Décorateurs were sleek and ultra-modern, the chromed tubular armchairs similar to earlier models by Mallet-Stevens and Sognot. A modular couch stretched the length of two walls, silk-upholstered bolsters providing the only sense of comfort. Not everyone approved, the critic for *Art et décoration* writing in 1930 of her 'abuse of straight lines. A little superfluity is not always useless. This designer has looked at Djo-Bourgeois without understanding, without understanding the lesson.'

Guiguichon continued to exhibit at the Salons in the 1930s, showing a range of rooms. Preferred woods were palisander, sycamore, and rosewood. She developed a private clientele and worked both through, and beyond, the Salons until the 1950s.

Guillemard, Marcel:

Born in Paris in 1886, Guillemard was a generation older than most of the young designers and architects in the vanguard of the 1920s style. Early training at the Kriéger furniture-manufacturing firm in the Faubourg Saint-Antoine, where he joined Louis Sognot, imbued him with a strong sense of the rich heritage and tradition of French furniture (Antoine Kriéger was a prominent manufacturer of all eighteenth-century styles). Guillemard later followed Sognot to Primavera, where he served as a top designer and decorator from the end of the First World War until his premature death in 1932 at the age of forty-six.

It appears that all of his interiors were marketed through the firm, Guillemard being credited both on his own and in collaboration with Sognot, Chauchet-Guilleré, and Georges Lévard.

Guillemard played an important role in furnishing the Primavera pavilion at the 1925 Exposition. Displayed were a dining room and office. The former, in particular, received wide coverage for its strikingly modern lemonwood furniture, executed by Olesiewicz; in particular, an oval table with flaring pedestal foot. Cubist murals by Chassaing brought warmth to the room's formality.

Sognot's influence showed increasingly, Guillemard introducing nickelled tubular furniture into his repertoire after 1925. Certain chairs, such as the models displayed in a tea-room at the 1929 Salon des Artistes Décorateurs, are indistinguishable from those of his colleagues. This is true also of the tubular hall furniture which he showed the following year, and of a modular metal bar, whose components could be adjusted to provide innumerable combinations of shelf space.

Guillemard's adherence to his classical training ensured neat, angular, and, above all, functional interiors. Sometimes he was even judged to have carried traditionalism too far. Yvanhoë Rambosson, for example, wrote in *Art et décoration* of an otherwise pleasing dining room at the 1922 Salon, that 'The table is perfect in its proportion. It is a shame that the subjects in marquetry in the middle of the sideboard and the dumb-waiter are at odds with the design. Surely there is something better than a Greek figurine to ornament a modern table? I have another objection directed at the whole set which, in my opinion, is rather serious: its elegance is a bit funereal. The furniture is made of palisander encrusted with maple flecked with silver speckles. This brings to mind an association with mortuary decoration, an association strengthened by the presence of motifs which suggest tombs of antiquity.' Coincidentally, the young girl's room which Guillemard exhibited the same year at the Salon d'Automne received identical censure in *Mobilier et décoration* for its use of marquetry decoration on rigidly modern furniture. The

lesson clearly did not require further reinforcement; from 1923 Guillemard eliminated all surface decoration.

Hamanaka, Katsu:

Hamanaka was born in Sappora, Japan. He was trained as a lacquer-worker and it is probable that he was lured to Paris in the 1920s by the prospect of ready employment. The revived vogue for lacquer – initiated in part in the prewar years by Eileen Gray – caused a shortage of qualified artisans. Dunand and Jallot, among others, looked to the East for extra technical expertise.

Little is known of Hamanaka's training, beyond that he emerged at the Salons in 1929 to exhibit a range of lacquered tables, screens, and boxes. In 1980, frail but elated, he walked into the gallery of a startled Left Bank Art Deco dealer to announce that he was the creator of the lacquered screen on display. Promising to return, Hamanaka left. The dealer read of his death shortly after. A part of Art Deco history had slipped elusively away, almost unnoticed.

It seems from Hamanaka's limited output that he worked alone. It is not even known if he himself manufactured the wood furniture to which he applied his lacquered decoration. His screens, especially the one depicting two bulls in combat, show powerful design allied to technical virtuosity.

Herbst, René:

Herbst was born in Paris in 1891. His education and career until the First World War are sketchy: on qualifying as an architect, around 1908, he gained experience in Paris, London, and Frankfurt. From 1919 he applied himself to the challenges of modern living, concentrating mainly on metallic furniture, shop window displays, and interior lighting, to the point that the critic André Boll referred to him in *Art et décoration* as *homo triplex*.

He made his début at the 1921 Salon d'Automne, displaying furnishings for a rest area (*coin de repos*) in the Musée de Crillon. Later came a wide range of architectural commissions: cinemas, shop façades, restaurants, offices, aeroplanes, and exhibition galleries. In 1924 the award of the Blumenthal prize enhanced his reputation, adding credence to his crusade for modernism.

Herbst participated widely in the 1925 Exposition, both as a member of the Jury and as an exhibitor. He took boutique 27 on the Alexander III bridge, designing both the building and its interior, the latter in collaboration with Les Etablissements Siègel (general installation), La Compagnie des Lampes Mazda (lighting), Coupé (carpets), L'Art du Bois (furniture), and Chatel et Tassinari (cushions). Elsewhere, he displayed a mahogany and nickelled metal piano in the Pleyel exhibit, and designed boutiques for Cusenier, Lina Mouton,

Les Etablissements Siègel et Stockmann Réunis, and Paul Dumas. For the last-mentioned he also designed the furnishings, in collaboration with G. Vernet.

In 1927 Herbst was appointed President of the Syndicated Chamber of Decorative Artists, a prelude to his cofoundership of the U.A.M. two years later. The 1930s brought increased renown: Herbst won the commission to decorate the Maharajah of Indore's palace in India. He also participated in the 1935 Brussels Exposition. At the outbreak of the Second World War, he volunteered, with Jules Leleu, for the French airforce, and was demobilized the following year. In 1946 he was elected President of the revived U.A.M.

From 1926 Herbst began to replace the earlier wood components in his furniture with metal, glass, and mirror. Mounts, in tubular nickelled metal, were often serpentine, leading a contemporary critic to label them 'bicycle handlebars', which, in turn, led to a Herbst soubriquet, 'Man of Steel'. Designs were rigorous, logical, and functional, the furniture devoid of mouldings and ornamentation. Herbst never fully renounced wood, however, retaining it for de luxe commissions such as his apartments in the early 1930s for the Aga Khan and the prominent art dealer, Léonce Rosenberg. As the *Mobilier et décoration* wrote of his furniture at the 1933 U.A.M. exposition, 'Réne Herbst, the champion of metal work, is not the intransigent enemy of wood, and he shows us this by exhibiting a table and chairs which have no metal.' Upholstery was in velours, cane, leather, or fabric by Hélène Henri. In 1929 Herbst introduced horizontal expandable metal straps on to the backs of his chairs.

By 1930 Herbst was in strong competition with Adrienne Gorska, Louis Sognot, Claude Lévy, and Emile Guénot for the metal furniture market. A desk illustrated in a 1933 article in *Art et décoration* emphasized his philosophy on mass-production: its rectangular top was flanked by filing racks, shelves, and drawers, each element an optional addition to the basic unit. If the piece did not exactly meet an individual client's needs, extra components could be added piecemeal.

Great emphasis was placed on interior lighting, both direct and indirect. Herbst retained André Salomon as his consultant, their designs executed, in most part, by La Compagnie des Lampes Mazda. Two models bear special mention: a dining-room chandelier displayed at the 1928 Salon d'Automne and, the following year, a curious floor lamp comprising a circular metal disc supported by twin rods. Herbst also pioneered the science of modern shop window illumination. Concealed lighting provided daytime nuances and night-time visibility.

One of Herbst's lesser-known achievements as an interior decorator was his modernization of the mannequins used in the dress shops which he furnished, especially those of Siègel and Luminex. These traditionally life-size wax models were transformed by Herbst into wood and glass silhouettes.

Iribe, Paul:

Recognized as the precursor of the 'pure' Art Deco style – Ruhlmann, Süe et Mare, and Groult all readily acknowledged his influence – Iribe's creativity was confined largely to four short years, from 1910 to 1914. His fame appears, in retrospect, to match that of Colonna: a brief, meteoric burst of brilliance followed by years of obscurity.

Born in Angoulême in 1883 as Paul Iribarnegaray – a name understandably contracted – he was trained as a commercial artist and became famous as a caricaturist for a range of Parisian journals, including *L'Assiette au beurre, Le Rire, Le Cri de Paris*, and *Le Témoin*.

At some stage in the early 1900s Iribe developed the related skills of interior decorating, no doubt with the encouragement of Paul Poiret, for whom he designed a range of jewelry, fabrics, wallpapers, and furniture. It was another couturier, however, who sealed his fame as a furniture designer: Jacques Doucet. Doucet decided in 1912 to offer his collection of eighteenth-century furniture at auction, and commissioned Iribe to furnish his new apartment at 46 avenue du Bois (now the avenue Foch). With his young assistant, Pierre Legrain, Iribe designed a marvellous range of modern furniture, three pieces of which – two *bergères* and a commode – were donated subsequently to the Musée des Arts Décoratifs, Paris. A further pair of *bergères*, bearing the broad, circular, snail-like, spiralled armrests which characterize his most spectacular work, were included in the celebrated sale of Doucet's collection at the Hôtel Drouot in 1972.

Iribe's style provided elegance in a quite unprecedented manner. Whereas a Louis XV flamboyance is evident in the fluid designs, the discipline is distinctly 1800. There is also a pleasing touch of femininity and comfort. Preferred woods were zebrawood, with its distinctive grain, macassar ebony, and mahogany. A favourite stylized motif was the rose, later to become the celebrated 'rose Iribe', a symbol of high Art Deco, despite its prewar conception.

In the winter of 1914, perhaps spurred by the outbreak of war, Iribe set sail for the United States for what became a sixteen-year sojourn. He settled in Hollywood, designing giant stage sets for Cecil B. de Mille. In 1930, at the age of forty-seven, he returned to France, where he took a studio at 4 avenue Rodin. He was engaged intermittently until his death in 1935 in designing jewelry for Coco Chanel.

Jallot, Léon-Albert and Maurice-Raymond:

Of the oldest generation of 1920s decorators, Léon Jallot was born in Nantes in 1874. Paris, however, was his training ground. He attended nightschool in Montparnasse before entering the Ecole des Beaux-Arts, from which he emerged with the basic technical skills that established him as a respected artist, wood sculptor, and engraver. His career

began around 1894. In 1899 he was placed by Samuel Bing at the head of the Studio which manufactured the furnishings for La Maison de L'Art Nouveau on the rue de Provence. Jallot therefore participated in the production of some of the *belle époque*'s most prized works – those designed by the firm's renowned threesome: de Feure, Colonna, and Gaillard. Despite this, Jallot later claimed that he had always reacted against the style's excesses. When the Maison Bing closed in 1903, he established his own studio at 17 rue de Sedaine. His versatility was immediately apparent; carpets, fabrics, lamps, and furniture being exhibited at the Société Nationale des Beaux-Arts the following year.

The prewar years saw him evolve into a master artist/craftsman. His furniture was traditional: formal eighteenth-century shapes decorated with heavily carved floral panels and mouldings.

From 1919 Jallot abandoned such cabinetry, relying for decoration on burled veneers, especially jacaranda and wild cherry, to provide contrasting compositions. Emile Sedeyn wrote in *Art et décoration* of his exhibit at the 1921 Salon des Artistes Décorateurs: 'His furniture has the easy elegance of ideas created in a flash and then mulled over – ingenuity, savoir-faire, and patience are all combined in his work.' Marquetry, in ivory or mother-of-pearl, enhanced the wood's rich grain.

Maurice Jallot was born in Paris during the 1900 Exposition, an auspicious beginning, certainly, for an intended career in the arts. On graduating from the Ecole Boulle, he joined his father's studio in 1921, leaving after a while to gain outside experience before rejoining in 1930. Imbued with the same energetic versatility as his father, he displayed a range of ensembles and individual pieces at the Salons. His most important commission was the Hôtel Radio, reviewed in many contemporary magazines.

At the 1925 Exposition father and son exhibited widely, both singly and in partnership. Furnishings were provided for the Hôtel du Collectionneur (*grand salon*), Ambassade Française (smoking room, man's bedroom, reception hall, and small *dégagement*), La Société Noël, La Maison de Bretagne, and Gouffé Jeune. It was clearly unnecessary, with such exposure, to retain their own exhibition stand.

Léon and Maurice displayed at the Salons for many years. Their furniture in the 1920s was in wood – palisander, walnut, amboyna, camphor – sometimes enhanced with *galuchat* or eggshell. Shapes were unimpeachable: sober and practical. The lessons of 1900 had been well learned. From 1926 they faced the problem common to all woodworkers: whether to adjust to, or fight, the revolutionary introduction of glass and metal. They chose the former, introducing a distinctive range of modern furniture: stainless steel card-tables with reversible tops, mirrored cabinets, and tea-tables. Lacquered doors, psyches, and screens were a perennial

favourite, motifs ranging from monkeys and angular fish to pure geometry.

It is often assumed that Dunand executed Jallot's lacquer-work, but the evidence is to the contrary. A 1920 article in *Art et décoration*, which traced the evolution of the medium, showed an Indonesian artisan applying lacquer to a table in Jallot's workshop. A further article by G. Rémon in 1929 analysed Léon's sculpted woods and lacquers. His long mastery of both media was cited, and emphasis given to lacquer's preservative effect on untreated wood. Decorative panels and screens were carved in bas relief with equatorial forests, deer, and monkeys, which were then defined in polychromed lacquers on a gold ground. These were produced into the mid-1930s.

Léon, retired since the 1940s, died in 1967. Maurice continued the family business until nearly 1950.

Jaulmes, Gustave-Louis:

An artist of considerable and varied talents, Jaulmes is known today for his Art Deco tapestries. Born in Lausanne in 1873, he trained as an architect. Between 1901 and 1905 came a transition to painting; and later, in collaboration initially with Messrs Menu and Boigegrain, the emphasis was increasingly on tapestry. In the interim, he exhibited regularly at the Salons, displaying a wide range of decorative objects. He made his tapestry début in 1915, abandoning his rigid painting tutelage for that of the eighteenth-century traditions of Gobelins, Beauvais, and Aubusson. His first works were in *petit point*. The emphasis was on multicoloured compositions, each a transposition into brightly tinted wool of his preliminary sketch. The Musée Rodin at the Hôtel Biron commissioned two tapestries during the First World War. Other commissions illustrated in a 1920 article by Léon Deshairs in *Art et décoration* show allegorical panels depicting Music, Abundance, and *Flóreal* (the period between 20 April and 19 May).

Furniture commissions included tapestries for Louis Süe. Jaulmes's designs were classical, inspired by Flemish prototypes from the 1780s: formal flower sprays and baskets of fruit interlaced with ribbons, matching the stiff Louis XVI forms of Süe's *canapés à corbeille*. A typical tapestry screen from 1919, depicting two pigeons and fruit on a pink ground, is in the collection of the Musée des Arts Décoratifs, Paris. A number of small-sized furnishings – chair backs, screens, etc. – were woven by his wife, Marie-Georges.

Jaulmes's versatility is evident in his participation at the 1925 Exposition. He was listed in the catalogue of the Hôtel du Collectionneur as an artist. Also shown were seven oils depicting 'Les Mois en Fête' in Süe's Salle du Grand Palais, murals for the Hall of Honour in the Sèvres pavilion, and tapestries for furniture in the Musée d'Art Contemporaine and the Ambassade Française.

Commissions, often monumental in size, were undertaken for, and by, Gobelins, with whom Jaulmes had a longstanding relationship. One project took ten years to complete. His sketches for 'The Rivers of France' were exhibited at the 1923 Salon des Artistes Décorateurs, the completed tapestries shown at the same Salon in 1933. His most celebrated work was commissioned by the French State as a gift to the City of Philadelphia in recognition of the rout of the English. The panel exemplified Deshairs' description of Jaulmes's style as 'filling every inch of cloth, leaving no "holes" in the decoration'. The primary intention was not, as it might at first seem, to cram all possible detail into the picture but rather to use such detail as a means of introducing infinite colour permutations, each an essential component of the total composition.

Jaulmes worked until the Second World War. He died in Paris in 1959.

Joubert (René) et Petit (Philippe):

The decorating firm of D.I.M. (Décoration Intérieure Moderne) was established in 1919 by René Joubert and Georges Mouveau at 19 place de la Madeleine. Joubert, born in Laval (Mayenne), had trained as an architect before moving to the decorative arts. Employment at La Maison Jansen, where he was instructed by the noted Art Nouveau cabinetmaker, Léon Benouville, was followed by further experience in furniture-making at Diot et Bouché. Mouveau brought a background of stage designing to the partnership, but returned to his chosen métier around 1923, when the theatre strike which had led him to seek employment at D.I.M. was over. Joubert ran the firm on his own for a year, with a M. Viénot as his technical director.

In 1924 he was joined by Philippe Petit, a younger man, who had worked briefly at Primavera after his studies at the Ecole Bernard-Palissy. Joubert was clearly the senior partner, designing most of the furnishings which he displayed at the Salons both under the firm's name and his own. Petit played a supporting role, creating the interiors which would soften Joubert's forceful lines by the introduction of muted grey and green carpets and wallpapers. A full eleven years later, in a tribute to Petit in *Mobilier et décoration*, the critic wrote of his role: 'Generally these artists are the unobtrusive and anonymous employees of architects' offices, design studios, and industrial firms. They ensure the continuity of the difficult tasks of study and patient research and bring them to technical and artistic fruition.'

Joubert's furniture designs were logical, the emphasis placed on what he described as a piece's longitudinal (i.e.,

horizontal) form. A rigid traditionalist, like Follot and Leleu, his inspiration was often Louis XVI or Restauration. He worked for an elite clientele. Editions were small as, on the whole, were the objects themselves, especially in the late 1920s when a range of phonogram cabinets, mobile cocktail cabinets, and plant stands were introduced.

Warm woods such as palisander, walnut, and macassar ebony imparted the desired sense of luxury. Decoration was provided most successfully by the incorporation of large panels of burled veneers, such as fernwood, which had a most pronounced grain. Marquetry, always understated, was confined to ivory or coralwood cross-banding or trim.

The firm took boutiques 37 and 39 on the Alexander III bridge at the 1925 Exposition, its furnishings supplemented by those of Desagnat (paintings and wallpaper), Tisseyre (wrought-iron), and Daum (light fixtures). The nearby Pleyel stand displayed a D.I.M. piano in palisander. It was their dining room in the Ambassade Française, however, which sparked the greatest excitement; the critics hailing it as a *tour de force* of sobriety and harmony.

D.I.M. moved to 40 rue du Colisée in the mid-1920s, the gallery's inaugural exhibition staged on 6 November 1926. The accompanying catalogues showed a wide range of furnishings, the firm's artisans listed as Messrs Rigoulot, Eckman, Martin, Deniau, Voellmy, and Ramadier. The range of carpets, in particular, was unanticipated: over one hundred designs, many cubist in inspiration.

Joubert yielded to the onslaught of metal furniture designs with equanimity. The first glimpses of its incorporation into his furniture came at the 1927 Salon; the next year a New York cafeteria commission was comprised entirely of tubular metal chairs and tables. By 1930 many nickelled metal desks and chairs were evident, the latter upholstered in leather. Elsewhere, radio cabinets and phonographs were made of lacquered metal and glass, the effect chic and modern. In the same year his dining-room table for the Countess A. de M. was in aluminium.

Joubert's death in 1931 led to Petit's resignation, he and D.I.M. continuing to exhibit independently at the salons. He died in 1945.

Jourdain, Francis:

Born in Paris in 1876, Jourdain was the son of Frantz Jourdain, an architect. Internship with Albert Besnard and Eugène Carrière led to his first painting exhibition, in 1897. His canvases, mostly landscapes, were shown for several years at the Druet, Salon des Artistes Indépendants, and Salon d'Automne. Feeling the need to diversify, he studied sculpture with Joseph Chéret and gravure with Jacques Villon, emerging after 1900 with a clear vision of the road ahead for twentieth-century decorative arts.

Jourdain's exhibit at the inaugural Salon d'Automne in 1902 included several very plain and geometric pieces of furniture, ample testament to his fierce opposition to the prevailing Art Nouveau idiom. He recalled his philosophy at the time in a 1922 interview with René Chavance published in *Art et décoration*: 'I went in the opposite direction. I said to myself that a table was essentially a plank on four legs. The first job was to carry this out. Any decoration would come afterwards if there was room.' Jourdain could lay claim to be the new century's first modernist, well ahead of the Bauhaus and de stijl schools. Commissions for his curiously stripped furnishings came gradually, until in 1912 he was able to open his modest Ateliers Modernes in which a single artisan was employed. Business grew during the war years despite Jourdain's brief mobilization in 1916. By 1919 he had opened a showroom, 'Chez Francis Jourdain', in the rue de Sèze in Esbly (Seine-et-Marne), the furnishings manufactured in a nearby workshop.

Jourdain's doctrine on the need to unfurnish a space in order successfully to furnish it is now well known. He remained implacably loyal to this belief throughout his career, speaking out against excess whenever possible, for example, in *Intérieurs-I*: 'The great designer of the future will be the person who knows how to keep to the strictly necessary components but establish between them such a just proportion, such a perfect balance, that there will not be a single "hole" or gap in their arrangement and no part of the room that he intends them for will seem bare.' A client's demand for a more lavish effect was met, at most, by the introduction of a contrasting veneer. Not surprisingly, many early commissions were commercial: restaurants, cinemas, train compartments, automobile accessory shops, nurseries, and offices. Later came a select group of private clients such as Princess Murat, President Barthou, the printer Draeger, Mallet-Stevens, and Grosclaude, several of whom were won over by a visit to Jourdain's own home at 26 rue Vavin.

Preferred woods in the early years were walnut, oak, zingana and maple; from 1925 Jourdain introduced steel, aluminium, lacquer, and wrought-iron.

At the 1925 Exposition, Jourdain showed a selection of furniture, light fixtures, and carpets in a boutique on the Alexander III bridge. He also decorated a library in the nearby G. Crès & Cie stand, and participated in the Ambassade Française, designing the pavilion's physical culture hall and smoking room in collaboration with Bastard, J. and J. Martel, Massoul, Lachenal, and Schenck. A cofounder of U.A.M., Jourdain continued to work until the Second World War. His drawing room in the group's exhibit at the 1937 Exposition was judged by the critic Georges Besson to be his *chef-d'oeuvre*. Included was a selection of modular furniture entitled 'Essai de désencombrement pour jeune travailleuse intellectuelle ou manuelle'.

continued on page 113

49 *Rousseau:* chair in rosewood, *galuchat*, and ivory (Collection of Sydney and Frances Lewis)

50 *Rousseau:* chair in rosewood, *galuchat*, and ivory (Collection of Sydney and Frances Lewis)

51 *Ruhlmann:* coffee-table in rosewood with mother-of-pearl veneer, *c.* 1928 (Photo: Christie's, NY)

52 *Ruhlmann:* corner cabinet in palisander, macassar ebony, and ivory, 1916. An identical model is illustrated in *Exposition rétrospective E.-J. Ruhlmann*, exhibition catalogue, Musée des Arts Décoratifs, Paris 1934 (Collection of Sydney and Frances Lewis)

53 *Ruhlmann:* fall-front secretary in palisander, *galuchat*, and ivory, *c.* 1926. Illustrated in *Petits Meubles modernes*, Paris 1929, pl. 40; and *Les Echos des industries d'art*, June 1926 (Collection of Galerie Vallois)

54 *Ruhlmann:* table in burl amboyna, *c.* 1925 (Collection of Galerie Vallois)

55 *Ruhlmann:* cabinet in burl amboyna and ivory, with silvered-bronze feet. Similar to the model commissioned by the Elysée Palace, 1920 (see pl. 221) (Collection of de Lorenzo Gallery)

56 *Ruhlmann:* cheval mirror in burl amboyna with ivory veneer (Collection of Steven Greenberg)

57 *Ruhlmann:* ensemble, including (left) a stele in violetwood executed by Porteneuve, *c.* 1934; (centre) a lady's desk with tambour top in macassar ebony and ivory, 1922 (the fifth example of model No. 1603 from the Atelier B, another example exhibited in the boudoir of the Hôtel du Collectionneur at the 1925 Exposition); illustrated in *Art et décoration*, Dec. 1922, p. 180; and *L'Art décoratif français 1918–1925*, Léon Deshairs, Paris 1926, p. 17; (centre back) silk wall hanging for a reception hall exhibited in the Hôtel du Collectionneur at the 1925 Expo-

sition, the design by Stéphany, and marketed by Cornille *frères*; illustrated in *Art et décoration*, Jan.–June 1928, p. 189; (right) chiffonière in burl amboyna with ivory veneer, model No. 2232, commissioned by the Musée des Arts Décoratifs, Paris, Nov. 1924. An identical model, exhibited at the Salon des Artistes Décorateurs, 1924, is illustrated in *Encyclopédie des métiers d'art*, Vol. I, Paris, pl. 29 (Photo: Sully-Jaulmes)

58 *Ruhlmann:* jewel cabinet in burl amboyna and ivory, *c.* 1913 (Collection of Jacques Mostini)

59 *Ruhlmann:* grand piano for Gaveau, 1924, exhibited in the *grand salon* of the Hôtel du Collectionneur at the 1925 Exposition. Illustrated in *Mobilier et décoration*, July 1925, p. 121; and *L'Hôtel du collectionneur*, Paris 1926, pl. 5. The sketch for the piano is illustrated in *Les Arts de la maison*, Spring 1924, p. 24, pl. 5 (Collection of Warren Cresswell and George Matheson Gerst)

60 *Ruhlmann:* cabinet in burl amboyna with ivory veneer and silvered-bronze medallion by Foucault, *c.* 1920 (Collection of de Lorenzo Gallery)

61 *Ruhlmann:* ensemble including a cabinet (*meuble de rangement*), armchair, and bronzes by Bourdelle. The cabinet exhibited in the *grand salon* of the Hôtel du Collectionneur at the 1925 Exposition with the original pair of doors shown on the floor to the right, illustrated in *L'Hôtel du collectionneur*, Paris 1926, pl. 6. The pair of doors shown in the cabinet were designed by Jean Goulden and substituted when the cabinet was exhibited at the 1929 Exposition in Barcelona (Photo: Sully-Jaulmes)

62 *Ruhlmann:* lady's desk in violetwood veneered in Moroccan leather and with ivory pulls, the interior in macassar ebony. Illustrated in *Art et décoration*, July–Dec. 1933. A similar dressing-table is illustrated in *Petits Meubles modernes*, Paris 1929, pl. 39 (Photo: Sully-Jaulmes)

63 *Ruhlmann:* liquor cabinet in macassar ebony, ivory, and tortoise shell, *c.* 1926. Illustrated in *Petits Meubles modernes*, Paris 1929, pl. 37. A similar model is illustrated in *Exposition rétrospective E.-J. Ruhlmann*, exhibition catalogue, Musée des Arts Décoratifs, Paris 1934 (Collection of Félix Marcilhac)

64 *Süe et Mare: meuble à linge* in palisander and burl wood, 1923, exhibited in the *grand salon* of the firm's Musée d'Art Contemporain at the 1925 Exposition. Illustrated in *Le Mobilier français d'aujourd'hui (1910–1925)*, Pierre Olmer, Paris 1926, pl. 13. The vase by Edgar Brandt (Photo: Sully-Jaulmes)

65 *Süe et Mare:* secretary in mahogany, 1922. Illustrated in *Les Arts de la maison*, Autumn 1923; and *Le Mobilier français d'aujourd'hui (1910–1925)*, Pierre Olmer, Paris 1926, pl. 13. The clock illustrated in *Intérieurs I*, Léon Moussinac, Paris, pl. 51; *L'Art décoratif français, 1918–1925*, Léon Deshairs, Paris 1926, p. 8; *Intérieurs de Süe et Mare*, Paris 1924, pl. 24; and *Mobilier et décoration*, Jan. 1926, p. 17 (Collection of Primavera Gallery)

66 *Süe et Mare:* table in macassar ebony with glass top, the sculpture by Scarpa (Collection of Galerie Lamouric)

67 *Süe et Mare:* settee in giltwood upholstered in Aubusson tapestry representing the story of Paul and Virginia from a design by Charles Dufresne. Exhibited in the *grand salon* of the firm's Musée d'Art Contemporain at the 1925 Exposition. Illustrated in *La Renaissance de l'art français*; *Intérieurs I*, Léon Moussinac, Paris, pl. 52; *Art et décoration*, 1925, p. 21; *Les Arts de la maison*, Autumn 1923; and *Mobilier et décoration*, Jan. 1926, p. 13 (Collection of J.-J. Dutko)

68 *Suisse:* four-panel screen in lacquer with incised decoration, *c.* 1928 (Collection of Mr and Mrs John Mecom)

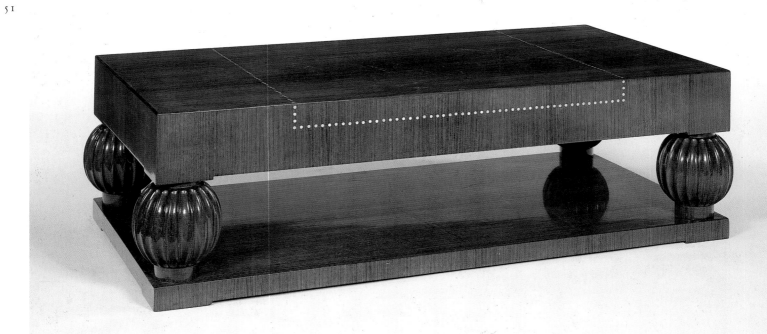

54

56

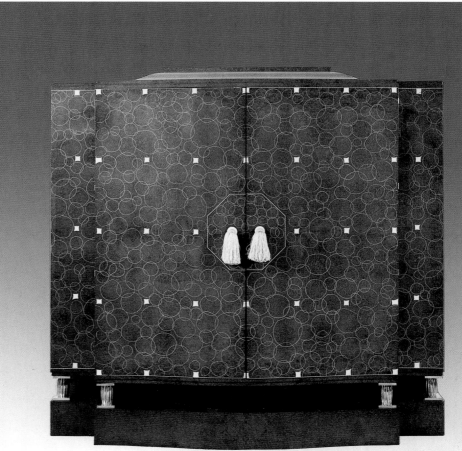

55

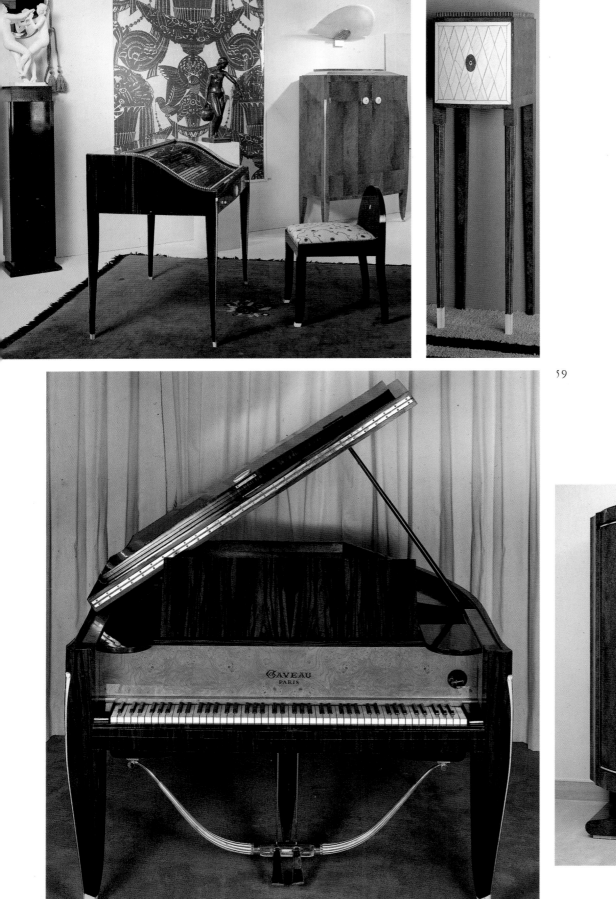

61

62

63

64

65

66

67

A year later Jourdain worked with Chareau, Sognot, and Adnet on a director's office and reception hall for the Collège de France. This was one of his last commissions; in 1939 he retired to concentrate on writing. He died in 1958.

Kinsbourg, Renée:

Born in Rouen, Kinsbourg moved to Paris where her address was listed in the mid-1920s as 85 rue de Longchamp. A decorator by profession, she designed interiors marketed by Les Arts de France. At the 1925 Exposition, she displayed a young woman's bedroom for the firm's stand on the Esplanade des Invalides in collaboration with A. Berger, with furniture executed by the cabinetmakers Taso and Molino, wrought-iron fixtures by Leblanc, and upholstery by Open & Cie.

A smoking parlour exhibited at the 1926 Salon d'Automne incorporated the angular lines which characterize Kinsbourg's furniture. A console table and chairs in macassar ebony show sharp, clean edges and corners. Veneers were sumptuous, mounts minimal. Today her work is often mistaken for that of Chareau.

In 1926 she displayed a lady's bedroom in palisander and lacquer at the Salon, again retailed by Les Arts de France. Two years later the critic Gabriel Henriot wrote in *Mobilier et décoration* of her exhibit at the Salon des Artistes Décorateurs: 'Mlle Kinsbourg has tried to fix the play of light on her screens. One receives the reflections from the lamps; the other, and in this it is very original, is devoted to a couple's intimate reverie. The carpets, which are exaggeratedly modern, are called "Sea of Clouds" and "The Quarry". They provide the pretext for a delicate symphony in grey.'

In the same year, she displayed at the Salon d'Automne a de luxe cabin for a transatlantic ocean liner. Practical and compact, the storage units were built into the room's panelling to maximize space. Drawers were housed underneath the bed and within the headboard, and a swivel table could be used for bedtime snacks. The bathroom included a concealed dressing-table which was lowered outwards from the wall. Colour and decoration were provided by a pale grey carpet with overlapping cubist motifs. Kinsbourg's thorough comprehension of the project's needs was evident at every point.

Kinsbourg's carpets formed an integral part of such displays, giving warmth and ambience where the furniture did not. In 1931 she designed several carpets for Saddier et ses Fils, using a muted palette of greys and beiges.

Kiss, Paul:

Kiss never fully stepped out of the shadow of Edgar Brandt, with whom he was initially associated, although he produced a substantial amount of very high-quality metalwork. Con-centrating on furnishings – consoles, light fixtures, radiator covers, gates, etc. – he exhibited through the Salon des Artistes Décorateurs, the Salon des Artistes Français, and the Salon d'Automne. His style, for a metal as anonymous as iron, is highly distinctive: martelé decoration became his hallmark. Hardly an object, however small, lacks this distinctive Kiss *imprimatur*, the deep hammered incisions accented with black patina.

Kiss was born in Balalfalva, Rumania. A 1925 article in *Mobilier et décoration* chronicles several years of itinerant jobs in Hungary and Germany before he settled on French citizenship, establishing his atelier and showroom at 2–4 rue Léon-Delhomme.

The 1925 Exposition provided fine exposure, Kiss took boutique 5 on the Alexander III bridge, alongside that of Sonia Delaunay. He displayed a wide range of wrought-iron objects, including a door for the Monument to the Dead at Levallois-Perret. He was also commissioned to provide the entrance door for the Fernand Savary pavilion. His floor lamps, in particular, caught the public's attention and impressed the critics. An article in *Mobilier et décoration* in December 1925 gave him high praise.

In 1926, in collaboration with Paul Feher, Kiss displayed wrought-iron ensembles at two Salons. He participated also in an exhibition at the Musée Galliera entitled, charmingly, 'Une petite Exposition après la grande'. His work was marketed by La Société des Toiles de Rambouillet.

Klotz, Blanche-J.:

Paris-born, Klotz was listed in the 1920s at 3 rue de Miromesnil. A self-taught decorator, her work received a remarkable amount of coverage for somebody who participated only once – in 1934 – at the annual Salons. The critic René Chavance traced her career in a 1928 article in *Art et décoration*: initial designs for lampshades, cushions, and curtains led to furniture and, finally, to architecture.

Klotz's early preference in furniture was for warm, richly grained woods – gaboon, palisander and walnut – without marquetry or prominent metal mounts. Logic predominated. An office illustrated in 1924 shows the essence of her evolving style: the desk sharply angular and functional, its chair with square arms and harmonious beige leather upholstery. Two years later, Léon Moussinac illustrated two Klotz interiors in his *Intérieurs IV*: a man's and woman's bedroom. The latter was a remarkable achievement – fresh and feminine – its chairs and bed with scalloped fan-shaped backs of Louis-Philippe influence, similar in inspiration to designs by Süe et Mare in the early 1920s. The man's bedroom provided a muted variation on the same decorative theme, the mahogany chairs with tiered crest-rails and buckskin upholstery. An example is to be found in the

collection of the Musée des Arts Décoratifs, Paris.

Klotz took a stand on the Esplanade des Invalides at the 1925 Exposition, displaying a hall/studio for a villa in Montagnac – in effect, a large lounge at the foot of a flight of stairs. The furniture, including a desk and X-shaped walnut stools upholstered in beige satin, was characteristically neat and angular. Large vases of white arum lilies added a fresh look, as did a panel of butterflies painted by Raoul Dufy. Other collaborators included Faucheur (cabinetry), Ducret (electricity), Monteaux (murals), Sapho (fabrics), and Devilliers (decorated plaster).

A 1928 article in *Art et Décoration* by René Chavance questioned the relatively small number of women interior decorators. Of Klotz he wrote: 'One can say of this artist that she was urged on by a natural inclination. The vocation came to her without the exertions normally associated with these housewifely qualities. She began by furnishing for herself before thinking of doing the same for others. Then her friends, beguiled by the good taste and ingenuity displayed in her own home convinced her not to keep to herself talents which she could utilize so successfully.' Illustrated were a wide range of Klotz ensembles – living room, library, salon, villa, bar, bathroom, bedrooms, antechamber – all characteristically functional, yet elegant and calm. The line – vertical and horizontal – ruled supreme. Curves were few, even in chairs, and there were few contours in armoires and cabinets. Preferred materials were gaboon, oak, and tussore silk.

A 1929 article by G. Rémon in *Mobilier et décoration* showed several further Klotz ensembles, some now difficult to distinguish from those of contemporaries, in particular, Sognot and Perriand. The emphasis was on colour harmony: warm woods upholstered in beige or maroon, with complementary walls painted in Stic-B and a screen in stained straw similar to a model by Jean-Michel Frank. The furniture was ultramodern, especially a hinged and shelved three-part coffee table.

In 1930, Klotz participated in the first Salon des Artistes Modernes, exhibiting an office for an executive in the chemical industry. Metal mounts appear for the first time in her furniture, the desk showing a strong Chareau influence, its stepped rectangular wood top mounted on stainless steel supports and stretchers. The room lacked any form of conventional light fixture; light came from sources designed by André Salomon within the ceiling and walls.

Why Klotz participated in only one of the annual Salons remains unclear: certainly the lady's desk which she exhibited at the 1934 Salon d'Automne was completely uncharacteristic: its top and frieze in *verre églomisé* engraved with zodiac symbols by Pierre and Jacques Lardin.

An article in *Art et décoration* by Gaston Varenne in 1935 reviewed a new departure: editions of furniture *en série* manufactured by the cabinetmaker Schmit on rue de Char-onne. Ten examples of each model were made. Klotz claimed, correctly, that no two sets were identical as the client selected his preferred veneer, upholstery (leather in various tones, or parchment) and fabric designs by Hélène Henri. To further disguise the concept of an edition, most pieces were bifunctional. An extension dining-room table, for example, became an elegant studio work-table on removal of its two leaves. Likewise, a buffet could be transformed into a *bibliothèque basse*. Varenne was favourably impressed: 'These multipurpose pieces of furniture are practical, the ingenuity with which they are presented, and the fine appearance that they maintain in these transformations, show that nothing is left to chance.'

In the same year an article on the ocean liner *Normandie* reviewed cabins which Klotz had designed in lacquered aluminium with stainless steel fixtures and furniture, the latter again upholstered by Hélène Henri.

Kohlmann, Etienne:

Parisian-born in 1903, Kohlmann came early to his chosen profession, working as a trainee cabinetmaker at the Nieuport aviation factory in 1916. A series of career changes followed in short order: apprenticeship in a technical cabinetry school, where he produced his first complete piece, a commode; a one-year enrollment at the Ecole Boulle; and a further twelve months with an *ébéniste* in the Faubourg Saint-Antoine. All this by the age of twenty, when he joined Le Studium Louvre as a cabinetmaker/decorator, soon to be appointed, with Maurice Matet, its codirector, a position he held until 1938.

Throughout the 1920s Kohlmann was acclaimed as much as a cabinetmaker as a decorator. In an article on the artist in the March 1928 issue of *Art et décoration*, H.-A. Martine reiterated a common critics' refrain: 'There are few furniture technicians as accomplished as Kohlmann.' Later in the article Martine noted one of his favourite forms of decoration: the use of pale grained veneers juxtaposed assymetrically to provide contrast within a single wood. The sections were edged in dark bands, the resulting designs compared by Martine to the *porte à faux* technique favoured by architects at the time.

Kohlmann contributed a woman's bedroom with adjoining office in the Grand Magasins du Louvre pavilion at the 1925 Exposition, the furniture and wall panelling in palisander and sycamore, the drapes, silk upholstery, and window shades by Max Vibert. The effect was neat, if nothing else, the critics settling on formality and refinement as its hallmarks.

A glance at the Appendix in this book indicates both the volume and range of Kohlmann's designs through many years. Many interiors were illustrated in reviews such as

Meubles du temps present and *Répertoire du goût moderne*, the mood always close to the vanguard of modern design. Tubular metal furniture mounts began to appear after 1925, their understatement due perhaps to Kohlmann's reluctance to forgo his cabinetry training.

The 1930s brought a chain of prestigious commissions, several reviewed in a 1934 article in *Art et décoration* by Paul Laroche, in particular an office for the Director of Social Sciences, the furniture marketed by Fournier. A mature Kohlmann emerges, his ensembles expressing clearly the *ésprit moderne*. He participated in several pavilions at the 1937 Exposition Internationale and again at the New York World's Fair, continuing independently after the Second World War as an interior designer.

Lahalle (Pierre) et Lévard (Georges):

A 1920 article in *Art et décoration* traced the evolution of the firm of Lahalle et Lévard from its first partnership, that of Lahalle and Maurice Lucet. Both had studied architecture at the Ecole des Beaux-Arts before joining the Studio Pascal. In 1903 they branched out on their own, designing both building façades and interiors. Their first essays in furniture design were markedly Art Nouveau, the pieces outlined in sinuous curves and arabesques. Soon, however, relief decoration – often carved by Léon Jallot – was replaced by polychromed marquetry medallions of fruit and flowers. Shapes were criticized for becoming too rigid. In 1907, Georges Lévard, a graduate of the Ecole des Arts Décoratifs, joined Lahalle and Lucet and the trio expanded their furniture production, in part to meet a growing South American market. Prior to the First World War they joined the search for twentieth-century furniture design, basing their models on the simple grandeur of the Directoire and Consulate styles.

In 1919 the three were still together, exhibiting at the Salons a range of interiors produced for clients such as Corbin and the hotel Kapferer. The collaboration, according to Pierre Olmer in *Le Mobilier française d'aujourd'hui (1910–1925)*, produced 'a sober and refined distinction, an excellent overall appearance, and one finds again here reminders of the beautiful furniture of the first part of the nineteenth century, though, happily, with less of its heaviness.'

The trio dissolved gradually within the next few years. Lahalle continued to participate, though less fully from 1922, when he was appointed Professor of Composition at the Ecole Boulle, the post vacated by Maurice Dufrène. Lucet departed shortly after, leaving Lahalle and Lévard to keep the business in operation even after Lévard joined Primavera. At the 1925 Exposition, the two architects took their own stand on the Esplanade des Invalides, displaying a vestibule in collaboration with Ruetsch and Berthelot (furniture), Morand (wrought-iron), da Silva Bruhns (carpets), and Mlle Chaplin (decorative paintings). The pair also participated with André Fréchet in Le Studium Louvre, exhibiting a boudoir and reception hall. In the Primavera pavilion Lévard presented a hallway, its furniture by Sognot and Claude Lévy. His most celebrated interior, however, remained the indoor swimming pool for a villa on the Riviera shown at the 1924 Salon d'Automne in collaboration with Ruhlmann and Primavera's director, Chauchet-Guilleré.

Lahalle et Lévard continued to design ensembles into the 1930s, special emphasis given now to Coramandel lacquerwork. A boudoir displayed at the 1928 Salon d'Automne proved especially chic, the arched chaise longue and tiered dressing-table, in sycamore, conveying a lavish *ésprit moderne*.

Their earlier furniture closely resembled that of Dufrène and Renaudot. Elegant and modern, its market appeal was clearly to the middle and upper-middle classes.

Lahalle and Lucet were both born in 1877 in Orléans (Loiret), the former dying in Versailles in 1956, the latter in 1941. Lévard was born in Bayeux (Calvados). His birth and death dates are unknown.

Lalique, René:

Lalique's accomplishments in jewelry and glass need no reinforcement here. His innovation and artistry bear witness to an unmatched genius through two of the most fertile, yet distinctly antithetical, periods in the history of decorative arts. Gallé and Tiffany matched his creativity at the end of the nineteenth century; others his chosen medium of glass in the postwar era. No one could begin to command such attention in both periods.

Lalique's transition to glass came around 1902. Experiments at Clairefontaine, near Rambouillet, led to the formation of a studio at Combs to manufacture moulded glass. A final move to Wingen-sur-Moder, in Alsace-Lorraine, came between 1918 and 1922. Lalique used a plaster-moulding process to produce glass which, in most cases, he did not colour; tonal gradations were obtained by varying its thickness. Sometimes, cutting and polishing operations were added, or specialized areas of the moulded design treated with acid to produce the desired limpid, frosted, or milky effect. The range of glassware seemed limitless – from every conceivable domestic accoutrement to monumental architecture. Glass furniture was a relatively late development, added to Lalique's repertoire in the second half of the 1920s, when he had perhaps tired of small domestic glassware.

The firm's pavilion at the 1925 Exposition included a dining room designed by the architect Marc Ducluzeau in

which the walls were decorated with a lavish hunt scene of hounds pursuing wild boar in a forest. The room's chandelier, candelabra, stemware, and illuminated ceiling panels were all in glass, but the table was in wood by Bernel. The critic for *L'Illustration* questioned the need for outside collaboration, censure which Lalique appears to have taken to heart, since in 1927 he exhibited two glass tables at the Salon des Artistes Décorateurs, each comprised of moulded panels housed in chromed metal mounts. The following year came a glass liquor cabinet containing sets of decanters and ice buckets, the interior with concealed lighting. The critic for *Art et décoration* approved of Lalique's inroad into the realm of conventional furniture, writing that the exhibit was, as always, 'astonishingly young and inventive'. The same year *Mobilier et décoration* illustrated a dining room which included a long glass dining-table supported by twin pedestal feet.

A range of tables and architectural elements – doors, ceilings, screens, fountains, and columns – now followed, illuminated, where possible, from within. Furniture forms were conservative, decoration provided by pressed decorative panels within the glass. It appears that Lalique stopped short of creating glass chairs and settees, though he would certainly have been aware of the prototypes produced by Baccarat to great acclaim in the late nineteenth century.

Born in Ay-sur-Marne in 1860, Lalique died in Paris in 1945.

Le Corbusier:

Le Corbusier was born Charles-Edouard Jeanneret in La-Chaux-de-Fonds, Switzerland, in 1887. He attended the town's Ecole d'Art before serving a fifteen-month internship with the renowned Paris architect, Auguste Perret, in 1908/09. During a trip to Germany in 1910 he met Tessenow, director of the German Werkbund, who introduced him to the problems of standardizing mass-production furniture. In 1917 he settled in Paris. He took the name Le Corbusier in 1920 on cofounding the review *L'Esprit nouveau* with the painter Amédée Ozenfant at 35 rue de Sèvres. Twenty-eight issues were published at irregular intervals within the next five years, the most celebrated being his 1921 manifesto, *Une Maison est une machine à habiter*.

At the 1925 Exposition the magazine's exhibit in the Cours-la-Reine on the Right Bank was entitled 'Le Pavillon de l'Esprit Nouveau'. Le Corbusier was joined in its design by his cousin, Pierre Jeanneret, an architect. Other collaborators were listed as Faure, Boyer, Emery, Stranik, Guilbert, and Nietscke, the metal furnishings executed by the Agencements Standards U.P. and Les Etablissements Réunis à Brno.

Replacing the word 'furniture' with the word 'equipment',

Le Corbusier offered new solutions to old problems: 'If we analyse the problem we find that the equipment is used for classifying the various utensils needed for domestic purposes. We replace the innumerable pieces of furniture, with their different shapes and names, with standard storage units incorporated into or standing freely against the wall. These units are placed in each spot in the flat where a precise function occurs daily, and the inside is designed according to their exact use. They are no longer made in wood, but in metal, in workshops where office furniture is still made today. The storage units alone constitute the furniture of the house, leaving the maximum amount of space free in the room. The study of tables and chairs leads to entirely new concepts, not of a decorative, but of a functional nature. Etiquette has been made redundant by the evolution of customs. It is possible to seat oneself in several ways, and the new shape of chair must correspond to these different ways. By using metal tubing or sheet metal to construct the new seat shape, the problems disappear; the traditional use of wood hindered initiative.'

The pavilion's interior consisted of standardized living units, in particular a series of bookcase components (*caisses métaliques*) manufactured by Thonet. These were 'standardized units designed to be combined in a multitude of ways, they could be sold at the Bazar de l'Hôtel de Ville or at the avenue des Champs-Elysées. They can stand to any height against a wall or form the wall itself.'

The public's reaction was predictable: everything was far too intellectual and surgical, even orthopedic. Besides, they expected to be shown how they should live *today*, rather than tomorrow.

Initially, Le Corbusier found few adherents even beyond the Exposition. In 1929 Léon Deshairs wrote of his display at the Salon d'Automne: 'M. Le Corbusier is not seeking to please. He has no preconceived aesthetic theory. I saw some visitors to the salon startled rather than charmed by this "interior equipment of a living space" which recalls nothing that they love.'

By 1930, however, the initial resistance and incomprehension had begun to soften. Max Terrier wrote in an article in *Art et décoration* on metal furniture that his models should be seen simply as a declaration of war on the stuffed and cushioned ideal of a bourgeois living room. The furniture's cold and impersonal lines were suddenly svelte, logical, and timeless. Within years the revolution was won and tubular metal furniture became *de rigueur*.

In the late 1920s Le Corbusier, Jeanneret, and Perriand designed half a dozen furniture models which were included subsequently in many of their interiors. These are today recognized as classics. Three chairs, in particular, have received universal recognition. These are the *grand confort* model (in large and small editions), credited generally to

Perriand, in which bulky square cushions are contained within a chromed tubular steel chassis by Thonet. The model, introduced in 1928, was reproduced in 1959 by H. Weber and in 1965 by Cassina.

The second model is an armchair with adjustable back (*siège à dossier basculant*), which resembled Marcel Breuer's 1925 'Wassily' chair. Comprising a tubular metal frame with leather or ponyskin upholstery and arm straps, it was introduced in 1929 and reoffered in 1959 and 1965.

The third is Le Corbusier's celebrated chaise longue, the prototype introduced in 1922 for his *Immeubles-Villas* and refined both for his 1928 *Villa à Carthage* and 1929 *Maison de Mr X* in Brussels. Its stepped shape matched the human form – a revolutionary concept at the time. The model consisted of two basic elements: a rocking chair and a detachable metal support. Its upholstery was in ponyskin.

Another important piece of furniture, again credited to Perriand, was a swivel chair (*siège tournant*) exhibited first in a dining room at the 1929 Salon d'Automne. The accompanying table consisted of a rectangular glass top resting on inverted U-shaped twin supports linked by a stretcher. It was described as a *table en tube d'avion, section ovoid*.

A founder-member of U.A.M., Le Corbusier remained active for the rest of his life, both expanding on the group's theories and researching functional solutions. In 1965, the year of his death, Cassina was granted the reproduction rights to certain of his chair models.

Legrain, Pierre:

Legrain's fame rests today not on furniture design but on his designs for book-bindings, though this was a skill which he used only reluctantly to tide him through the austere First World War years.

He was born 10 February 1887, in Levallois-Perret, to a prosperous distillery owner and a mother of Belgian origin. He attended school at the Collège Sainte-Croix in Neuilly before entering the Ecole des Arts Appliqués Germain Pilon around 1904 to study painting, sculpture, and theatre decoration. The collapse of his father's business forced him to leave school and help support the family. He found work selling cartoons to the popular press, augmenting a meagre income by long hours of painting theatre sets. In 1908 his cartoons came to the attention of Paul Iribe who asked him to contribute to his satirical reviews, *L'Assiette au beurre, Le Témoin,* and *La Baïonette.* Impressed by Legrain's creative skills, Iribe invited him to collaborate on various projects, including a 1912 commission to decorate in the modern style Jacques Doucet's apartment at 46 avenue du Bois.

The meeting with Doucet was to seal Legrain's future after Iribe left for the United States at the beginning of the war.

Legrain volunteeered for action, and after his demobilization in 1916, when work was scarce, he sought out the wealthy Doucet, and in 1917 was offered a salary of Fr300 per month to design modern bindings for Doucet's renowned book collection. Legrain was forced to accept, though he had never before designed a book cover. A studio was set up in his patron's dining room, where Legrain revolutionized the art of bookbinding in 365 designs executed by Doucet's binders. In 1919, now married and living at 9 rue du Val-de-Grace, he left Doucet's exclusive employment and began to accept other commissions. He continued, however, to design a range of unique pieces for Doucet which he exhibited at both the 1923 Salon des Artistes Décorateurs and, more importantly, the following year in an interior designed by Pierre Chareau entitled 'La Réception et l'Intimité d'un Appartement Moderne'. These items were later incorporated in the studio Saint-James which Paul Ruau designed for Doucet in Neuilly in 1926.

In 1923 Legrain established his own workshop within that of the decorators Briant et Roberts at 7 rue d'Argenteuil, from where he moved first to a basement in the avenue Percier and then to 304 rue Saint-Jacques. Feeling the need to maintain his reputation as a bookbinder, he planned yet another move, this time to a larger building, the Villa Brune, in which he could house a bindery. On 17 July 1929, the day of the scheduled move, he suffered a fatal heart attack.

Legrain's courtship of the avant-garde was described by Léon Moussinac in *Interieurs IV*: 'Pierre Legrain's personality allows him to be seduced by the problems of organization and interior decoration for a particularly rich social minority, which wishes to appear informed about what is best. The results of this, because they are particularly rich, are particularly exceptional pieces of furniture. Pierre Legrain's art is exclusive.' Commissions came by word-of-mouth. Legrain therefore needed to exhibit only intermittently; at the Salon des Artistes Décorateurs (until 1926); the 1925 Exposition (bookcovers in the Hôtel du Collectionneur); 'Les Cinq'; and the inaugural U.A.M. exposition in 1929.

Doucet afforded Legrain an expanding clientele, which allowed him to earn a living from his twin passions, furniture design and interior decoration. Jeanne Tachard, a noted milliner and friend of Doucet through their mutual interest in ethnic art, became an important patron, commissioning Legrain to furnish two apartments at 41 rue Emile-Menier. So well did his African-inspired furniture complement her tribal art collection that she retained him to decorate her villa and grounds at Celle-Saint-Cloud, a triumph discussed at length by Gaston Varenne in a 1924 article in *L'Amour de l'art.* Other noted clients were Pierre Meyer, for whose house on the avenue Montaigne Legrain designed the celebrated glass and copper Pleyela piano shown at the 1929 exhibition of 'Les Cinq' at the Galerie de la Renaissance; Maurice

Martin du Gard (a suite of rooms); the Viscount de Noailles (a bedroom); the Princess G. de G. (a house on the rue Villejust and another at Celle-Saint-Cloud); Mme Louise Boulanger; and Suzanne Talbot. Small commercial commissions filled in the gaps: leather camera cases for Kodak, cigarette box designs for Lucky Strike and Camel; and a desk set for the Elysée Palace.

Doucet's Neuilly collection was divided posthumously between a 1958 gift by Jean Dubrujeaud to the Musée des Arts Décoratifs, Paris, and the auction held in 1972 at the Hôtel Drouot. The wide range of pieces showed Legrain's pursuit of luxury through lavish materials and contrasting colours. Palmwood, with its coarse, open grain, was particularly suited to African-inspired furniture, while highly buffed palisander and ebony brought opulence to cubist pieces. Legrain also exploited the tactile qualities of his materials, juxtaposing metal or glass with sharkskin or animal hides. Colour was added by expanses of lacquer or small detailing in enamel and mother-of-pearl. His walls complemented the furniture, their surfaces panelled in cork, parchment, corrugated card, or oilcloth.

Legrain left the execution of his designs to others: Dunand for lacquer; Miklos for enamelling; Vuitton for leather-upholstered furniture; Keiffer, Canape, and Noulhac for bookbindings.

Legrain's furniture was at once energetic, masculine, architectural, and theatrical. His inspiration was drawn primarily from two sources: African tribal art and cubism. The former had a considerable vogue in the early 1900s as France's West and Central African colonies were pillaged by profit-minded trophy hunters, their booty rushed to eager collectors in Paris and Marseilles. Legrain was exposed first to Doucet's collection, later to that of Mme Tachard. He drew on various Ashanti and Dahomey pieces for furniture – thrones, neck-rests (to protect elaborate hairstyles), and chieftain's stools – to create his own modernized blend of primitive designs. Léon Rosenthal referred to this influence in a 1923 article on Legrain in *Art et décoration*. Later, a 1972 article by Lynn Thornton in *The Connoisseur* included an illustration of the throne of Ghèzo, King of Dahomey (1818–1858), its seat an undeniable prototype for Legrain's famous curule-shaped tabouret in black lacquer and *galuchat* (see ill. 144).

Doucet's contemporary art collection included cubist paintings by Picabia, Modigliani, Picasso, and Braque. Legrain applied the concept three-dimensionally to certain pieces of furniture, as did two other Doucet artists, Miklos and Czaky. Powerful angular and stepped forms underlined Legrain's essays in this style. Another influence was Howard Carter's discovery in 1922 of Tutenkhamen's tomb, the block feet on a library chair for Doucet, *c.* 1923, resembling those on an Egyptian throne.

Leleu, Jules:

Leleu was certainly descended in spirit, if only tenuously in lineage, from France's great eighteenth-century Leleu cabinetmaking family. A strict traditionalist, he adapted the unimpeachable sobriety and elegance of his predecessors to the dictates of modern good taste. The *Mobilier et décoration* critic, Gaston Derys, touched directly on the link in a 1933 article: 'I will not be telling anyone anything new by proclaiming that Jules Leleu is one of our best decorative artists. ... I imagine that in time people will seek out the work of Jules Leleu just as they seek the work of Charles Cressent, Jean-François Oeben and Jean-Henri Riesener today.' Strong words, indeed, which should not go unexamined. Today, the numerous illustrations of Leleu ensembles in contemporary reviews suggest that such praise is unwarranted. Many pieces, especially seat furniture and commodes, are clearly derivative of Ruhlmann. Some examples, among many, of this influence are a *canapé* illustrated in *Sièges contemporains*; and several commodes in the catalogue of an auction of Leleu furnishings at the Hôtel Drouot on 24 November 1981. These last show an unashamed resemblance to a bedroom model incorporated by Ruhlmann in his Hôtel du Collectionneur at the 1925 Exposition. It should be stressed that the issue here is not Leleu's cabinetry – of a quality, always, that defies censure – but his originality as a designer. The contours, selection of materials, and even his manner of using ivory marquetry for decoration, show an unquestionable Ruhlmann influence.

Nevertheless, there is much in Leleu's dual role as cabinetmaker/decorator which pleases. Harmony, sophistication and prudence abound. Raymond Escholier expressed the feelings of many in his assessment in *Art et décoration* of a dining room at the 1922 Salon d'Automne: 'Here nothing is skimped or unwholesome. This is not a decor that is fitted to exceptional or abnormal beings, but to a well-to-do domestic way of life, concerned about comfort and bursting with health.' Later monographs in *Mobilier et décoration* attested to the esteem in which Leleu was held.

He was born in Boulogne-sur-Mer in 1883. In 1909, after tuition under Théophile Deman, he succeeded his father in the family painting firm, where he was joined by his brother Marcel. The addition of a showroom and adjoining cabinet works allowed the brothers to make inroads into the decorating field. In 1914, they were both mobilized, Jules enrolling in the airforce. Returning home in 1918, he decided to specialize in furniture-making. Participation in the 1922 Salon d'Automne led him two years later to open a gallery on the avenue Franklin Roosevelt, Marcel remaining in Boulogne to manage the atelier. Soon lamps, carpets, and fabrics were introduced. By 1929 Leleu had moved to 65 avenue Victor Emmanuel, where he remained until after the

Second World War, his sons Jean and André succeeding him some years later. He died in Paris in 1961.

Leleu participated in the annual Salons from 1922. At the 1925 Exposition he took stand 46 on the Esplanade des Invalides, displaying a dining room, the carpet by da Silva Bruhns. In the Ambassade Française pavilion he contributed furniture for the reception hall and the music room.

Warm woods became Leleu's hallmark – walnut, macassar ebony, amboyna, and palisander – the furniture's richness derived from the material itself. Marquetry decoration, never extensive, was in ivory, *galuchat*, or horn. Lacquer was introduced in the late 1920s, Raymond Cogniat noting in a 1934 article in *Art et décoration* that it was applied for Leleu by a team of local Oriental artisans. Elsewhere, articles listed Bobot, Dunand, and Hamanaka as collaborators. In the late 1930s smoked glass panels were introduced into furniture, with etched floral decoration by Schwartz. Metal and glass were restricted, wherever possible, to furniture mounts, Leleu believing that, unlike wood, they did not beautify with age. However, chromed metal was permitted for floor lamps, whose inverted shades provided indirect lighting.

Leleu's commissions included ensembles for embassies and ministeries, and even a dining room for the Elysée Palace. In 1936 he furnished the Grand Salon des Ambassadeurs at La Société des Nations, Geneva. The room, still in existence, is known as the 'Salon Leleu'. Ocean liners provided further prestige and publicity. Leleu designed for the *Ile-de-France*, *L'Atlantique*, *Pasteur*, and *Normandie*, providing the last-mentioned with its de luxe 'Trouville' apartment (the word 'cabin' was clearly inappropriate for opulence on this scale). Included were a drawing room and dining room with lacquered seat furniture and ash piano, Aubusson murals, and ivory-coloured Moroccan leather wall panelling.

A wide range of collaborators was listed through the years, among them Leleu's wife, sons, and daughter, Paule. Da Silva Bruhns was his foremost coexhibitor, supplying carpets for numerous interiors. Kasskoff was also important, executing murals, tapestries, and leather upholstery. Further furniture decoration was provided by J. Calliet (cabinetry), E. Letessier (chairs), L. Gigou (metal mounts), and Bastard, Brayer, Despierres, and Chapelain-Midy (wood finishing and painted decoration).

Lévy, Alfred (see Majorelle)

Lucet, Maurice (see Lahalle et Lévard)

Lurçat, André:

Born in Bruyères (Vosges) in 1894, Lurçat attended the Ecole des Beaux-Arts, emerging as one of the theorists of the rationalist movement which transformed furniture design in the late 1920s. He was the brother of Jean Lurçat, a noted carpet and tapestry designer of the period.

Though trained as an architect, Lurçat interested himself also in the interiors of his buildings, the furnishings matching the strict geometry of their environment. A 1929 monograph by the critic J. Porcher in *Art et décoration* described the ambience: 'A study designed for the modern man, composed of four walls, two chairs, and a table. Everything is bare. There is nothing to see. The modern man pushes a button or turns a key and the table reveals a typewriter, just like every other typewriter. The walls open revealing cupboards stuffed with books and papers no better organized than anywhere else. The passion for order has become so urgent that order itself had to be transcended.' Porcher issued a clear, though understated, caveat: too much rationalism would deny the inhabitant his humanity and innate *joie de vivre*. Illustrated were bookcases, desks, and showcases, all devoid of curves, mouldings and marquetry. The effect was sober and clean.

An earlier article on Lurçat by Jean Galliotti in a 1927 issue of *Art de décoration* reviewed his modernization of a traditional couturier's gallery on the rue Vignon. Again, the impact was severe, the writer citing the rooms 'nudism'. Colour was evident, however, in the abstract carpets of Jean Lurçat and Marcoussis. The furniture was in bleached sycamore upholstered in grey silk. The overall pleasing effect was credited, however, more to the interior's architectural lighting than to the furnishings themselves. In 1928 a young man's bedroom, marketed by Les Etablissements Leford, included a selection of mass-production furniture. Lurçat was a founder-member of U.A.M., exhibiting well into the 1950s. His metal furniture was executed and marketed by Thonet.

Majorelle, Louis:

The undisputed master cabinetmaker of the 1900 era – the first in a hundred years, the critics felt, to measure up to the most splendid *ébénistes* of the eighteenth century, Louis Majorelle survived the First World War despite the 1916 bombing of his Nancy atelier at 6 rue de Vieil-Aître. He returned from Paris in 1918 to rebuild both his workshop and his confidence, the latter undermined by the ferocious postwar obloquy heaped on the same Art Nouveau movement which had swept him to international celebrity. Many in a similar situation would have quietly bowed out, but Majorelle, whether out of economic necessity or buoyed by the challenge of the new modernism, continued to design and manufacture furniture. But the 1920s did in fact belong to a new generation, and the master cabinetmaker slipped into

obscurity. Pierre Olmer, in *Le Mobilier français (1910–1925)*, provided an accurate summary of Majorelle's predicament: 'Perhaps he did not disengage himself quickly enough from the errors of the Ecole de Nancy, in which one must acknowledge, though, his courage as a pioneer. His most recent work is a little dated . . . a fact explained by its origins.'

Following the war, Majorelle exhibited sporadically at the Paris Salons, preferring, as he had in the prewar era, to offer his furniture directly to the public through the firm's outlets in Nancy (20 rue St. Georges), Paris (53 avenue Victor Emmanuel and 22 rue de Provence), Lyon (28 rue de la République), and Lille (55 rue Esquermoise). Majorelle turned sixty in 1919 and seeing the need for continuity appointed Alfred Lévy, one of his students, codirector of the firm.

Lévy's collaboration is first listed at the 1920s Salon d'Automne in a silver cabinet with wrought-iron mounts. The following year came a dining room in macassar ebony and amaranth. The critic for *Art et décoration* found it to have a solid and logical opulence, despite its monumentality. The latter censure was predictable: Majorelle had suffered it intermittently for thirty years. In 1923, Gaston Varenne touched on the issue from a slightly different viewpoint, writing in *Art et décoration* that Majorelle designed furniture 'for men only'.

Majorelle's evolving style can be traced in his choice of materials. Gone as early as 1908 were the boldness and sumptuousness of his Art Nouveau ormolu waterlily and orchid furniture mounts; in their place by 1920 were heavy wrought-iron models, either black or in unpatinated grey. The early preference for dark hardwoods – mahogany, purpleheart, rosewood – remained, joined in the 1920s by macassar ebony. Decorative marquetry – floral or landscape – was phased out, in its place ivory stringing or cross-banding.

As a member of the Jury for the 1925 Exposition, Majorelle exhibited two ensembles *hors concours*: the first an office library in the firm's stand on the Esplanade des Invalides. Large Louis XVI-style furniture decorated only with wrought-iron mounts was shown against herring-bone veneered walls beneath a painted frieze. Daum vases with Majorelle wrought-iron mounts placed at random on desk tops and *guéridons*, and a wrought-iron radiator grill, provided the only identity to the largely anonymous setting. Collaborators were listed as Jeanès (artist-painter), Mahier (wrought-iron), Steiner (sculpture), Burtin (carved plaster), Janin (stained-glass windows), and Steinmetz and Dicop (cabinetry). Also exhibited was a dining room marketed by Chambry. The critics were harsh: bourgeois, soulless, and, yet again, a trifle too heavy.

The 1925 Exposition must have brought painful memories to the aging Majorelle, now close to death. Gone were the fanfare and limelight afforded his splendid Art Nouveau bedroom suite twenty-five years earlier, in its place virtual obscurity among the era's new generation of cabinetmakers. Absent, too, were the bulk of his old Ecole de Nancy furniture cohorts: Gallé, Prouve, Vallin, and Gauthier. Jacques Gruber had survived, but solely as a stained glass artist.

Majorelle died 15 January 1926, Alfred Lévy assuming the firm's directorship. Retrospective exhibitions at both the annual Salons paid tribute to Nancy's master cabinetmaker. The first, at the 1926 Salon d'Automne, displayed a mahogany and locustwood desk and chair *aux nénuphars* from the 1900 Exposition Universelle alongside a buffet in amaranth, macassar ebony, and American walnut from the 1922 Salon d'Automne. Total luxuriance versus total constraint, the opposing lodestars of Art Nouveau and Art Deco philosophies, made especially significant when viewed in the work of a single cabinetmaker.

The Salon des Artistes Décorateurs had a similar retrospective the following year: turn-of-the-century examples *aux orchidées* and *aux algues* were displayed with one of Majorelle's last works: a 1925 smoking room in coralwood, in collaboration with Alfred Lévy, Janin (stained-glass windows), and Francin (carpets).

Les Ateliers Majorelle continued to exhibit at the Salons, in 1929 participating also in the 3rd Exposition of La Décoration Française Contemporaine. Lévy was joined at this time by Louis Majorelle's nephew, Pierre, a graduate of the Ecole des Beaux-Arts, Paris, and the family's cabinet shop in Nancy. The two participated in an office shown at the 1930 Salon d'Automne. Other collaborators included Paul Colin (paintings), Guénot (sculpture), Dunand (vases), Décor et Lumière (lamps), and Lehucher (window shades). The room appeared curiously cold and stark, lacking the fullness and warmth which had been the hallmark of Majorelle interiors for so many years. Pierre died unexpectedly shortly after. Yvanhoë Rambosson reviewed the firm's recent furniture in a 1933 article in *Mobilier et décoration*. Illustrated were ultramodern tables, bars, and cabinets with glass shelves, similar to contemporary designs by Jules Leleu. Rambosson saw in all this a prevailing continuity: 'The founder's impetus and the disciplines he imposed still go on. In this house you can live in the past without losing sight of the present and even the future. It is a good example of a tradition whose lessons have been well learned.'

Mallet-Stevens, Robert:

Mallet-Stevens was born in Paris 4 March 1886 and took the surnames of his father, Maurice Mallet, a painting appraiser, and his maternal grandfather, Arthur Stevens, a Belgian. Childhood in Maisons-Lafitte was followed in 1905 by

enrolment at the Ecole Spéciale d'Architecture, to which he returned in 1924 as a professor. He graduated in 1910, spending the remainder of the prewar years preparing architectural sketches and interiors. Very little actual constructional work was completed, Mallet-Stevens limiting himself to projects such as his 'Une Cité Moderne' shown at the 1912 Salon d'Atumone, and a thesis published in the Belgian magazine, *Le Home*. An important work at this time was a music-room project for a villa in Deauville. An early and enduring influence throughout his work was Josef Hoffmann who, in 1905, had designed the famous palace for Mallet-Stevens's uncle, Adolph Stoclet, in Brussels.

Mallet-Stevens established himself after the war, designing a wide range of private residences, theatres, cinemas, shops, offices, and public gardens, the most renowned of which were a villa for the Viscount de Noailles in Hyères (1923–25), six villas in a street in Auteuil which bears his name (1926–27), and a casino at Saint-Jean-de-Luz (1928).

In the 1925 Exposition Mallet-Stevens had a resounding success, participating in five diverse projects: a studio for La Société des Auteurs de Film; a winter garden in which the brothers Jan and Joel Martel constructed 'cubist' trees in reinforced concrete; the pavilion for Le Syndicat d'Initiative de Paris; the Pavillon du Tourisme; and a hall in the Ambassade Française.

In a 1933 article in *Architecture d'aujourd'hui*, Mallet-Stevens discussed with great clarity the role that he perceived for his furniture, which was of simple form and without ornamentation: 'There is no technical reason why furniture and the applied arts should change. It is generally architecture which inspires the so-called decorative arts. They act in harmony with architecture and adapt to it, becoming one with it. They evolve as architecture evolves, but always following its lead.' Among the most notable of his furniture designs were garden chairs in green-painted tubular steel and canvas for the Noailles villa (*c.* 1924); furniture for his office in Auteuil – a desk, chairs, and table – in lacquered sheet metal and nickel-plated tubular steel; and furnishings for the Cavroix house in Roubaix (1934). However, he did not design all the furniture in his interiors, but invited others, such as Djo-Bourgeois (a student of his at the Ecole Spéciale d'Architecture), Chareau, the Bauhaus, Prou, Dominique, and Klotz to provide individual pieces. Dufy contributed fabrics, and Gray and D.I.M carpets.

Mallet-Stevens used a combination of woods and metal, the latter sometimes executed by Labormétal, for his furniture. Warm veneers or lacquered finishes compensated for the severity of design. The introduction to *Une Demeure 1934*, published by *Architecture d'aujourd'hui*, explained the effect: 'Finally, all the furnishings and interior decoration are in different woods. Some of the doors, the panelling, the *armoires*, the libraries, the ceilings in the smoking room, the

tables, the chairs are made from oak, pear wood, sycamore, zingana, etc. There are few rare elements but the work is exquisite. The chosen materials are usually very simple: the meticulous working turns them into luxury items.' Upholstery was in leather or a rubberized fabric.

Illumination played a significant part in Mallet-Steven's interiors. Natural lighting was provided by Louis Barillet's stained-glass windows, the selection of colours limited to opalescent whites and pale greys. Artificial illumination, often on the advice of the lighting engineer, André Salomon, was commissioned to Jean Perzel, Genet and Michon, or Jacques Le Chevalier.

In 1930, Mallet-Stevens was appointed president of the newly formed U.A.M. He participated in the 1935 Brussels Exposition and also in the 1937 Exposition Universelle, at which he was awarded numerous architectural commissions. With the advent of the Second World War he virtually ceased work, moving with his family to south-west France, where he died 8 February 1945 of a protracted illness.

Mare, André (see Süe et Mare)

Martine School (see Poiret)

Matet, Maurice:

Matet was born in Colombes on the Seine in 1903. By 1925 he was an established decorator at Le Studium Louvre, the art atelier of the Louvre department store on the rue de Rivoli. He participated in the firm's pavilion at the 1925 Exposition, showing a dining room in which he had the distinguished cooperation of Jacques Gruber (stained glass), and Edgar Brandt (wrought-iron). Mlle Chameaux designed the carpets. The décor was tropical, leopard-skin upholstery was matched by paintings of jungle scenes. The walls' upper frieze depicted athletes in competition.

In late 1928, Matet and Kohlmann, collaborators for the previous five years, were listed in *Buying Antique and Modern Furniture in Paris* by T. and L. Bonney as codirectors of Le Studium Louvre. It appears that Matet may have left the firm within months, since his exhibit at the 1929 Salon des Artistes Décorateurs was marketed by Saddier et ses Fils. He accepted a professorship at the Ecole des Arts Appliqués, and continued to design furniture until after the Second World War.

Matet exhibited regularly at the Salons from 1923 to 1929, showing a range of ensembles and individual pieces. Early furniture – in woods such as pearwood, wild cherry, *gaiac*, and locustwood – was neat but bland, vibrancy and femininity provided by Max Vibert's carpets and delightful panels. His most distinctive furniture was included in a 1928

boudoir: open armchairs in tubular steel upholstered in a ribbed rubber fabric. An attempt at such chic the previous year had met with censure from the *Mobilier et décoration* critic: 'The whole dining room set is made of lacquer. This is another fashionable whim which has to be borne while regretting the tyranny it exercises. Anyway, given the circumstances, I do not believe that this fashion will last.'

Several Matet interiors were illustrated in reviews such as *Répertoire de goût moderne*. Since health was a very saleable commodity in the late twenties, it is no surprise that a 1929 issue showed a sketch of a 'gentleman's gymnasium', complete with punching-bag, dartboard, dumb-bells, and parallel bars.

Mercier frères:

Claude Mercier's furniture-manufacturing firm at 100 Faubourg Saint-Antoine was well-established by 1850. A wide range of eighteenth- and early nineteenth-century styles was reproduced – everything from Louis XVI to Empire – the shameless stock-in-trade of most of the quarter's cabinet-makers. In turn, both Art Nouveau and Art Deco furniture were made. By 1900 the firm was called 'Mercier Frères' and was presumably managed by two or more of Claude's sons.

Mercier Frères adapted readily to the prevailing Art Deco Style, offering a range of 'modern' interiors in addition to its traditional wares. An office displayed at the 1924 Salon des Artistes Décorateurs included a full range of lamps, furniture, paintings, and wall panelling. The effect was powerful. The September 1926 issue of *Les Echos des industries d'art* illustrated a commode in palisander veneered with ivory and ebony. Its contours – fundamentally Louis XVI, down to the elongated *toupie* feet – was adapted judiciously to the modern style by the application of a central ivory panel depicting two kneeling maidens among flowers. Further interiors, such as studios designed by H. Aribaud and Eric Bagge for the firm's exhibits at the two 1929 Salons, remind the viewer that Mercier was by tradition a manufacturer of *wood* furniture; sleek settees and chairs incorporate cylindrical pearwood frames more economically and fashionably made in tubular metal.

Mercier took stand 48 on the Esplanade des Invalides at the 1925 Exposition, under the same roof as other commercial manufacturers such as Sormani, P. A. Dumas, and Evrard Frères. Displayed was a dining room designed for the firm by Raymond Quibel, the neat furniture enhanced by murals of mountainous forests. The effect was striking, far more so, in fact, than many interiors shown by professed Art Deco proponents.

In the late 1920s Mercier opened a gallery, 'Palais de Marbre', at 77 Champs-Elysées.

Mère, Clément:

Born in Bayonne in 1870, Mère apprenticed in Gérôme's Paris atelier, returning afterwards to family life in the provinces. Landscapes painted in the Basse-Pyrénées and Franche-Comté were displayed at the Salon Nationale. His style was calm, if undistinguished. Visits to old colleagues at the Ecole drew him back to Paris at the turn of the century, and he began to produce leatherware and fabric patterns. He joined Meier-Graefe's La Maison Moderne, working closely with Franz Waldorff, a designer of bookcovers and embroidered silks.

Some time later came small examples of Mère's new *métier*: letter openers, toiletry items, fans, and bookcovers in *repoussé* leather, *galuchat*, and ivory. A 1912 article by Emile Sedeyn in *Art et décoration* traced this evolution from the fine to the applied arts. The objects, exquisitely rendered, showed refinement and femininity. An Oriental influence was evident, particularly in his patinated leather floral designs.

Mère introduced furniture into his repertoire at the Salon des Artistes Décorateurs and Société Nationale, *c.* 1910. Preferred woods were macassar ebony, maple, and rosewood. His style revealed a rigid Louis XVI discipline which cramped inspiration. Clearly, the emphasis was on the object's materials rather than its shape. The critic Yvanhoë Rambosson drew attention to this imbalance in a 1922 article in *Art et décoration*: 'There are a large number of knick-knacks which are decorated without regard for the intrinsic beauty of the materials that were used. He tries to prettify a commonplace shape with unnecessary additions, and he forgets that the decoration should enhance the lines and surfaces of the objects and not cover them needlessly. I saw a little powder box that was successfully worked, but otherwise there were so many pieces with bits of colour stitched in randomly with no apparent reason. These are good examples of false luxury, to be avoided at all costs.'

Around 1924, Mère received two important commissions: a cabinet for Lord Rothermere and a desk, now in the Musée des Arts Décoratifs, Paris, for Robert de Rothschild, an ardent patron of contemporary furniture.

Little is recorded of Mère after 1925. He no longer participated in the Salons and appears to have retired.

Mergier, Paul:

Born in Orthez, Basse-Pyrénées, in 1891, Mergier moved to Paris where he studied engineering at the Ecole Brequet, following this with graduate studies at the Ecole Supérieure d'Aéronautique and the science faculty at the Sorbonne. Conscripted in the First World War, he was demobilized in 1920 and began his work in cabinetmaking and *dinanderie*, in which his knowledge of science and metallurgy stood him in good stead.

He exhibited a wide range of objects at the Salons from 1925: vases, paintings, screens, doors, and furniture. A preferred medium was enamelled copper, frequently used in vases made to his designs by Goetz or La Monaca Guy. Lacquered screens with *repoussé* decoration were also displayed, some encrusted with mother-of-pearl, *coquille d'oeuf*, pewter, gold, or silver.

In his furniture, too, Mergier showed his expertise in metalware. Cupboards in palisander incorporated copper doors inlaid with semiprecious metals. One such work caught the discerning eye of Jacques Doucet, the period's foremost collector of modern furniture, who commissioned a filing cabinet for his studio in Neuilly. The piece, now in the Musée des Arts Décoratifs, Paris, includes every aspect of Mergier's metalware repertoire, in addition to leather doors and a parchment-lined interior.

The themes for Mergier's screens were drawn from classical mythology – Nessus, Neptune, Bacchante, etc. – and seem tired and outmoded in comparison to the range and sophistication of his materials.

Montagnac, Pierre-Paul:

Montagnac was born in 1883, references in the 1920s listing both Paris and Saint-Denis as his place of birth. He obtained his painting and decorative skills through two municipal academies, Carrière and La Grande Chaumière, making his début at the Salons in 1912. His address from 1919 was given as 58 rue de Rome.

Montagnac designed a wide range of commercial and domestic interiors, choosing a select group of artists, including da Silva Bruhns, Subes, and Perzel, to provide ancillary furnishings. Magazines such as *Nouveaux intérieurs français* and *Petits Meubles modernes* show a sober, but anonymous, modern style inspired by the late eighteenth century. His furniture was, at first, somewhat too robust and large. Léon Moussinac described it in *Intérieurs IV* as incorporating the trappings of comfort without being too bourgeois. Preferred woods were palisander, sycamore, and oak. Decoration was provided largely by contrasting veneers, rather than marquetry. Various furniture-makers in the Faubourg Saint-Antoine were approached to execute his designs, Montagnac settling finally on Robert Sangouard at 116 avenue des Batignolles, Saint-Ouen. Commissions were also marketed by Le Confortable and Galeries Lafayette.

At the 1925 Exposition, Montagnac took a stand next to Sangouard's on the Esplanade des Invalides and displayed a hallway and gallery. He also participated in the *grand salon* of the Ambassade Française and, to show his diversity, designed a selection of chased bronze key escutcheons, window bolts, and hinges for Fontaine & Cie, a Parisian locksmith.

The 1930s brought two prestigious ocean liner commissions: in 1931 a de luxe bedroom and drawing room for the *Atlantique*, and four years later the 'Caen' suite on the *Normandie*. Montagnac rose to the challenge, the quality of the cabinetry, in particular, pleasing the critics. A 1934 article in *Mobilier et décoration* traced other recent interiors, placing heavy emphasis on architectural lighting. He was appointed President of the Société des Artistes Décorateurs in 1930 and organized its pavilion at the 1937 Exposition. He died in 1961.

Moreux, Jean-Charles:

Moreux was born in Mont-Saint-Vincent in 1889. On moving to Paris he established himself at 11 *bis* rue de Rome. A renowned architect, he designed for all income groups a wide variety of private residences, villas, and hotels, occupying himself increasingly with every aspect of interior decoration.

Ultramodern, if not 'minimalist', his furniture can be defined as fiercely rational and formal. Well constructed, it allowed for no ornamentation beyond the selection of suitable veneers.

Despite the fact that he exhibited only once at the Salons (in 1924), Moreux received frequent magazine coverage, especially in *Les Arts de la maison* and *Répertoire du goût moderne*. Illustrated were a wide range of rooms in which to work or not to work, the distinction often blurred. A welcome variation was a summerhouse containing wicker chairs and table, with cushions by Sonia Delaunay and glassware by Jean Luce.

In a 1927 article in *Art et décoration*, Moreux maintained that he had solved the problems of modern construction by 'the maximum use of space, with sliding doors, sash windows, folding tables on the walls, and furniture hung from the ceiling by rope.' Superficial decoration was proscribed, Moreux professing to have 'banished high fantasy and extreme audacity'. Gone was every semblance of ornamentation, in its place razor sharp angles and functionalism.

Despite these minimalist tendencies, Moreux was persuaded to design a lavish table for Jacques Doucet's studio in Neuilly. The result was the opposite of spartan, combining macassar ebony, crocodile skin, ivory, *galuchat*, and crystal, all within a small illuminated table probably made for him by Pierre Legrain. At the 1925 Exposition he provided the furniture in a library exhibited by Auguste Perret.

Mouveau, Georges (see Joubert et Petit)

Nathan, Fernand:

Born in Marseilles, Nathan studied architecture, painting, and sculpture before settling on a career as an interior

decorator. Moving to Paris, he made his Salon début in 1913, establishing his studio at 112 boulevard de Courcelles.

Nathan designed entire rooms, the furnishings manufactured for him by a wide range of artisans. His furniture was a mélange of English Regency, Restauration and Louis-Philippe influences. Pieces shown at the Salons in the early 1920s were light and charming, praised by the critics for their unpretentious forms and light floral marquetry. Preferred was a pale base wood inlaid in palisander or amaranth with trailing flower sprays, the petals and stamen embellished with mother-of-pearl; this at a time when veneered ornamentation was largely proscribed for modern furniture. The critic Léon Moussinac found it necessary to defend Nathan in *Intérieurs II*: 'It would be illogical to use an unnecessary embellishment, but is it unnecessary when it enhances a composition? And should we be deprived of the resources of the noble profession all because of a theory?'

Other furniture decoration appears over-ornate. A dining room illustrated in *Décors et ameublements au goût du jour* used a recurring Nathan motif: broad crest-rails carved with fruit. The same theme was repeated elsewhere on pilasters and cornices, generating an unintended rustic effect. By 1926, Nathan's furniture had lost its earlier appeal, and the critics no longer reviewed it in their Salon coverage.

Nathan's wallpapers and carpets provided the vibrancy which his furniture lacked. They dominate nearly every interior, a repeating pattern of large flowers used to impart colour in a manner similar to that used by the Martine School and Süe et Mare.

Nathan was an independent designer and negotiated with various retailers to market his furnishings: Primavera, Bianchini, Cornille Frères, and Galeries Lafayette.

The 1925 Exposition drew on Nathan's skill as an architect. He designed boutiques for both Les Etablissements Florina and Compagnie des Perles Electriques, in both instances participating also in the interiors, his furniture executed by Jeist and Art du Bois. In the Ambassade Française he joined a host of Salon co-members in the decoration of the pavilion's *grand salon*.

Nics frères:

Nothing is known of Michel and Jules Nics' early years beyond that they were born in Hungary, became at some point naturalized Frenchmen, and opened an atelier at 98 avenue Félix-Faure in the early 1920s. Because they participated in the Salon des Artistes Français – geared almost exclusively to paintings – their work was not reviewed by the decorative arts critics at the Salon des Artistes Décorateurs or the Salon d'Automne. The historian, therefore, is left with little sense of their output or relative importance at the time. Certainly a large percentage of their work was architectural:

gates, interior grills, elevator cages, ramps, and shop fronts, one of the last-mentioned for La Société Anonyme des Gants Alexandre at the 1925 Exposition.

Two editions of *La Ferronnerie moderne* included illustrations of their work, commissioned by architects such as Sebille, Azema, Petit, and Grossard. Smaller items included light fixtures, consoles, guéridons, and fanlights.

Light fixtures were a major part of their output. Never over-ornate, the Nics gave the angularities and symmetrical volutes of their chandeliers a deeply hammered finish which imparted to their work a measure of identity in a field which had by 1925 become largely uniform. Opalescent glass shades softened the light, directing its diffused glow towards the ceiling.

In 1935 Jules Nics alone was listed as the founder-successor of the firm.

Pascaud, Jean:

Born in Rouen in 1903, Pascaud graduated in engineering in 1924 from the Ecole Centrale des Arts et Manufactures. An interest in the decorative arts led him into furniture design and increasingly, from the late 1920s, into the broader field of interior design. His address was listed as 1 rue de la Villa L'Evêque.

Pascaud was a traditionalist. Not for him the chromed tubular metal and glass slabs of Dufet or Dupré-Lafon. The history of furniture, both past and future, lay in proven design and in the judicious selection of rich veneers – violetwood, palisander, and American walnut, accented with parchment and *galuchat* or understated metal banding. Raymond Cogniat analysed Pascaud's philosophy in a 1935 article in *Art et décoration*: in simplicity and technical virtuosity lay the accord which represented both contemporary taste and the non-imitative continuation of tradition. Illustrated were individual pieces and ensembles: commodes, cabinets, dining rooms, and *salons*. To today's reader these appear ultramodern, even anonymous. Without signature or documentation, Pascaud's furniture is indistinguishable from that of Royère, Arbus, Dominique, or Pascal.

Pascaud presented his conservative, restrained furniture in surroundings which gave it the necessary warmth and ambience. The walls of a 1935 bedroom were lined in mauve fabric, its doors lacquered in gold, its linens and upholstery were in grey silk. Reactions were mixed. *Mobilier et décoration* cried out against such preciosity; *Art et décoration* praised the room's warmth and luxuriance. A year earlier Brunon Guardia assessed Pascaud's prevailing style in an article on the Salon d'Automne: 'M. Pascaud has worked over the decor with love. There is a wall lined in pearlish-grey. The interplay between the colours of the carpet and the brown and white curtains set off a tall writing-desk distinguished by

its clean lines and which would belong to the finest tradition of cabinetmakers were it not for a small round piece of veneer dead in the centre of this handsome piece of furniture which fatally detracts from our well-founded admiration for it.'

Pascaud's participation at the Salons was limited to the early 1930s. Later he concentrated on developing an elite clientele which included government officials and foreign ambassadors. Commissions for the ocean liners *Pasteur* and *Normandie* brought further prestige. Collaborators included Mme Bouissou (decorative glass panels), Pierre Lardin (engraved mirrors), and Léon Lang (panelling).

Perriand, Charlotte:

Born in Paris in 1903, Perriand attended the Ecole de l'Union Centrale des Arts Décoratifs. There is no record of any exhibit by her in the 1925 Exposition. Her début as a decorator appears to have taken place at the 1926 Salon des Artistes Décorateurs, where she displayed a living-room corner, the furniture in burl amboyna and palisander, with a carpet by Marianne Clouzot. Although functional and 'modern' the ensemble is unremarkable except for the fact that the furniture resembles certain Printz models at the time. The following year, however, Perriand's decision to join Le Corbusier and Jeanneret catapulted her from obscurity to world attention.

She displayed an attic bar (*un bar sous le toit*) at the 1927 Salon d'Automne, the previous year's veneered woods abruptly replaced by sheets of chromed steel, aluminium, and slabs of glass. Early readings of Le Corbusier's 'Vers une architecture et l'art décoratif d'aujourd'hui' had made her a fervent disciple. Furniture was stripped to its essentials, 'purified of everything that was simply an embellishment'.

Perriand remained with Le Corbusier and Jeanneret until the end of the 1930s. The three exhibited, in most part, as collaborators so it is difficult to credit furniture designs individually. Perriand, still living in Paris, and until recently an adviser to Cassina, has always stressed the collaborative effort. To a recent question on this issue, she replied: 'It really was team-work, a symbiosis. We talked things over together. Sometimes one word was enough to modify a plan and give it its final shape.' Contemporary magazines, on occasion, contradict this modest recollection, crediting the introduction of certain models, especially the *grand confort* armchair and a 1928 dining room with swivel chairs, directly to Perriand.

In 1930, Perriand became a founder-member of U.A.M., and was still listed as a member in 1955. Certain interiors and individual pieces are credited to her in the Society's literature; for example an 'Habitation d'Aujourd'hui' at the 1936 Salon des Arts Ménagers. A modern house, illustrated in *Répertoire de goût moderne, II*, incorporates a favourite theme:

facilities for both work and recreation. Functional kitchens, office space, and bathrooms juxtapose with an exercise room, bar, and solarium. A spartan phonograph and typewriter stand remind the reader of the prevailing architectural idiom.

At the outbreak of the Second World War, Perriand accepted an invitation from the Japanese Minister of Commerce and Industry to exhibit in Tokyo and Osaka. She remained in self-exile until 1946, returning then to France to work both with Le Corbusier and independently. She continued to experiment with metal furnishings, her designs manufactured in Jean Prouve's studios.

For a detailed discussion of furniture designed by Le Corbusier, Jeanneret, and Perriand, see LE CORBUSIER.

Petit, Philippe (see Joubert et Petit)

Petit, Pierre:

Petit was born in Paris in 1900. He entered the Ecole Boulle in 1914 to study cabinetry, a skill which he never actually practised. At the end of the war he joined Siègel, a firm specializing in hotel and shop installations, and worked for them until 1927 designing a range of furniture, light fixtures, wallpapers, and grillwork. In 1928 he established himself at 4 Place Gambetta, continuing to exhibit independently at both annual Salons up to and after the Second World War. He died in 1969.

The critics described Petit as an architect/*ensemblier*. His interiors were modern, the furniture in a combination of woods – sycamore, oak, walnut, and palisander – and chromed metals. A wide range of accomplished artisans were commissioned to execute his designs, in particular, Stéphany (fabrics), Coudyser (carpets), Lehucher (drapes), and Straub and Vagniat (lacquered furniture). An interesting characteristic of his interiors was the incorporation of stained-glass windows and room partitions executed by J.-K. Ray and A. Chanson. A travel agent's office, illustrated in *Intérieurs modernes*, included a typical example: a collage of exotic holiday venues, trains, ships, and buses in a combination of textured and clear glass, the adjoining room furnished with bicoloured chairs and angular desks.

Petit's palette was bright: the furnishings juxtaposed contrasting colours; the walls and carpets were in red and grey. Indirect lighting accentuated the interplay of tones.

Poiret, Paul:

As much by his dress designs as by his celebrated feasts and orgies, the couturier Paul Poiret gave Paris its pre-First World War lustre. Surrounded by artists such as Paul Iribe, Georges Lepape, Brissaud, and Raoul Dufy, it is not

surprising that Poiret's boundless creativity overlapped into the field of interior decoration. In April 1911, following visits to the Wiener-Werkstätte and the Palais Stoclet, Poiret founded the Martine School. Named after one of his daughters, the school took in its first class of twelve-year-old girls recruited from the Parisian working class. Poiret's individualism is reflected in the school's charter: the students were assigned rooms in his own house where he personally instructed them in the study of nature. There was no formal tuition, no teaching staff. The girls were encouraged to visit the Jardin des Plantes and to make sorties into the countryside, sketchbooks in hand. Progress was measured in competitions set and judged by Poiret himself, the best designs being converted into fabrics printed on cylinder presses by Paul Dumas or into carpets manufactured by Fenaille. Poiret described the reason behind the school's *modus operandi* in his 1930 autobiography, *En habillant l'époque*: 'I have seen the "Herr Professor" in Berlin and Vienna twisting the brains of their pupils in order to make them fit into a new mould as if it were an iron straitjacket. . . . I found this working and disciplining of minds utterly criminal.'

The results were spectacular. Nature's spontaneity and freshness were captured and retained: daisies, poppies, cornflowers, baskets of begonias, and massive hortensias soon blossomed in kaleidoscopic profusion on carpets, curtains, wallpapers, and upholstery fabrics. Poiret saw his role as that of a moderator: to stimulate and encourage the students without imposing his own ideas. The flower became the pretext for conveying colour, the students' untutored imaginations the means of creating it in unprecedented combinations. Surprisingly for a commercial venture launched on such a modest financial scale, Poiret was hard put to keep the school profitable. He blamed the public's lack of aesthetic sophistication for several unsuccessful editions.

Raoul Dufy both shared Poiret's enthusiasm for the Ecole Martine and participated in many of its design projects. The two worked together for many years – initially in a teacher-protégé relationship and then as partners – renting a studio in the avenue de Clichy to print their fabric designs, the chemist Zifferlin developing preferred colour, lithographic inks, and aniline dyes. By the early 1920s, Dufy's talent had been noticed by the prominent fabric retailer Bianchini, who placed him under contract, bringing to an amicable end his fruitful relationship with Poiret.

Poiret participated at the annual Salons for many years, both independently and, from 1912, in association with the Ecole Martine. Carpets predominated, either as individual exhibits or as part of entire rooms. In the 1920s came a wide range of new furnishings: pianos, lampshades, cushions, vitrines, and lacquered and marquetry tables. The furniture was largely cubistic in shape, the wood painted in single vibrant colours without further decoration. Occasionally,

richly grained woods remained unpainted: peroba, maple, and varnished sycamore. Chairs, sofas, and beds were piled high with sumptuous tasselled cushions and bolsters. Light fixtures were concealed, their diffused rays catching the gold and silver sheen on silk curtains or playing softly on the edges of crystal tableware. Furniture designers for the Martine School included Mario Simon, Léo Fontan and, of course, Poiret himself.

Many complete ensembles were exhibited. The influence of the Ballets Russes and Bakst, in particular, was omnipresent. A dining room for a hunting lodge was shown at the 1923 Salon d'Automne, the chairs with charming double scroll crests, despite their somewhat Directoire formality. The following year Poiret participated with Mallet-Stevens, Ruhlmann, Legrain, and others in Chareau's 'La Réception et l'intimité d'un appartement moderne' at the Salon des Artistes Décorateurs, designing the apartment's veranda. Jean Badovici illustrated nine Poiret ensembles in his *Intérieur français 1925*: an atrium, hallway, stairwell, telephone alcove, bedrooms, and dining rooms. The author's assessment was favourable: 'The work of Poiret has a lively spontaneity and reveals an overflowing imagination, a naïve sincerity, and a hint of hesitant grace which calls to mind the primitives, who have an indisputable charm. This graceful fantasy which comes out in the invention of ingenious and delicate ornaments for the smoking room or the library, this poetry of colours, these prettily painted pieces of furniture and these carpets all bring to today's world of design an appealing and valuable elegance in style which is rarely found.' Other critics found the displays less enduring and described them as 'puerile', 'circus-like', 'languid' and – disapprovingly – 'Baudelarian'.

Poiret devised a masterly means of capturing the limelight at the 1925 Exposition: three barges, entitled *Amours* (Love), *Délices* (Delights) and *Orgue* (Pipe Organ), anchored in front of the quai de la Seine. Fitted with plush interiors which he designed in collaboration with Dufy, La Maison Rosine, and La Maison Martine, the vessels drew wide acclaim, providing Poiret with a fitting capstone to his career. *Amour* was comprised of a bedroom, *Délices* of a *salon* and dining room, and *Orgue* of an immense illuminated organ.

Painted furniture, characteristically exotic in style, was set off against plush carpets decorated with vibrant flower sprays on warm green and orange/red grounds. Visitors flocked to the barges, finding whimsical relief from the neighbouring mainland exhibitions, many of which were didactic in theme.

Poiret and the Ecole Martine continued to exhibit at the Salons after the 1925 Exposition, showing a variety of furniture and light fixtures and large numbers of carpets. In 1927, Poiret designed a de luxe cabin 'Chantilly' for the ocean liner *Ile-de-France*. The following year, the school displayed a dining room designed by Yves Chudeau. Disciplined and

unspectacular, the angular furniture and glass tableware lacked the spontaneity and flamboyance of earlier work.

Porteneuve, Alfred:

Trained as an architect, Porteneuve lived and worked in the awesome shadow and celebrity of his uncle, Ruhlmann. He appears to have joined the family firm in the early 1920s. He participated in the Hôtel du Collectionneur at the 1925 Exposition, responsible with two other architects, Bourquin and Haranger, for the pavilion's interior architecture. He soon gained his uncle's confidence, collaborating on various interiors from 1926, his special responsibility being to design the settings of Ruhlmann's interiors and to coordinate the firm's participation in local and international Expositions.

On Ruhlmann's death in November 1933, Porteneuve was charged with the liquidation of the remaining inventory. Ruhlmann had left explicit instructions both that the office at 27 rue de Lisbonne be closed and that the name of Ruhlmann and Laurent be discontinued. Porteneuve installed himself nearby at 47 rue de Lisbonne and continued to work under his own name. He designed his own furniture models, reproducing, in addition, a range of models which Ruhlmann had authorized be manufactured posthumously with the qualifying identification, 'modèle de Ruhlmann édité par Porteneuve'. His own models bear a branded signature, 'A. Porteneuve'. His designs from 1934 are virtually indistinguishable from earlier Ruhlmann prototypes so it is difficult to determine whether his own preferred style happened to match that of his uncle or whether he continued as he did for commercial reasons.

Porteneuve sometimes exhibited independently at the Salons before 1934, at the 1930 Salon des Artistes Décorateurs, for example, he collaborated with Henri Rapin on the Exhibition Hall, the interior furnished by P. Beucher, Lalique (illuminated fountains), Thonet (garden furniture) and Brunet et Meunié (fabrics and carpets). At the 1937 Exposition he displayed an office for the President of the Syndicat des Soiereries de Lyon and collaborated with Jean Dunand in an ensemble in the Société des Artistes Décorateurs pavilion.

Printz, Eugène:

Printz was born in Paris in 1889, the son of a cabinetmaker in the Faubourg Saint-Antoine, where he served his apprenticeship. The firm reproduced a range of *ancien régime* styles, especially Louis XV and XVI. Printz later opened his own atelier at 12 rue Saint-Bernard, where he continued to manufacture 'style' pieces, mostly for interior decorators. He even drew on the eighteenth-century tradition of providing maquettes – his were in cardboard – for the client's approval.

The decision to switch to contemporary furniture appears to have come at the time of the 1925 Exposition, in which Printz participated only minimally, sharing the credit with Pelletier and James for the furniture in Chareau's office/library in the Ambassade Française. He made his début as a modernist, with a bedroom in rosewood, at the 1926 Salon des Artistes Décorateurs. His reputation grew rapidly; by 1930 his highly personal style attracted praise from the critics. Printz showed his work in most of the decade's major exhibitions, for example, the 1935 Brussels Exposition and the 1937 Exposition des Arts et Techniques. After the Second World War, he joined Leleu, M. Jallot, Dominique, and Prou in the group, 'Décor de France'. He died in 1948.

Printz's style shows great energy and innovation. A charming interplay of arches and perpendiculars predominates, the crispness of design accentuated by the contrast between dark woods and bright metal mounts. He is quoted by Bernard Champigneulle in a *Mobilier et décoration* article as saying: 'I admire the seductive harmony between the straight lines and the curves and this originality which is at one and the same time daring and discreet.' Few, if any, of his contemporaries could claim to have developed a more distinctive range of furniture, many fine examples of which were illustrated in magazines such as *Sièges contemporains* and *Petits Meubles du jour*.

Two aspects of Printz's designs bear special mention: his modular tables, with three, five, or six hinged elements, which could be positioned in a straight line or compressed to form a bookcase, and his system of folding doors (*portes-accordéon*) on large cupboards.

From his gallery at 81 rue de Miromesnil in the fashionable 8th *arrondissement*, Printz sought out an elite clientele, including the Princess de la Tour d'Auvergne (a Paris apartment and her château de Grosbois), the Princess de Wagram (a Paris townhouse), the Viscount de Richemont (a Paris apartment), and Baron Rudolphe d'Erlanger (a house in Tunisia). State commissions included the Musée Permanent des Colonies in Vincennes, the Cité Universitaire in Paris, and interiors for the Société Générale. Other distinguished customers were Marshall Lyautey, Jeanne Lanvin, and the theatrical producer, Louis Jouvet, for whose productions of *Jean de la lune* and *Domino* Printz designed the sets.

Printz's preferred woods were *palmier*, Gabonese ebony, kekwood, sycamore, and violetwood. Furniture mounts were selected from a similarly diverse range of metals: copper, steel, bronze, and wrought-iron, their surfaces oxidized, silvered, patinated, lacquered, or incised. Dunand was a frequent collaborator, providing a range of lacquered and chased decorative finishes to cabinet doors. Chair upholstery was in silk or Lutetia velvet.

A catalogue published by the firm in 1934 showed a wide selection of furniture. Customers were invited to choose their favourite woods, ranging from *palmier*, the most expensive,

through palisander and *bois des îles*, to walnut. Editions ranged from five – for the firm's most elaborate cabinets, listed at Fr40,000 – to thirty for small tables and lamps. Items were stamped 'E.P.'. The catalogue also offered a range of decorative objects by Cros, Dunand, Mayodon, Methey, Pompon, and others, incorporated by Printz in his interiors.

A distinctive aspect of Printz's interiors was his use of a circular ceiling cupola to provide indirect lighting.

Priou, Gaston:

Priou remains relatively unknown. Born in Paris, he emerged in 1922 at the Salon des Artistes Décorateurs as an accomplished artist in lacquer. Ten years later he was still exhibiting the same range of screens, trays, and small furniture in lacquer and *coquille d'oeuf*, this time for de luxe cabins on the ocean liner *S.S. Félix-Roussel*. Why Priou remained unnoticed is uncertain (only one brief reference appears to have been made to his work – a black lacquered dressing table – in a 1922 article in *Art et décoration*). Although his output was less than that of lacquerwork contemporaries such as Louis Midavaine and Etienne Saïn, his designs incorporate a careful interplay of lavish dark lacquers accented with crushed eggshell. The lacquer was applied thickly with a drip technique. The few pieces which have survived show excellent workmanship. Tropical landscapes were popular Priou themes, as were mountain citadels and enchanted isles.

Prou, René:

Prou was born in Nantes (Loire-Inférieure) in 1889. He settled in Paris after graduating from the Ecole Bernard Palissy in 1908, joining La Maison Gouffé, of which he was appointed artistic director. In 1912 he was awarded two prestigious decorating commissions: the Salle de Conseil du Comptoir d'Escompte de Paris and the residence of the Paraguayan ambassador. Although the war interrupted his career, he continued his research into new materials and techniques. In 1919, listed at 26 rue de Lyon, he exhibited his first-class cabin for the ocean liner *Paris* at the Salon d'Automne, the furniture executed by Schmit & Cie.

A string of ocean liner commissions followed in the next four years: the *Paris, Volubilis, Roussillon, Cuba*, and *De Grasse*, several of the interiors shown at the Salons. Further important exposure at the time was afforded by the Exposition Coloniale de Marseille.

The 1925 Exposition drew widely on Prou's skills as an architect and decorator. He had a hand in numerous exhibits, not only for his own boutique on the Esplanade des Invalides, but for Fontaine et Cie, L'Art du Bois, Le Pavillon de L'Art Colonial, La Société des Chaussures 'Cécil', the boutique Elégance, the Pavillon des Alpes-Maritimes, Le Palais de la Ville de Paris, a governor's apartment in the Pavillon de l'Indo-Chine, and, in the Ambassade Française, a boudoir and bathroom in collaboration with Eric Bagge. Furniture, key escutcheons, silks, fabrics, shop fixtures, and chandeliers showed that Prou's modern style, better known in the 1930s, had already matured.

In 1928 Prou succeeded Paul Follot as artistic director of Pomone, where he remained until 1932. The appointment of a rationalist to replace the traditionalist Follot signalled the firm's changing philosophy, immediately noticed by the *Mobilier et décoration* critic Gabriel Henriot in his review of the 1928 salon: 'What M. René Prou calls "Little Salon for Ladies in a Palace" made photographers despair. They stood there in front of the display discussing it endlessly. It seemed that Pomone had changed direction. Need I say that I was not greatly struck by this gooseberry suite, although each piece is pleasing enough on its own? Maybe it was the lighting, which was switched off each time I saw it, that gave me this impression.'

Prou's principal collaborators at Pomone were Henri Martin and Albert Guénot. Others, listed in early 1929, were Jean C. Colosiez, Pierre Paschal, and Jean Mérot de Barré.

Prou made the transition from wood – especially macassar ebony, amaranth, palisander, and *bois des îles* – to metal furniture in the late 1920s. He had a special liking for wrought-iron (for doors and furniture mounts), executed for him by Yung, Brandt, or Subes. Veneers were sumptuous: tortoise shell, lacquer, Duralumin, and pigskin.

A booklet published by the firm in the 1930s, *Le Secret de succès de l'atelier René Prou*, listed his architectural and decorating commissions in the previous twelve years: 300 apartments, 60 private residences, 30 banks, 400 train compartments for La Compagnie Internationale des Wagon-Lits, and 15 ocean liners (in addition to the ones mentioned above, these included the *Ile-de-France, Atlantique, Normandie, Champlain, La Fayette, Florida*, and *Colombie*). Commissions in the 1930s included a dining room for the Waldorf Astoria, New York, and other interiors in Geneva, Tokyo, and Le Havre.

From the late 1930s until he died in 1947, Prou taught part-time, most notably at the Ecole Nationale des Arts Décoratifs.

Rapin, Henri:

Born in Paris in 1873, Rapin studied under Jean-Léon Gérôme. He emerged as an accomplished painter, illustrator, and decorator, exhibiting at the Salons from about 1903. The early furniture, in oak, was over-large and bourgeois: stiff contours carved with floral mouldings and panels by Charles Hairon and Le Bourgeois gave way later to ceramic and marquetry medallions. Other preferred woods were *bois de vikado*, walnut, mahogany, and burl amboyna.

continued on page 161

125 *Klotz:* dressing table and chair in macassar ebony, illustrated in *Petits Meubles du jour*, Paris, pl. 28. The chair illustrated also in *Sièges contemporains*, pl. 21

126 *Klotz:* sketch for a bedroom for Mme R., Paris. Illustrated in *Intérieurs IV*, Léon Moussinac, Paris, pl. 20

127 *Kohlmann:* end-table in walnut, marketed by Le Studium Louvre, *c.* 1928. Illustrated in *Petits Meubles modernes*, Paris 1929, pl. 13; and *Intérieurs d'aujourd'hui*, Waldemar George, Paris 1928, pl. 25

128 *Kohlmann:* cabinet included in an office marketed by Le Studium Louvre, *c.* 1930. Illustrated in *Mobilier et décoration* (Collection of de Lorenzo Gallery)

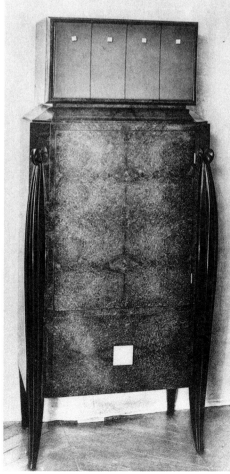

129 *Lahalle et Lévard:* dressing-table in sycamore and Coromandel lacquer, with silvered-bronze mounts, in collaboration with Mlle de las Cazas, exhibited at the Salon d'Automne, 1928. Illustrated in *Petits Meubles modernes,* Paris, pl. 17; *L'Art décoratif français en 1929,* Pierre Olmer, Paris 1929; and *Mobilier et décoration,* Dec. 1928

130 *Lahalle et Lévard:* dressing-table in marquetry with eight fluted feet, with matching tabouret. Illustrated in *Petits Meubles modernes,* Paris 1929, pl. 16

131 *Lahalle et Lévard:* secretary in burl walnut, lemonwood and mahogany with ivory and palisander marquetry, exhibited at the Salon of the Société des Artistes Décorateurs, 1924. Illustrated in *Les Arts de la maison,* Spring 1924, pl. XI; *Mobilier et décoration,* June 1924; and *Petits Meubles modernes,* Paris 1929

132 *Lahalle et Lévard:* secretary in burl wood, illustrated in *Petits Meubles modernes,* Paris 1929, pl. 15

133 *Lalique:* rectangular table in glass, exhibited at the Salon of the Société des Artistes Décorateurs, 1927. Illustrated in *Mobilier et décoration*, May 1927, p. 139

134 *Lalique:* oval table in glass, exhibited at the Salon of the Société des Artistes Décorateurs, 1927. Illustrated in *Mobilier et décoration*, May 1927, p. 139

135 *Le Corbusier, Jeanneret, et Perriand:* Ensemble illustrated in *Intérieurs*, Frantz Jourdain, pl. 17

136 *Le Corbusier:* chaise longue in chromed tubular steel, black-painted steel, and pony skin, designed in collaboration with Pierre Jeanneret and Charlotte Perriand in 1928 for a villa in Ville d'Avray. Exhibited at the 1929 Salon d'Automne and marketed by Thonet. Illustrated in *25 années U.A.M.*, René Herbst, Paris 1956, p. 111; *Intérieurs XI*, Léon Moussinac, Paris, pl. 17; and *Art et décoration*, Jan.–June 1930, p. 41 (Photo: Christie's, NY)

137　*Legrain:* Pleyela piano in glass and copper, marketed by Pleyel, collection of Pierre Meyer. Illustrated in *Art et décoration*, March 1929; and *Mobilier et décoration*, April 1929, p. 125

138　*Legrain:* dressing-table, in black lacquer and *galuchat*, marketed by Louis Vuitton. Illustrated in *Le Style moderne dans la décoration intérieure*, Henri Clouzot, Paris, pl. 28

139　*Legrain:* chair in brown lacquer decorated with incised gold triangular motifs, for Jacques Doucet, 1923. Illustrated in *The Connoisseur*, November 1972 (Photo: Sully-Jaulmes)

Opposite

140　*Legrain:* desk in ebony and *galuchat* for Jacques Doucet, *c.* 1923, the model included in a modern apartment designed by Pierre Chareau and illustrated in *Art et décoration*, June 1924; and *L'Art décoratif français 1918–1925*, Léon Deshairs, Paris 1926, p. 18 (Photo: Sully-Jaulmes)

141　*Legrain: table-desserte* in *galuchat*, bone, and maple (Photo: Sully-Jaulmes)

142　*Legrain:* console table in snakeskin and giltwood, exhibited at the first Salon of the Union des Artistes Modernes, 1929 (Collection of Galerie Vallois)

143　*Legrain:* bench in stained oak, ebony, and gold lacquer, for Jacques Doucet. Exhibited in 1923 (Photo: Sully-Jaulmes)

144　*Legrain:* tabouret, curule-shaped, the seat and central column in *galuchat*, the four feet and base in black lacquer. Exhibited at the 1923 Salon of the Société des Artistes Décorateurs. Illustrated in *Art et décoration*, 1923; *Femina*, Jan. 1925, p. 30; *L'Illustration*, May 1930, pp. 17–20; *La Gazette des beaux-arts*, March 1930, p. 79; *L'Oeil*, Dec. 1961, pp. 45, 47; *The Connoisseur*, Nov. 1972; and *Le Meuble français moderne*, Léon Moussinac, Paris 1952, p. 151 (Photo: The Brooklyn Museum)

145　*Legrain:* armchair, *c.* 1928. A similar model is illustrated in *Intérieurs IV*, Léon Moussinac, Paris, pl. 32

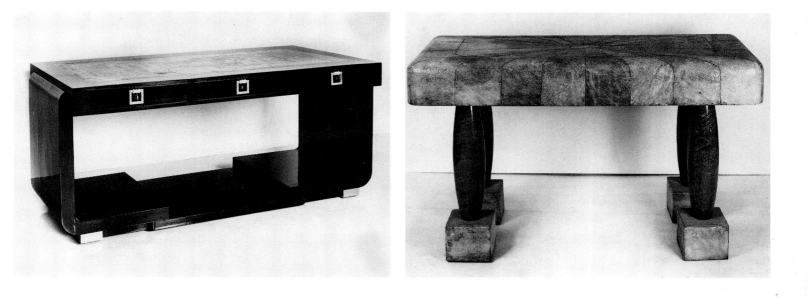

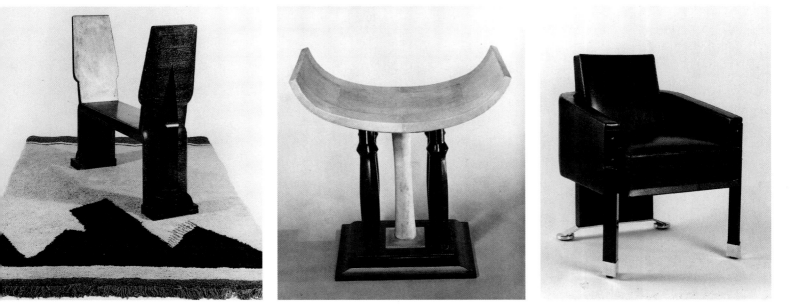

146 *Leleu:* desk and tabouret in burl amboyna, exhibited at the Salon of the Sociéte des Artistes Décorateurs, 1927. Illustrated in *Petits Meubles du jour*, Paris 1929, pl. 8

147 *Leleu:* grand piano marketed by Régy, illustrated in *Le Arti D'Oggi*, Roberto Papini, Casa Editrice d'Arte Bestetti e Tumminelli, Milan 1930, fig. 256

148 *Leleu:* armchair, illustrated in *Le Arti D'Oggi*, Roberto Papini, Casa Editrice d'Arte Bestetti e Tumminelli, Milan 1930, fig. 264

149 *Leleu:* dressing-table chair veneered in *galuchat*, *c.* 1928 (Collection of Barry Friedman, Ltd., NY)

150 *Leleu:* armchair in mahogany inlaid with ivory. The model produced also in amboyna, *c.* 1922. Illustrated in *Mobilier et décoration*, 1922 (Photo: Christie's, NY)

151 *Leleu:* music cabinet veneered in tortoise shell, with steel banding, the interior in sycamore (Collection of Félix Marcilhac)

152 *Leleu:* cabinet in macassar ebony with ebony and mother-of-pearl veneer, the feet with ivory *sabots*, 1938 (Photo: Sully-Jaulmes)

153 *Leleu:* psyche mirror and stool in amboyna, illustrated in *Petits Meubles du jour*, Paris 1929, pl. 22

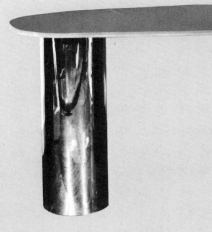

154 *Lurçat: salon* ensemble for M. P. D.-W., Paris 1928. Illustrated in *Art et décoration*, Sept. 1929; and *Répertoire du goût moderne II*, Paris, pl. 3

155 *Lurçat:* desk with chromed foot and drawers, the top in glass

156 *Majorelle:* cabinet in teak with rosewood and mother-of-pearl veneer, *c.* 1927 (Photo: Christie's, NY)

157 *Majorelle:* cabinet illustrated in a firm's advertisement in *Les Echos des industries d'art*, June 1926

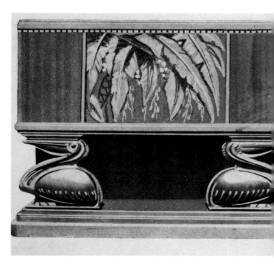

158 *Mallet-Stevens:* furniture for a room with two beds. Illustrated in *Répertoire du goût moderne IV*, Paris, pl. 22

159 *Martine School:* armchair and ottoman in ebony, maple, and green velvet, designed by Paul Poiret, 1912. The model illustrated in *Le Style 1925*, Yvonne Brunhammer, Paris, p. 69. A matching vitrine illustrated in *Art et décoration*, July–Dec. 1920, p. 144

160 *Martine School:* commode in silvered-wood with incised decoration by Leó Fontan, the interior in ebony, 1923 (Collection of Warren Cresswell and George Matheson Gerst)

161 *Martine School:* dining room for a hunting lodge in peyroba and polished sycamore, exhibited at the Salon d'Automne, 1923. Illustrated in *Les Arts de la maison; Intérieurs français*, Paris 1924, pl. 25; and *Art et décoration*, Nov. 1923, p. 177

162 *Matet:* *torchère* in mahogany, marketed by Le Studium Louvre. Illustrated in *Intérieurs III*, Léon Moussinac, Paris, pls. 39, 42. An identical pair exhibited at the Salon d'Automne, 1924, were illustrated in *Art et décoration*, Dec. 1924, p. 191

168 *Montagnac:* hall marketed by Robert Sangouard, *c.* 1927. Illustrated in *Ensembles mobiliers*, Paris, pl. 1

169 *Montagnac:* lady's desk and stool exhibited at the Union Centrale des Arts Décoratifs, 1927. Illustrated in *Art et décoration*, Jan.–June 1928; *Petits Meubles modernes*, Paris 1929, pl. 26; *Les Echos des industries d'art*, Feb. 1928, p. 31

170 *Moreux:* sketch of a room, illustrated in *Répertoire du goût moderne IV*, Paris, pl. 23

171 *Moreux:* table in ebony, crocodile skin, and *galuchat* with ivory veneer and internal illumination, probably executed by Pierre Legrain. Commissioned by Jacques Doucet, *c.* 1923. Illustrated in *L'Illustration*, 3 May 1930, p. 18; *Les Echos des industries d'art*, Jan. 1927, p. 11; and *La Gazette des beaux-arts*, Jan.–June 1930, p. 79

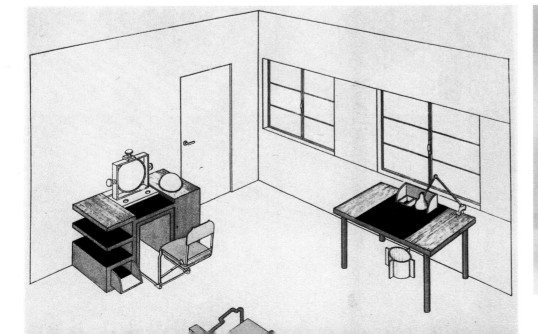

172　*Nathan: salon* chair, table, and armchair for M. M., Paris. Illustrated in *Intérieurs II*, Léon Moussinac, Paris, pl. 46

173　*Nics frères:* wrought-iron console, mirror, and compotes, all with hand-hammered *martelé* finish. Illustrated in *La Ferronerie moderne*, 3rd series, Henri Clouzot

174　*Pascaud:* dining-room, illustrated in *Ensembles mobiliers V*, Paris 1930, pl. 13

175 *Perriand:* silver cabinet in violetwood, illustrated in *Mobilier et décoration*, June 1927, p. 172

176 *Perriand:* mirrored and metal card table, 1926. A similar table is illustrated in *Art et décoration*, July–Dec. 1927, p. 173

177 *Perriand:* swivel chair in chromed tubular steel and leather, 1928, marketed by Thonet and exhibited at the Salon d'Automne, 1929. Illustrated in *Répertoire du goût moderne II*, Paris; *25 années U.A.M.*, René Herbst, Paris 1956, p. 111; *Art et décoration*, Jan.–June 1930, p. 157, and May 1928, p. 161; and *Mobilier et décoration*, July 1928, p. 22 (Collection of Jacques Mostini)

178 *Perriand:* salon in burl amboyna and palisander with fabric by Marianne Clouzot, 1926. Illustrated in *Les Echos des industries d'art*, June 1926

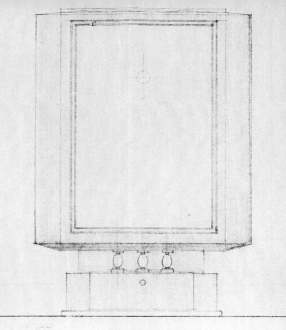

179 *Petit:* industrialist's office, marketed by Siègel. Illustrated in *Mobilier et décoration*, Nov. 1926, p. 127

180 *Porteneuve:* design for a cabinet, *c.* 1935

181 *Porteneuve:* liquor cabinet in macassar ebony, burl amboyna, and ivory, 1930s (Collection of Homeculture Gallery, Toronto)

182　*Printz: secrétaire à abattant* in walnut with lacquered and incised metal panels by Jean Dunand (Photo: Primavera Gallery)

183　*Printz:* armchair upholstered in silk with copper feet. Illustrated in *Intérieurs présentés au Salon des Artistes Décorateurs*, H. Rapin, Paris 1930, p. 129; and *Sièges contemporains*, Paris, p. 110

184　*Printz:* chair, *c.* 1929. Illustrated in *Sièges contemporains*, Paris

185　*Printz:* magazine holder in wood and metal (Collection of Maria de Beyrie)

186 *Printz:* living room including an armchair in black lacquer with velours upholstery, designed for Marshall Lyautey's reception hall at the Musée des Colonies. Illustrated in *Nouveaux Intérieurs français*, Paris, pl. 10

187 *Printz:* table in walnut with hinged components: closed forming a hexagon, open three attached tables. Exhibited at the Salon of the Société des Artistes Décorateurs, 1928. The model was also produced with five or six linked sections (Collection of Galerie Vallois)

188 *Printz:* table with red lacquer by Jean Dunand, illustrated in 'Eugène Printz et son atelier', *Mobilier et décoration*, 1938, p. 8

189 *Printz:* desk in polished palmwood for the Princesse de la Tour d'Auvergne's château de Grosbois. Illustrated in *Petits Meubles du jour*, Paris 1929, p. 11; and *Intérieurs présentés au Salon des Artistes Décorateurs*, H. Rapin, Paris 1930, pl. 36

190 *Printz:* bedroom in palmwood exhibited at the Salon of the Société des Artistes Décorateurs, 1926. Illustrated in *Intérieurs français au Salon des Artistes Décorateurs*, P. Follot, Paris 1927, pl. 34

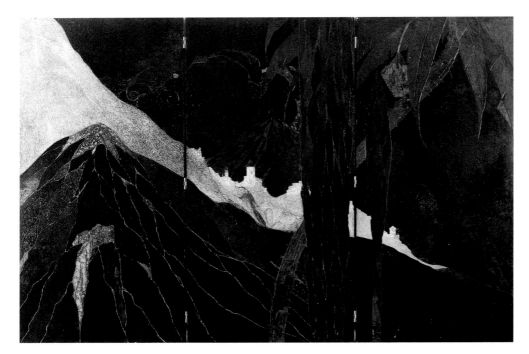

191 *Priou:* three-panel screen in lacquer and eggshell, 1928. Illustrated in *Decorative Folding Screens*, J. W. Adams, New York 1982, pp. 170–71 (Collection of The Brooklyn Museum)

192 *Prou:* fall-front desk in burl wood, illustrated in *Petits Meubles modernes*, Paris 1929, pl. 29

193 *Prou:* cabinet-on-stand for a library, illustrated in *Intérieurs IV*, Léon Moussinac, Paris, pl. 44

194 *Prou:* lady's desk and chair in burl wood, part of a bedroom ensemble illustrated in *Sièges contemporains*, Paris, pl. 15; and *Ensembles nouveaux*, Paris, pl. 15

Opposite

195 *Rapin:* bedroom exhibited at the Salon of the Société des Artistes Décorateurs, 1926. Illustrated in *Intérieurs français au Salon des Artistes Décorateurs*, P. Follot, Paris 1927, pl. 32

196 *Rateau:* armchair in ebonized wood (Photo: Sully-Jaulmes)

197 *Rateau:* ensemble exhibited at the Metropolitan Museum of Art, New York, 1926, including a bronze chair with interlacing fish decoration; a pair of bronze floor lamps with alabaster shades; a bronze toilet table with mirror; and a bronze stand. The chair was designed for Mrs G. Blumenthal's swimming pool, New York, *c.* 1914

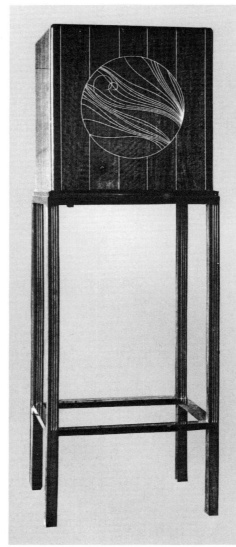

198   *Rateau:* ensemble exhibited at the Metropolitan Museum of Art, New York, 1926, including a six-panel screen in engraved gold lacquer entitled 'Coursing in the Forest'; seat furniture in carved oak upholstered in tapestry by Braquenié & Cie; a bronze low-table; a pair of bronze floor lamps with alabaster shades; and a small leopard-skin rug. The *canapé* in Aubusson tapestry designed by Paul Plumet

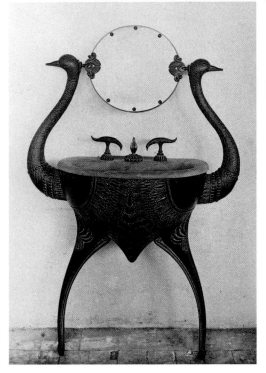

199 *Rateau:* commode, veneered *sans transverse*, with ormolu mounts. The model displayed in the Pavillon de l'Elegance at the 1925 Exposition (Photo: courtesy of F. A. Rateau)

200 *Rateau:* wash stand, bronze and marble, *c.* 1925 (Photo: courtesy of F. A. Rateau)

201 *Rateau:* chaise longue, bronze, model No. 1385 for the terrace in Jeanne Lanvin's boudoir. Also displayed in La Maison Callot Soeurs at the 1925 Exposition (Photo: courtesy of F. A. Rateau)

202 *Rateau:* guéridon, bronze and marble, *c.* 1925 (Photo: courtesy of F. A. Rateau)

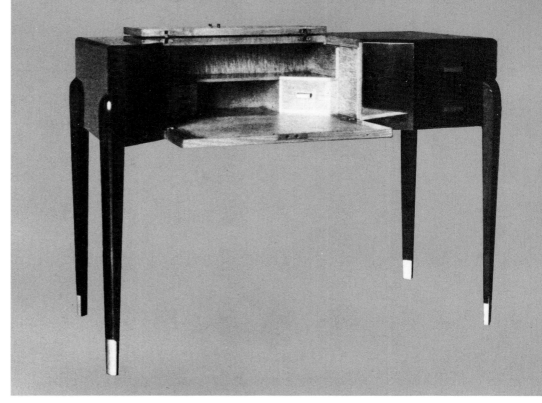

203 *Renaudot:* games table and chair, marketed by P. A. Dumas, *c.* 1923. Illustrated in *Intérieurs III*, Léon Moussinac, Paris, pl. 49; *Art et décoration*, March 1923; and *Décors et ameublements au goût du jour*, Gaston Fleury, Paris 1926

204 *Renaudot:* lady's desk in macassar ebony with gilt-bronze *sabots*, marketed by P. A. Dumas. Illustrated in *Art et décoration*, Jan.–June 1928

205 *Renaudot:* bedroom in tones of grey, black, green, and old gold; the lacquered green furniture with gold trim, the chairs in palisander with maroon upholstery. Illustrated in *Mobilier et décoration*, July 1923; and *L'Art décoratif français 1918–1925*, Léon Deshairs, Paris 1926

206 *Renouvin:* chair in grey lacquer with matching velours upholstery. Illustrated in *L'Art décoratif français 1918–1925*, Léon Deshairs, Paris 1926, p. 80; and *Art et décoration*, Oct. 1924, p. 124

207 *Rousseau:* cabinet in palmwood with *galuchat* and ivory veneer

208 *Rousseau:* table in palmwood and *galuchat* (Private Collection)

209 *Ruhlmann:* tallcase clock, 1922. Illustrated in *Les Arts de la maison*, Autumn 1924, pl. 13 (Collection of Sydney and Frances Lewis)

210 *Ruhlmann:* furniture sketches, illustrated in *Croquis de Ruhlmann*, Léon Moussinac, Paris, pl. 3

211 *Ruhlmann:* loggia for Jacqueline Francell, the furniture in palisander. Illustrated in *Intérieurs présentés au Salon des Artistes Décorateurs 1930*, H. Rapin, Paris 1930, pl. 39; *Le Salon des Artistes Décorateurs*, Paris 1930, pl. 34; and *Art et décoration*, Jan.–June 1930, p. 5

212 *Ruhlmann:* salon for the architect Molinie, the furniture in macassar ebony and amboyna. Illustrated in *Intérieurs I*, Léon Moussinac, Paris, pl. 36

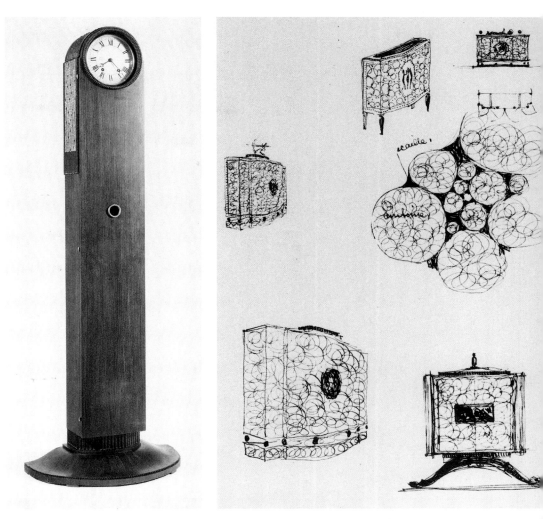

213 *Ruhlmann:* office ensemble, including a desk in amboyna, ivory, and *galuchat*, the model illustrated in *Art et décoration*, Jan. 1920, pp. 10–11; the chair in amboyna with silvered-bronze *sabots*; the filing cabinet in amboyna with ivory veneer (Photo: Lillian Nassau, Ltd.)

214 *Ruhlmann:* armchair in macassar ebony and ivory, 1913 (Collection of Barry Friedman, Ltd., NY)

215 *Ruhlmann:* chaise longue in macassar ebony with silvered-bronze feet, the model exhibited in the Hôtel du Collectionneur at the 1925 Exposition (Collection of Peter and Sandra Brant)

216 *Ruhlmann:* table with ivory *chutes* and *sabots*, the eggshell top by Jean Dunand (Collection of Barry Friedman, Ltd., NY)

217 *Ruhlmann:* ambassador's desk in palisander, *galuchat*, ivory, and silvered-bronze, executed by Adolphe Chanaux, 1925. The model (No. 1501) exhibited in the office/library of the pavilion Une Ambassade Française, designed by L.-H. Boileau and L. Carrière, at the 1925 Exposition. Illustrated in *Une Ambassade française*, Paris 1925, pl. 3 (Collection of French & Co., NY)

218 *Ruhlmann:* central motif of the celebrated 'Commode à char', 1919, depicting a charioteer. The model was manufactured with both four and six feet. For the four-legged variety see *Exposition rétrospective E.-J. Ruhlmann*, exhibition catalogue, Musée des Arts Décoratifs, Paris 1934; for the six-legged variety see *Harmonies Intérieurs de Ruhlmann*, Paris, pl. 17; and *L'Art décoratif français 1918–1925*, Léon Deshairs, Paris 1926, p. 49

219 *Ruhlmann:* office exhibited at the Exposition Coloniale, Paris, 1931. The pair of large bronze *vases réflecteurs* are by Subes

220 *Ruhlmann: grand salon* in the Hôtel du Collectionneur at the 1925 Exposition, the carpet by Gaudissard, fabric designs by Stéphany, the painting over the fireplace by Jean Dupas. Illustrated in *Ensembles mobiliers*, 1st series, Paris, pl. 26; *Ensembles mobiliers*, 2nd series, Paris, pl. 1; and *Art et décoration*, July 1925, p. 118

221 *Ruhlmann:* ensemble, including a pair of pedestals and tabourets, and a cabinet in burl amboyna with ivory veneer and central silvered-bronze medallion by Foucault entitled 'La Nuit et le Jour'. Commissioned by the Elysée Palace, 1920. Exhibited in the same year at the Salon d'Automne and in the Ambassade Française at the 1925 Exposition. Illustrated in *Une Ambassade française*, Paris 1925, pl. 4; and *Exposition rétrospective E.-J. Ruhlmann*, exhibition catalogue, Musée des Arts Décoratifs, Paris 1934

222 *Saddier:* dressing-table in sycamore, *c.* 1928. Illustrated in *Mobilier et décoration*, July 1929, p. 7 (Photo: Areta Adler)

223 *Sognot:* lady's desk and chair, marketed by Primavera and exhibited at the Union Centrale des Artistes Décorateurs, 1928. Illustrated in *Art et Décoration*, 1928

224 *Sognot:* desk and chair, in collaboration with Charlotte Alix. Illustrated in *Petits Meubles du jour*, Paris 1928

225 *Sognot:* chest of drawers and filing cabinet, in collaboration with Charlotte Alix. Illustrated in *Petits Meubles du jour*, Paris 1928

226 *Sognot:* side-table in oak with metal foot, marketed by Primavera. Illustrated in *Petits Meubles modernes*, Paris 1929

227 *Subes:* table in wrought-iron and marble, the lamp with an alabaster shade. Illustrated in *Art et décoration*, Nov. 1924

228 *Subes:* mantel clock in wrought-iron and marble, exhibited at the Exposition de la Décor Moderne de l'Horlogerie at the Musée Galliera, 1921. Illustrated in *Art et décoration*, July 1921

229 *Subes: vase réflecteur* in bronze, exhibited at the Exposition Internationale, 1937. Illustrated in *Le Luminaire III*, Guillaume Janneau, Paris, pl. 46

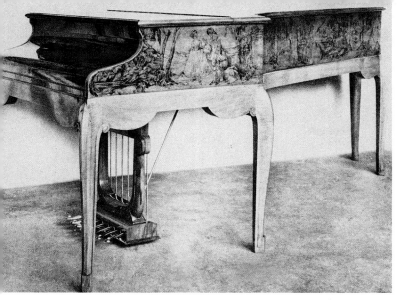

230   *Süe et Mare:* Pleyel harpsichord with seven pedals, in varnished natural pearwood, decorated by Bernard Naudin. Illustrated in *La Renaissance de l'art français et des industries de luxe*

231   *Süe et Mare:* Pleyel grand piano, exhibited in the firm's Musée d'Art Contemporain at the 1925 Exposition. Illustrated in *Mobilier et décoration*, June 1925, and July 1927, p. 8; and *Ensembles mobiliers*, 2nd series, 1925

232   *Süe et Mare:* view of the *grand salon* in the firm's Musée d'Art Contemporain at the 1925 Exposition. Illustrated in *Ensembles mobiliers*, 2nd series, 1925

233   *Süe et Mare:* sketch for the Gaveau grand piano in palisander and burl walnut exhibited at the Salon d'Automne, 1921. Illustrated in *Art et décoration*, Dec. 1921; and *Les Arts de la maison*, Autumn 1923

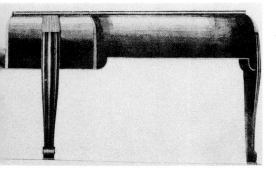

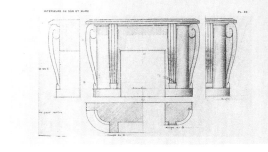

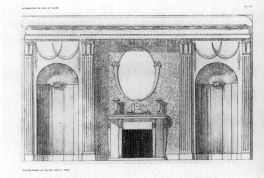

234   *Süe et Mare:* commode in macassar ebony veneered in mother-of-pearl, the feet carved as stylized palm fronds (Collection of de Lorenzo Gallery)

235   *Süe et Mare:* ensemble including a cheval mirror in macassar ebony with gilded frame; armchair in macassar ebony upholstered in pink satin; and crystal sconces; part of the firm's display at the Exposition of Modern French Decorative Art at Lord & Taylor, NY, 1928

236   *Süe et Mare:* sketch for a chimney, 1920, incorporating a well-known scrolled furniture motif. Illustrated in *Intérieurs de Süe et Mare*, Paris 1923, pl. 30

237   *Süe et Mare:* sketch of a *salon*, 1919, by Sue

238   *Süe et Mare:* cabinet in ebonized and silvered wood with tooled and painted leather doors (Collection of Robert Greene)

239 *Suisse:* wood panel in lacquer with incised decoration, *c.* 1928 (Photo: Christie's, NY)

240 *Szabo:* chandelier in wrought-iron for an exhibit in the Bernaux stand. Illustrated in *La Ferronnerie moderne*, Henri Clouzot, Paris

241 *Vera:* design for a lacquered and giltwood commode by Sue et Mare, *c.* 1921. The model was exhibited at the 1925 Exposition. Illustrated in *Exposition internationale des arts décoratifs et industriels modernes 1925*, Vol. 1, New York 1977, pl. XL; *Art Deco*, Katherine McClinton, New York 1972, p. 17; and *Feuillets d'art*, May 1919, p. 46

Miscellaneous ensembles and an anonymous piece

242   *Henrich (Gaston):* An interesting *salon* exhibited in Paris, *c.* 1927, and marketed by H. Wymphen. Illustrated in *Décors et ameublements au goût du jour*, Gaston Fleury, Paris 1926, pl. 16. The ensemble is illustrated to show that a great many decorators, beyond those known today, responded readily and effectively to the Art Deco style. Nothing appears to be known of Henrich

243   *Unattributed: semainier* with graduating drawers, the bronze bust by Gustave Miklos (Photo: Sully-Jaulmes)

244   *L'Atelier Français: salon* ensemble, *c.* 1913. The basic elements of the post-WWI high Art Deco style are already evident

Rapin's importance as a decorator diminished steadily from 1919. Interiors, awash with colour and detail – wallpapers, silk fabrics, pilasters, and painted friezes – appeared almost Victorian. The Salon critics found room for criticism at a time when popular dictates demanded a movement towards diminished decoration. He was blamed for 'an excess of verve'. As the critic Emile Sedeyn wrote in *Art et décoration* in 1921, 'His designs are never smooth and bare. You can sense that he fears the cold and boredom and that he spares himself no trouble to avoid or contend with them.'

His furniture, executed in the early 1920s by Evrard Frères, combined painted and varnished detail with ivory and exotic wood veneers. Here, too, Rapin was found delinquent, not only in his choice of decoration, but in the pieces' impracticability and construction. Yvanhoë Rambosson wrote in *Art et décoration* of the furniture in a girl's bedroom displayed at the 1922 Salon des Artistes Décorateurs: 'At first sight it is welcoming, but it is not based on practicality. A woman likes to be able to see herself in a freestanding or a wardrobe mirror. She needs to be able to hang or lay out her dresses somewhere. Manufacturers and businessmen can help artists in these matters. From a technical point of view I noticed that the table top is made to recede and as a result the legs and crossbars come into view. This will present a problem in the future, because of the difficulty of hiding the gaps which will necessarily appear as the wood settles down. Overhanging table tops are designed to conceal joins, among other things.'

By 1924 Rapin had been appointed artistic director of both the Sèvres Manufactory and the Ecole des Arts Décoratifs. He continued to apply himself to all aspects of the decorative arts and architecture. Two addresses were listed: 274 boulevard Raspail and 99 rue de Bac. The magazines *Intérieurs modernes* and *Décors et ameublements du goût du jour* show a wide range of contemporary interiors. The previous tendency towards over-ornamentation had now been checked. His ministerial office at the 1924 Salon des Artistes Décorateurs included a monumental cabinet carved by Hairon, with metal mounts by Georges Capon. Rapin also designed the Salon's exhibition hall and rotunda.

Rapin participated widely in the 1925 Exposition. For the Ambassade Française he designed both the *grand salon* (the architecture in collaboration with Pierre Selmersheim) and the dining room. Elsewhere he decorated the pavilion of the Librairie Industrielle et des Arts Décoratifs, the Arthur Goldscheider and Paul-René stands, and the Ecole du Comité des Dames de l'Union Centrale des Arts Décoratifs. He also designed furniture for the *grand salon* of the Hôtel du Collectionneur. For the Sèvres pavilion, he designed carpets, ceramics, lamps, and furniture, the last-mentioned executed by the Association des Anciens Elèves de l'Ecole Boulle.

Rapin continued to exhibit into the late 1930s, collaborating on some commissions with Jacques Rapin, presumably a son. Their exhibit at the 1935 Exposition de Bruxelles was one of his last. He died in 1939.

Rateau, Armand-Albert:

Born in Paris in 1882, Rateau attended the Ecole Boulle from 1894 to 1898. On graduating he established himself in a small studio, in 1900 accepting a position in the atelier of the renowned Art Nouveau ceramicist, Georges Hoentschel, where he probably collaborated on the furniture and *boiserie* displayed by the firm at the 1900 Exposition. In 1905 he took over the directorship of the Ateliers de Décoration de la Maison Alavoine, and remained there until the First World War. As director, he oversaw the commission to furnish the New York townhouse of George and Florence Blumenthal, later to become important private clients. Other prewar clients included Cartier, Georges Fouquet, and Tiffany's.

In 1919 Rateau became an independent decorator, opening his Atelier Levallois in Neuilly. He took a showroom on the boulevard Berthier, moving, *c.* 1930, to the quai de Conti. Employed in Neuilly was a team of skilled artisans and cabinetmakers, plasterers, sculptors, metalworkers, painters, and gilders, the most noted of whom was Paul Plumet, who was responsible for the crisply carved decoration on Rateau's furniture and panelling, initially in wood and then increasingly in bronze.

On a boat trip to the United States in 1919, Rateau became reacquainted with the Blumenthals, winning commissions to redecorate the family's French residences: the château de Malbose in Grasse, a townhouse on the boulevard Montmorency in Paris, and Le Vieil Arbre, a late-eighteenth-century hunting lodge in Passy.

The 1920s saw a host of prestigious commissions, beginning in 1920 with Jeanne Lanvin's apartment at 16 rue Barbet-de-Jouy. Rateau decorated a bathroom and bedroom, the latter's walls in Lanvin-blue silk embroidered with yellow and white roses, animals, pheasants, and palmtrees, themes reproduced as mounts in the room's furniture. The bathroom, in Siennese yellow marble with a central sunken tub, incorporated several of Rateau's now celebrated bronze furniture models – a chaise longue, dressing-table, sconces, and floor lamps – which he reused in later commissions. A repeating motif was the marguerite (the name of Mme Lanvin's daughter). The association was fruitful, leading in 1922 to Rateau's appointment as a director of Lanvin Décoration at 22 Faubourg Saint-Honoré. The firm was commissioned in the same year to redecorate the auditorium of the Danou theatre, undertaking, simultaneously, the decoration of a new venture, Lanvin-Sport.

Although he never exhibited at the annual Salons, Rateau did participate in the 1925 Exposition and also, the following year, in a retrospective exhibition at the Metropolitan Museum of Art, New York. At the Exposition, he provided a range of furniture for both the Maison Callot Soeurs exhibit in the Pavillon de l'Elégance and La Renaissance de l'Art Français et des Industries de Luxe.

In the second half of the 1920s interiors were completed for the Duchess of Alba (a bathroom in her Palais Livian in Madrid), Baron Eugène de Rothschild (the château de la Croë in Cap d'Antibes), Dr Thaleimer, and Mlle Stern.

Rateau's style was distinctive, its inspiration the Orient and antiquity. Trips before the First World War to Granada and Naples, where he visited Pompeii, helped his development of a very personal neoclassical style. Pheasants, butterflies, gazelles, and acanthus were recurring themes. Early oak furniture gave way to bronzeware exhanced with a *verde antico* patina.

Rateau mostly limited his furniture production to editions of three. Several of the most important models are now in the Musée des Arts Décoratifs, Paris; for example, a chaise longue (model 1385), a low table (model 1209), a pair of floor lamps (model 1318) and an oval tea-table (model 1463).

Rateau was active until his death in Paris in 1938, but the 1930s generated less interesting work than earlier.

Renaudot, Lucie:

Renaudot received substantial magazine coverage throughout her career. In addition to the major monthly reviews, numerous other publications illustrated individual pieces of her furniture or ensembles; for example, *Meubles du temps présent* and *Petits Meubles modernes*.

No record appears to have survived, however, of either her maiden name or early years. Salon catalogues list her place of birth as Valenciennes. It seems that she emerged unannounced on the Paris scene at the end of the First World War, making her début as a decorator at the 1919 Salon d'Automne. A fruitful liaison was immediately formed with the cabinetmaker Paul-Alfred Dumas, of 24 rue Nôtre-Dame-des-Victoires, for whom she designed furnishings until her death in 1939. Her style was classically inspired, part English Regency and part Louis XVI. A gentle formality predominated. Léon Moussinac described the effect in *Intérieurs III*: 'For a wealthy society caught up by elegance and which wants to use solid furniture, this artist creates suites of extreme distinction. . . . Thanks to a simple but subtle play of surfaces and lines, light adds to the effect of precious substances and to the grace of a curve in a piece of well-proportioned furniture.'

It is hard, in fact, to find adverse contemporary criticism of her interiors. The desk and chair which she entered in the 1928 competition at the Union Centrale des Arts Décoratifs precisely met the critics' requirements, though today the desk appears remarkably like an earlier Ruhlmann prototype. Only one mildly dissenting voice found its way into print, that of Louis Chéronnet, in a 1931 article in *Art et décoration*, who found 'in general an agreeable feminine disorder, yet a little too theatrical'.

Renaudot preferred a combination of woods, often a light burl veneer in juxtaposition with a dark one. The contrast drew attention where the piece's conservative contours could not. Alternative decoration was achieved by patterning within a veneer, the unusual grain in Brazilian jacaranda, for example, providing an arresting effect when running the vertical length of adjoining drawers on a commode.

A distinctive aspect of Renaudot's interiors lay in her ceilings. Many of these contained circular or square recessed frosted panelling to provide concealed lighting.

Renaudot received broad coverage at the 1925 Exposition: a studio for the Dumas stand on the Esplanade des Invalides and a child's room in the Ambassade Française, the latter in collaboration with Laure Albin-Guillot, Paule Marrot, and Evelyn Dufau. In the early 1930s came commissions for cabins on the *France* and *Normandie* and, in 1935, participation in the seventh exhibition of Artistes de ce Temps.

Renouvin, Georges:

Little is known of Renouvin beyond that he exhibited only infrequently at the Salons. He considered himself an independent decorator, above the fray of public exhibitions. He made the following distinction concerning his furniture in a 1924 article in *Art et décoration* by Guillaume Janneau: 'There are two types of room: there are those that bring out the conversation in the visitor crossing them, and then there are those where the visitor stands still and lingers, as if it were a haven, without really paying much attention to the pleasing aspect of the decoration. But he instinctively knows that he likes it. Undoubtedly the first type of room has a greater effect: it has achieved the aesthetic required by exhibitions. It is on display. However it is the second that I like to arrange. It is in this discreet setting that people live. A lived-in room can never be too soothing in its decoration.'

Renouvin's furniture was indeed 'calm'. It was, in fact, as purely neoclassical as is possible in the twentieth century. The same *Art et décoration* article illustrated a wide range of pieces in an unashamedly Louis XVI style, the shapes fundamentally unchanged in spirit from their late eighteenth-century forebears, except that they were devoid of all parquetry and ormolu mounts. Their interest came from fine quality veneer, lacquer, or Moroccan leather panelling.

Renouvin had a particular infatuation for the Louis XVI fluted *toupie* foot. It appears on most of his furniture, often charmingly transposed from the bottom of a furniture leg to its capital.

Favourite woods were macassar ebony, palisander, mahogany, and amaranth. Metal mounts, pared down to their functional essentials, were provided by P. and A. Picard. The 1924 article shows the technique used by Renouvin to generate an atmosphere of sumptuousness in a room containing stiff and traditional furniture; the ceiling was painted in gilt-speckled orange, the fabrics and linens were in orange and gold *lamé*, the drapes in grey velours.

Collaborators are listed as da Silva Bruhns (carpets), Soudbininne (ceramics), and Jean Renouvin, presumably a son, who was credited with a range of covered wood boxes.

Rousseau, Clément:

An air of excitement greets the infrequent arrival of a piece of Rousseau furniture on the auction block. No major Art Deco collection is considered quite complete without an example of his work. These are so rare that almost anything will do – table lamp base, pedestal, or small *meuble barbière*. The magic lies both in the form of his pieces – they show a very personal, somewhat whimsical, interpretation of late eighteenth-century furniture styles – and in the superb interplay of his preferred materials. Richly grained palmwood or rosewood provide the framework for furniture veneered with stained sharkskin intersected by thin ivory banding, a technique adopted by Rousseau in 1912.

Most of these pieces are thought to have been commissioned by private clients but, unfortunately, little firm information on any aspect of his cabinetry has survived. Born in Saint-Maurice-La-Fougereuse (Deux-Sèvres) in 1872, he was trained as a sculptor by Léon Morice, exhibiting at the Société des Artistes Français. Furniture appears to have been a natural extension of his sculptural abilities, one given respectability in the early 1920s by commissions from Jacques Doucet and Baron de Rothschild, examples of which are now in the Musée des Arts Décoratifs, Paris, and the Metropolitan Museum of Art, New York. Each piece is a miniature object of virtu, each in dark wood, especially *palmier*, that contrasts with tinted or bleached *galuchat* and snakeskin veneers above ivory *sabots*. Rousseau's workmanship is easily mistaken for Chanaux's, but luckily the pieces are invariably signed in an incised wavy scrawl, often with the year of manufacture.

Rousseau exhibited a selection of furniture and objects at La Galerie Charpentier in 1925. No later reference to him appears in contemporary reviews. He died in Neuilly-sur-Seine in 1950.

Ruhlmann, Jacques-Emile:

Had France of the 1920s been a monarchy, Ruhlmann would certainly have held the position of *ébéniste du roi*. No work as fine as his had been seen for 125 years. He was unswayed by the prevailing Art Nouveau idiom, and drew his inspiration directly from the eighteenth century. A strict traditionalist, he kept his forms elegant, refined, and above all simple. Although many of his most celebrated works were designed before 1920, Ruhlmann's furniture is today considered to be the epitome of Art Deco style and its finest expression.

Ruhlmann was born in Paris 28 August 1879. His parents, François and Valentine Ruhlmann, were from Alsace and of Protestant extraction. In 1900, after completing his studies and three years of military service, he joined his father's painting, wallpaper, and mirror business at 6 rue du Marché Saint-Honoré. His early responsibilities were primarily to oversee the firm's timber inventory and to coordinate its business negotiations. But by 1903 he was interested enough in furniture design to pay visits to various cabinetry shops in the area, such as Gevens, Stauffacher and Laberthe. The year 1907 brought two significant events: marriage to Marguerite Seabrook (1886–1957), and the death of his father.

He made his début with a selection of wallpaper designs at the 1910 Salon d'Automne and the following year exhibited a similar display at the Salon des Artistes Décorateurs. In 1912 he moved the family business to larger quarters bordering on two streets, its address listed as 10 rue Maléville and 27 rue de Lisbonne. Although the firm's previous stock-in-trade – paintings, mirrors, and light fixtures – continued to be manufactured, Ruhlmann set aside special facilities for his deepening interest in furniture design. His first furniture models were displayed at the 1913 Salon d'Automne – an inauspicious moment, with the war only months away.

The 1914–18 hiatus provided Ruhlmann with the opportunity both to refine his furniture design and to obtain a significant headstart on those of his contemporaries who saw active service. He was intensely productive during this period and designed such masterpieces as the 1916 corner-cupboard (*encoignure*) in ebony, its door veneered with a large basket of stylized blooms. This model, reproduced in both three- and four-legged versions, stands today as the acme of Art Deco taste.

In 1919 Ruhlmann went into partnership with Pierre Laurent, a friend and paintings specialist, and they formed Les Etablissements Ruhlmann et Laurent. Laurent was placed in charge of the rue Maléville decorating works and Ruhlmann retained the rue de Lisbon section as a furniture showroom. In the same year they purchased an industrial building at 14 rue d'Oussant in the 15th *arrondissement* and installed a cabinetry workshop on the third floor. Over the next nine years, they expanded slowly, recruiting artisans

with the assistance of André Fréchet, the director of Ecole Boulle, and Fenot, a noted *ébéniste*. Eventually the entire building was taken over for workshops, storerooms and offices. A new and more modern cabinetry shop employed thirteen artisans and two machinists, headed by M. Avon. M. Schlesser was in charge, among other things, of the selection of veneers.

At this point it is important to stress that Ruhlmann had no formal training in cabinetmaking and his technical knowledge was never more than superficial. He made drawings in ink, often at a scale of 2/100th, which provided front, elevation, and profile views of his furniture. These were then passed on to a draughtsman to be rescaled at 1/10th, and from there into the cabinetmaker's blueprint. Numerous examples of Ruhlmann's preliminary sketches were reproduced by Léon Moussinac in his 1924 *Croquis de Ruhlmann*. The fifty-four plates bear brilliant witness to Ruhlmann's ingenuity, but unfortunately no dates or chronology were given.

From 1913 to 1924 – more than half his entire career as a furniture designer – Ruhlmann's designs were executed by a range of *ébénistes* in the Faubourg Saint-Antoine; in particular, Haentges Frères and Fenot.

The 1925 Exposition catapulted Ruhlmann to the forefront of the modern French decorative arts movement. The nation heaped accolades on the man who demonstrated to the world France's superiority in its most prized tradition, furniture. It may have surprised Ruhlmann, after nine long years of cabinetmaking celebrity, to be pronounced an overnight success! But in fact, during those years he had been known only to a privileged minority, a situation that was radically changed by his Hôtel du Collectionneur. Hundreds of thousands of Exposition visitors flocked through its monumental doors to gaze in awe at the majestic interior described in the firm's catalogue – with more than a little understatement – as a 'Residence for a Rich (Art) Collector'. The pavilion, designed by Ruhlmann's close friend, the architect Pierre Patout, consisted of a vestibule, gallery, living room, bedroom, dining room, office, bathroom, and boudoir. Its success derived in part from the talents of the celebrated group of artists who had assisted Ruhlmann in the project: Bourdelle, Pompon, Bonfils, Dupas, Jaulmes, Jallot, Jourdain, Rapin, Puiforcat, Brandt, Decoeur, Mayodon, Dunand, Linossier, Décorchement, and Legrain, to list only the better known. The firm's own principal decorators were credited in the introduction to Jean Badovici's 1924 *Harmonies 'Intérieurs de Ruhlmann'* and included Stéphany, Huet, Bougenot, Picaud, Lardin, Lautelin, and Denise Holt.

In addition to the Hôtel du Collectionneur, Ruhlmann provided paintings for the Exposition's Gate of Honour; a range of decorative items for the Neubauer Jacques boutique; a piano for the Pleyel stand; and the architectural blueprint of the A. LeRoy boutique.

Apart from the 1925 Exposition and the two annual Salons, Ruhlmann exhibited in Madrid, Milan, New York, Athens, and Barcelona, as well as at the 1931 Exposition Coloniale where he furnished an office for Marshall Lyautey. In 1934, a year after his death, a retrospective exhibition of his works was staged at the Pavillon de Marsan. The accompanying catalogue provided a long list of prestigious clients headed by the Elysée Palace, David-Weill, Jacqueline Francell, the *Ile-de-France*, M. Molinié, the Paris Chamber of Commerce, the Maharajah of Indore, and numerous public dignitaries.

Ruhlmann used only the rarest and most exquisite of materials for his furniture. Rich veneers, such as palisander, amboyna, amaranth, macassar ebony, and Cuban mahogany, were inlaid with ivory, tortoise shell, or horn. Dressing-tables were embellished with leather, *galuchat*, or parchment panelling, and silk tassels on drawer pulls added a further touch of elegance. On rare occasions, a piece was sent to Dunand to be lacquered, and in the late 1920s and early 1930s, pieces were sometimes sprayed in the rue d'Ouessant workshops with a protective coating of cellulose.

Ruhlmann reacted with remarkable equanimity to the post-1925 advent of metal, in view of the fact that his reputation rested in part on the use of sumptuous veneers. Metal mounts appeared on his furniture from the mid-1920s, and their use was analysed by Léon Deshairs in a 1927 article in *Art et décoration*, in which Ruhlmann justified his adoption of metal as a way of countering the problems inherent in the modern centrally-heated house, particularly the damage caused to wood veneers by dry heat. The magazine showed a selection of desks and pivoting chairs, with functional, but not brutal, forms. Ruhlmann's 1932 desk for the Maharajah of Indore is a fine example of the successful incorporation of metal, its princely proportions embracing such chromed accessories as a telephone, swivel lamp, and wastepaper basket.

Ruhlmann's furniture was beyond the means of all but the most prosperous. He justified his exclusiveness repeatedly by arguments such as that quoted in the catalogue for the 1928 Lord and Taylor exhibition: 'The movement to develop a contemporary style in interior decoration will only come fully into its own when people of moderate incomes become interested, but owing to the fact that costly experiments must first be made in furniture de luxe, before this Renaissance in decoration can be effected, it is necessary that this art be developed under the patronage of the wealthy, just as the art of the older epochs was developed under the patronage of the courts.' Ruhlmann left to others the challenge of producing well-designed but inexpensive furniture for the middle-classes.

Individual pieces, especially from 1928, were given a branded number and alphabetized to register them within an

edition. Finally, a certificate, correspondingly numbered and signed by the master himself, accompanied each purchase.

Ruhlmann died at the relatively young age of fifty-four on 15 November 1933. The firm was dissolved, Laurent retaining the paintings side of the business and Ruhlmann's nephew, Porteneuve, establishing his own decorating firm.

Saddier et ses fils:

Little information exists on the decorator and furniture wholesaler, Saddier *père*, prior to the First World War. In 1919, he appears to have turned the management of the family firm at 29–31 rue des Boulets over to two sons, Fernand and Gaston.

Saddier et ses Fils began to receive attention from the critics in the early 1920s. A dining room entitled 'Les Cerises' in contrasting Ceylonese lemonwood and coralwood was displayed at Paris's first Exposition Décorative Française Contemporaine. The critic for *Art et décoration* found it discordant: 'He forgets that a decorative motif should not be cut off by a drawer, especially when the motif acts as a support. The cherries in marquetry look like transfers and the general harmony is full of discordances.' The room's lighting was provided by Dunaime through the firm of Gagnon. At the second Exposition Décorative Française Contemporaine in 1924, Saddier again displayed a dining room.

The firm took stand 39 on the Esplanade des Invalides at the 1925 Exposition, displaying a bedroom in *bois des îles*. It was certainly 'modern', as advertised; the dressing-table was especially interesting, with its twin tapering pedestal feet. Collaborators included Gagnon (bronze light fixtures), Coudyser (carpets and fabrics), and Lappara and Gabriel (silverware).

Saddier was also represented in the Colonial section at the 1925 Exposition by the Tunisian retailer Boyond, who exhibited a dining room designed for Saddier by the Rouen painter Raymond Quibel. The room's decorative theme – the countryside surrounding Rouen – called for a rustic appearance far removed from the modernism of the bedroom mentioned above, but well-suited to a French colony.

In 1926 Saddier presented a bedroom in mahogany and sapelli at the Salon d'Automne. Pastel wallpapers by Marianne Clouzot added femininity and elegance to the neat composition. In the same year, *Les Echos des industries d'art* illustrated two ensembles: a dining room in mahogany, with light fixtures by Dunaime, a carpet by Marcel Coupé, silverware by Lappara, decorative panels by Lehucher, and ceramics and glassware by Jean Luce; and a suite of furniture in palisander and burl walnut designed for the firm by Ghislain Rinquet. Other designers for Saddier in 1926 were J. and J. Adnet and Raymond Quibel.

The following year, Saddier displayed a bar at La Société des Artistes Décorateurs. Positioned at the end of a dining room, the theme for the bar was based on the triangle and circle: three-legged stools with triangular seats fitted into matching recesses within the bar counter, stemware by Jean Luce stood on elongated triangular shelving, and a table housed three wedge-shaped chairs beneath its circular top. The effect was original, even lighthearted. The furniture critic for *Mobilier et décoration*, however, found it no laughing matter: 'Sadly, when one has a drinks cabinet as striking as this at home, it must be easy to succumb to alcoholism.' Either the Prohibition mentality was at hand or his tongue was firmly in his cheek.

In 1927, Saddier also displayed a palisander and thuya bedroom and 'Studio on the Côte d'Azur', both designed by Rinquet, and a studio by J. and J. Adnet. The latter room was modern and lacked identity, except for its frosted tubular glass chandelier, the most recognizable of the Adnets' creations. Also marketed by Saddier was a walnut and palisander storage cabinet by Jean Betaille.

Nineteen-twenty-eight saw the creation of Saddier's *chef d'oeuvre*: a coiffeuse in sycamore shown at the Salon d'Automne. Part of a boudoir, the piece was conceived within a circle; the large central mirror extending on its right in a full semicircular sweep to a cylindrical stool with cushioned seat, and on its left to a chest-of-drawers on top of which was placed a spherical lamp by Dunaime. The model appears to precede by several months a nearly identical piece designed by Paul Poiret for Lord and Taylor, New York. The concept was at once avant-garde and feminine, its self-containment, however, making it a difficult item to place within an ensemble.

A 1929 article in *Mobilier et décoration* by G. Rémon on the third Exposition Décorative Française Contemporaine at the Pavillon Marsan underlined the celebrity status acquired by Saddier at that time. Illustrated were ensembles and individual pieces, often in collaboration with Edgar Brandt (wrought-iron), André Adam (decorative panels), and Lehucher and Chabert Dupont (window shades). Everything was ultramodern and sumptuous. Rémon was unequivocal: 'The Saddier brothers have the worry of keeping ahead of all the best cabinetmakers of their time.' Brave words, indeed, about any Ruhlmann contemporary.

From 1930, Saddier interiors were anonymous: clean, angular furniture in Honduras mahogany or burled cherry, often with pronounced metal mounts. The firm was quick to draw on the talents of others to complement their furniture. In 1931, for example, Raymond Quibel (decorative panels) Renée Kinsbourg (carpets), Mlle Cettier (wall hangings and curtains), Sabino (lighting), and Marcel Goupy (tableware marketed by Rouard) cooperated in a dining room retailed by Brunet, Meunié & Cie.

Sognot, Louis:

Sognot was born in Paris in 1892 and educated at the Ecole Bernard Palissy. Training, presumably as a cabinetmaker, at Kriéger, a well-known furniture manufacturer on the Faubourg Saint-Antoine, was followed in the early 1920s by a move to Primavera.

Sognot's designs were given individual credit at the Salons from 1923.

Sognot's importance is linked to the introduction of metal into interior design in the late 1920s. His style, always impeccably sharp, matched exactly the bold and clean sweep which tubular chrome brought to furniture. His quick grasp of the medium's aesthetic potential propelled Primavera to the forefront of the modern movement. At the firm, Sognot worked closely with Chauchet-Guilleré and Guillemard, but his principal collaborator for many years was Charlotte Alix. Of the numerous works they designed together, the chairs, in tubular or flat metal, were the most exciting, their high and angular frames upholstered in leather or rubberized fabric.

Sognot decorated two rooms in the Primavera pavilion at the 1925 Exposition. His boudoir, with paintings by Madeleine Sougez, was less successful than the adjoining bedroom which imparted an air of intimacy and femininity. The angular furniture was in warm woods to which Goujon's carpets brought additional colour. Elsewhere, he showed a piano designed for Gaveau, and several chairs.

A cofounder of U.A.M. in 1929, Sognot displayed a range of innovative furniture at the group's yearly exhibitions, several examples of which were illustrated in *Répertoire du goût moderne*, *IV* and *V*. Whenever possible, a piece was designed to serve more than one function: desk tops opened to interiors fitted as dressing-tables; pedestals enclosed compartments which housed smoking accessories, such as pipe racks, tobacco jars, and ashtrays. Even walls were movable; his administrator's office at the 1930 U.A.M. exhibition could be converted into a recreation room.

Notable commissions included an interior for Jean Carlu, the illustrator and poster artist (1930); furniture for his Highness Y.R. Holkar, the Maharajah of Indore (1931); offices for the newspaper *La Semaine de Paris* (1930); and the first-class cabin for the resident doctor on the *Normandie* (1935).

Sognot's celebrated 1931 double bed for the Maharajah of Indore, in Duralumin with twin glass end-tables, evolved from two earlier models: the first a single bed for a Colonial house shown at the 1930 La Semaine de Paris exposition; the second, with a coverlet by Hélène Henri, for a first-class cabin on the *Atlantique* the following year. In 1932 Sognot tried a new material; his set of dining chairs at the Salon des Artistes Décorateurs were in moulded and lacquered *Lakarmé*, an incombustible plastic.

Little further information has survived on Sognot beyond that he lectured part-time as a professor of Decoration at the Ecole Boulle from 1926. He died in 1970.

Subes, Raymond Henri:

The Appendix to this book gives an indication of the volume of Subes's work; individual articles on him in 1930 and 1935 issues of *Mobilier et décoration* and in *Art et décoration* stress his standing with contemporary critics. Subes inherited from Brandt the mantle that had been passed down by Emile Robert.

Born in Paris in 1893, Subes attended the Ecole Boulle, where he studied metal engraving, and the Ecole National Supérieure des Arts Décoratifs. His first employment set the seal on his career: a three-year apprenticeship in Robert's atelier in Enghien-les-Bains. Here, theories of metallurgy were put into practice. Here, also, the traditions of the medium were absorbed, to be later adapted by Subes as he led his metalware colleagues into 1930s design. He learned quickly, and in 1919 was appointed by Borderel and Robert, a prominent architectural construction company, as director of their metal atelier. Business flourished. Commissions poured in from architects throughout France. A cursory glance at Subes's architectural commissions in the 1920s shows the range of work undertaken: churches, cemeteries, monuments, exhibition halls, and hotels. Production was geared in large part to these commissions, and though Subes displayed a range of furnishings at the annual Salons, his importance cannot be measured by these smaller items; most of his *tours de force* remain unidentified on building façades and in the bold sweep of a hotel's stairway balustrade. Many more were stripped and scrapped when the ocean liners *Ile-de-France*, *Atlantique*, *France*, and *Normandie* met their ignominious ends.

Subes's displays at the Salons included commissions for other exhibitors: in 1927, for example, the steel frame for a Ruhlmann bookcase and a wrought-iron doorway for Michel Roux-Spitz. Later came work for Maurice Jallot and Porteneuve. The 1925 Exposition generated ironwork in the Ambassade Française, Hôtel du Collectionneur, and the pavilion of La Société de l'Art Appliqué aux Métiers.

Subes's choice of metals matched that of Brandt: a basic preference for wrought-iron interchanged occasionally with bronze, patinated copper, and, in the 1930s, aluminium and steel, the latter either oxidized or lacquered in Duco.

Süe (Louis) et Mare (André):

The partnership of Süe and Mare brought together two dissimilar talents and temperaments, out of which came a strong accord, described by Jean Badovici in his introduction

to *Intérieurs de Süe et Mare* as an 'admirable association of two dissimilar minds which combined the best of their qualities to put them at the service of Beauty. One provides a sure and precise knowledge and a rigorous sense of geometry; the other a refined and delicate sensibility. Süe is the architect who plays with numbers and spaces; Mare is the artist whose emotional richness makes the abstract constructions and austere equations live and smile.'

Mare was born in Argentan in 1887. Tuition in painting at the Académie Julian was followed in 1903–04 by participation at the Salon d'Automne and Salon des Indépendants. By 1910 Mare had begun to place an increasing emphasis on the decorative arts, including bookbindings, furniture, and complete ensembles in his Salon exhibits. From 1911 to 1913, he collaborated with an imposing list of artists – Duchamp-Villon, Marie Laurencin, Jacques Villon, and others – exhibiting his controversial 'Maison cubiste' in 1912. Association with Süe came came immediately before the war though their relationship was not formalized until the establishment of La Compagnie des Arts Français in 1919. With the outbreak of war, Mare volunteered for action, and his wife, Charlotte, executed his furniture, carpet, and fabric designs until the armistice. On the dissolution of his partnership with Süe in 1928, Mare returned to painting. He died in 1932.

Süe was born in Bordeaux in 1875. His father, Eugène Süe, was a doctor, and persuaded Süe to pursue a medical career at the city's *polytechnique*. But Süe's passions lay in the arts, and he left in 1895 for Paris, where he discovered impressionism, then all the rage. He enrolled at the Ecole Nationale des Beaux-Arts and received his diploma in 1901. Further studies in architecture completed his education. He was now ready to put his diverse talents to the test, exhibiting paintings at the Salon des Indépendants and the Salon d'Automne, and designing houses in the rue Cassini (1905) in collaboration with Paul Huillard. In 1910 he formed an association with Paul Poiret, decorating the latter's houseboat *Nomade* and his residence on the avenue d'Antin. In 1912, after Poiret had formed La Maison Martine, Süe established his own decorating firm, L'Atelier Français (see ill. 244), on the rue de Courcelles. Süe served on the Eastern front during the war, returning to form with Mare the Belle France at 22 avenue Friedland, a prelude to their Compagnie des Arts Français at 116 Faubourg Saint-Honoré. Numerous commissions followed immediately, both architectural and decorative, including that of the cenotaph in the Arc de Triomphe.

The partnership lasted until 1928, when Jacques Adnet assumed the firm's directorship. Süe continued independently, as an architect and *ensemblier*, until the Second World War. During the 1930s, Süe's commissions included shops, stage sets, offices, and private houses. He settled in Istanbul during the war, lecturing at the Academy of Fine Arts. He later returned to France and retired to Gascogne, near Bordeaux, where he died in 1968.

One key to the firm's success lay in its team of collaborators, which included Jaulmes, Vera, Dufresne, Drésa, Poisson, Marinot, Desvallières, Martin, Boutet de Monval, and several others, each free either to create individual works or to participate in group projects. A complete list of participants is given in *The Extraordinary Work of Süe et Mare*, the catalogue of a 1979 exhibition at the Foulk Lewis Gallery, London.

Süe et Mare produced a wide range of furnishings and objects: clocks, ceramics, lamps, fabrics, wallpapers, carpets, and silverware. For their furniture they used many different woods: macassar ebony, mahogany, palisander, burl walnut, ebony, and ash. Some pieces were in pale woods, such as beech or birch.

Important clients included the director of the Danou theatre (a villa in Saint-Cloud), the Duke of Medina Coeli (a living room for his palace in Madrid), the Countess of Goyeneche (a townhouse in Madrid), Charles Stern, M. Kapferer, M. and Mme Girod, and even several pieces of furniture for Jacques Doucet.

Süe et Mare's furniture was traditionally inspired. Traces of Louis XIV, Louis XV, Restauration, and Louis-Philippe are evident, particularly the latter, which they considered to be the most recent legitimate style. As Mare explained in a 1920 interview with Léon Deshairs published in *Art et décoration*, 'The Louis-Philippe style, for a long time favoured in the provinces, is the most recent to date of French styles. It is rather clumsy, but earnest, logical, welcoming. It responded to needs which we still have. Its forms are so rational that the motor-car designer of today who draws the interior of a car uses them unconsciously. We are not reviving it; we are not deliberately continuing it, but we find it while seeking out simple solutions, and through it we bind ourselves to the whole of our magnificent past. We are not creating a merely fashionable art.' The partners developed their theories further in a 1921 manifesto, *Architectures*. From the 1830–48 years they took the comfort that the period's cabinetmakers had built into its austere furniture. Süe et Mare's armchairs were lush and inviting, their tufted, colourful velours upholstery offering comfort and luxury. Other models were Baroque, even theatrical. Their imposing desk in Gabonese ebony, purchased directly by the Museum of Modern Art, New York, from the 1925 Exposition, incorporated ormolu feet cast as elongated fronds – an updated version of rococo cabinetry.

Few if any designers of 1920s furniture developed a more distinctive style. There is no mistaking the squared scroll foot on mid-1920s chairs, or the mother-of-pearl and silver veneered bouquet of summer flowers on a matching ebony commode and cabinet. Not only did their furniture echo the past, but it was profoundly French, a fact emphasized in the

firm's advertisements. Süe et Mare described their broader philosophy in a note in the catalogue for the 1928 Lord and Taylor exhibition: 'Our Art is essentially "human". We believe that our dwellings are made essentially for human beings and not for automatons. Therefore we strive for warmth and harmony, supple lines and reposeful forms, in order that the home be restful and in contrast with an ever more exacting and harassing type of existence.'

The 1925 Exposition eclipsed all Süe et Mare's earlier work. Un Musée d'Art Contemporain, their pavilion on the Esplanade des Invalides, received almost as much attention as Ruhlmann's nearby Hôtel du Collectionneur. Comprised of a rotunda and gallery, the interior was decorated by a wide team of collaborators, including sculptors, carpet and textile designers, and painters. Colour and sumptuousness abounded, the furniture in carved giltwood upholstered in Aubusson tapestry. Elsewhere, the firm displayed furniture in the Ambassade Française, the Parfums d'Orsay boutique, and the Salle des Fêtes; a harpsichord in the Pleyel stand; silver ornaments for Christofle-Baccarat; and decorative key plates and furnishings in the Fontaine & Cie pavilion.

Suisse, Gaston:

Suisse was born in Paris on 1 December 1896. Known primarily for his lacquer work, he described his paintings as 'après Nature'. Themes included lush equatorial forests inhabited by lemur monkeys, and birds of paradise above streams teeming with tropical fish.

Suisse entered the Ecole Nationale des Arts Décoratifs in 1913, enlisting the following year in the French infantry. Demobilized in 1918, he returned to complete his diploma under Paul Rénouard and David. He graduated in 1925, making his début the following year at the Salon d'Automne, where he exhibited for many years. Shown was a wide selection of screens, panels, étuis, and boxes in lacquer and eggshell. Private commissions included furniture in both modern and Oriental styles. Suisse frequently worked on wood or masonite, applying a base coat of gold or silver lacquer to which were added polychromed or incised decoration. In the early 1930s he switched from lacquer to nitrocellulose, a synthetic varnish which proved quicker-drying and easier to work with than traditional lacquer.

Suisse's atelier in the 1920s was at 42 rue de Tolbiac, and later at 47 boulevard Saint Marcel, conveniently near the Jardin des Plantes. He exhibited frequently outside of the Salons in the 1930s, providing, for example, the mural decoration for the Temple Ankor at the 1931 Exposition Coloniale and a reception hall in the Palais de Tokio at the 1937 Exposition Universelle, the latter in collaboration with the artist Cottet. Touring musuem exhibitions at the time included Brussels, Zurich, and Cairo.

Szabo, Adelbert:

Hungarian-born, Szabo became a naturalized Frenchman, establishing his metalwork atelier at 15 rue Emile-Dubois in Paris. His career in the decorative arts spanned thirty years: as early as 1907 he exhibited his ferronnerie at the Salon des Artistes Décorateurs; as late as 1938 he showed a wrought-iron door commissioned by a charity institution in Angoulême. His pre-First World War works were inspired by historicism rather than the prevailing Art Nouveau style. From 1919 they showed an accommodation for le style 25.

Szabo's range of metalwork was both small in volume and size: chandeliers, grills, radiator covers, mirror frames – even key escutcheons – were the norm. Only occasionally did he accept commissions for architectural projects; for example, a clock for the façade of the newspaper Le Temps building in 1921, and elevator doors and stairway ramps for La Banque de l'Union Parisienne ten years later. A major undertaking both in size and importance was the door of the first-class dining room on the Normandie.

Wrought-iron was his standard medium, though he occasionally used bronze or wrought-copper.

Vera, Paul:

Vera was born in Paris in 1882. Nothing is known of his upbringing and education but it can be assumed that he attended one of the city's fine art schools, since he emerged after 1900 at the Salons as an accomplished artist/decorator. A mural, 'Les Trois Grâces', displayed in 1913, shows both a technical proficiency and a sharp awareness of the prevailing fashion.

Vera explained his style, which depicted young women and flora in a whimsical Art Deco manner, as one which stressed the link between interior design and architecture. He wrote in Les Arts de la maison: 'The future belongs to architecture. Insofar as the great social and economic problems have an artistic or aesthetic expression, they will have to be solved in the first instance by architecture, by it and with it, but never without it.'

In the 1920s Vera produced a wide range of interior decorations: painted panels and murals, bas reliefs, tapestries, wallpapers, fabrics, and wood engravings for book illustrations. Favourite themes included the Four Seasons, garlanded flowers, fruit-filled cornucopia, and allegorical and mythological figures. Orpheus, in particular, was reproduced in various media. The critics approved, listing among the artists's talents an irrepressible optimism and joyous humour.

Vera is best known today for the wallpaper and tapestry designs which he exhibited at the annual Salons alongside examples by competitors such as Raoul Dufy, René Gabriel,

Tinota, and J.-E. Laboureur. The wallpapers were printed and marketed by La Compagnie des Arts Français, the tapestries executed by Aubusson.

A long-standing arrangement was established in the early 1920s with Louis Süe, who designed tapestry furniture mounts executed by Poisson, a cabinetmaker at La Compagnie des Arts Français. Vera also provided painted decoration for some of Süe's furniture, for example, a lacquered dining-room screen entitled 'Le Pain, le vin, les fruits, la viande', shown at the 1922 Salon d'Automne.

Two Paris addresses were listed in the Salon catalogues: 72 rue Blanche and 61 rue de Rome. Vera died in 1958.

APPENDIX

The Appendix consists of lists of the furniture displayed between 1920 and 1935 at the two foremost annual Paris Salons by most of the cabinetmakers, designers, and architects whose biographies appear in this book. Entries have been drawn from the Salons' catalogues to provide a chronological record of each decorative artist's exhibits. Although a substantial proportion of an individual's yearly output was not shown at the two Salons, many exceptional works were included in an attempt to catch the attention of both the Salon Jury and the press. In addition to a description of the type of furniture exhibited, the lists detail the artists' choice of materials, their collaborators, and their retailers.

Four Salons were held every year in Paris: those of La Société des Artistes Décorateurs, La Société du Salon d'Automne, La Société des Artistes français, and La Société Nationale des Beaux-Arts. Two of these gave special emphasis to the decorative arts: first, the Salon des Artistes Décorateurs, which from its inaugural exhibit in 1904 moved back and forth between the Pavillon de Marsan (now the Musée des Arts Décoratifs at the Louvre) and the Grand Palais; and second, the Salon d'Automne at the Grand Palais. The former was held in May–June, the latter in October–November.

Both Salons were given extensive coverage by Paris's leading fine and applied arts magazines, in particular *Mobilier et décoration* and *Art et décoration*, but it was not for this reason alone that most furniture exhibitors felt the need to participate. Just as important were the opportunities the Salons afforded to measure the progress of coexhibitors within the preceding six months and to keep abreast of new developments. Very few furniture designers – most notably, Coard, Dupré-Lafon, and Frank – declined to participate at all. Others exhibited intermittently at either one or both Salons.

Adnet, Jacques and Jean

Salon des Artistes Décorateurs
1926: Furniture, marketed by La Maîtrise
1927: Salon corner in collaboration with Schenck (nickel and glass), and J. and L. Bernard (paintings); furniture in peroba marketed by Saddier and Olivier-Desbordes
1932: Small furniture in mirror and metal, chair in white leather; marketed by La Compagnie des Arts Français
1933: Chimney in white stone with andirons, tongs, and shovel; cabinet covered in white sheep's leather; chair in white sheep's leather; low table with feet in slabs of glass; marketed by La Compagnie des Arts Français
1934: *Salon-studio* in collaboration with Jean Besnard (ceramics), Marie Chauvel (bird cage), P. Bertin and A. Lapeyre (walls painted in Stic-B); marketed by La Compagnie des Arts Français
1935: Bedroom including carpets and fabrics by Léoné Huet; marketed by La Compagnie des Arts Français

Salon d'Automne
1923: 4 paintings (Jacques)
    2 watercolours (Jean)
1924: 'Vulcain' carpet; marketed by La Maîtrise
    3 watercolours
1927: Library and smoking room, the furniture in 'Duco' varnish; marketed by La Maîtrise
    Sketch for a child's room
1932: Photographs of completed ensembles: dining room, living room, 2 libraries, and stage set
1933: Cupboard in smoked glass and chromed metal (metalware by Louis Gigou)
1934: Lacquered cabinet
1935: Cabinet with 3 doors, in lacquer and leather with metal foot; marketed by La Compagnie des Arts Français

Arbus, André-Léon

Salon des Artistes Décorateurs
1932: Small lady's desk and chair in ebony upholstered in grey satin
1935: Commode in parchment, ivory, and ebony

Salon d'Automne
1926: Bonheur-du-jour
1929: Black lacquered desk
1930: Ebony furniture, in collaboration with Henry Parayre (sculpture), and Marc Saint-Saëns (design); marketed by 'L'Epoque', 22 rue la Boétie
1931: Dining room; the table and console in ebony with polished glass tops, in collaboration with Marc Saint-Saëns (decorative panels), and La Société Industrielle des Pyrènées; marketed by 'L'Epoque'
1934: Corner bed in mahogany, the headboard decoration by W. Androusow

Bagge, Eric

Salon des Artistes Décorateurs
1920: Nursery in painted wood
1921: Dining room in stained pearwood and silvered amaranth
1922: Dining room in silvered amaranth and pearwood, in collaboration with Bernard Huguet

1923: Bedroom in maple and acacia
    2 perfume burners
    Bronze desk clock
1924: Dining room ensemble; marketed by Saddier et ses Fils
1926: Library in palisander with ivory inlay; marketed by G. E. and J. Dennery
1927: Architectural presentation
1929: Console in amboyna and thuya

Salon d'Automne
1920: Ensemble including a *boudoir-toilette*
1921: Ensemble for a library in speckled grey maple and ebony
1922: Bedroom in carved mahogany and patinated oak
    Dining room in patinated mahogany
    Salon corner
1923: Vitrine including ceramics; marketed by La Manufacture de Sèvres
1924: Commode and 2 sconces
1926: Dining and smoking room; marketed by Mercier Frères
1927: Dressing table and chair
    Jewelry cabinet by Paul Brandt
1928: Ensemble of seat furniture embroidered by Cornely (116 rue Réaumur), and a commode marketed by 'Le Palais de Marbre' (77 Champs-Elysées)
    Furniture fabrics and a carpet; marketed by Lucien Bioux (7 rue du Mail)
1929: Fabrics and carpets
1930: Ensemble, including a dressing table, chair, and screen; marketed by l'Atelier des Champs-Elysées; the furniture, silk, and tapestries marketed by Lucien Bioux

Barret, Maurice

Salon des Artistes Décorateurs

1932: Equipment for a small kitchen including metallic furniture, marketed by Les Etablissements L. Lelièvre & Cie; electric water heater by Les Etablissements Lemercier frères; electric oven by La Société Alsthom; refrigerator by Electro Lux; plumbing by Georges Guéneau et Fils; table on wheels and chair, marketed by Flambo (51 bis, avenue de la République)

1934: Equipment for a study including metallic furniture, working table, swivel chair, and filing accessories; marketed by Flambo

1935: An intellectual's studio, including equipment for a 'studio-minimum', including a work corner, relaxation corner, and an electric kitchen, the metallic furniture with standardized elements

Beaumont, Jean

Salon des Artistes Décorateurs

1929: 'Spring': panel in pencil and watercolour
Armchair in wood with Aubusson tapestry; marketed by Hamot Frères

1930: Ensemble including decorative panels in Aubusson tapestry, carpet in point noué, 2 chairs designed by René Prou with Aubusson tapestry; tapestries and carpets marketed by Hamot Frères

1933: 'Le Feu de brousse': lacquered screen by Eltine in collaboration with Louis Midavaine

1935: 'Les Phéniciens introduisent le vin en France': tapestry cartoon
Mural for a swimming pool
'Panthères': lacquered panel

Salon d'Automne

1919: 'Premières Neiges': screen
Printed screens
8 sketches for stage sets

Block, Robert

Salon des Artistes Décorateurs

1929: Restaurant, in collaboration with Delpuech, Havard, Brodovitch, Mito Block, Douce Guit, Stark, Desnos, Devilleneuve, Huehon, Rischmann, Marguerite Gros, and Miss Y. Barain; marketed by Studio 'Athélia', Studio d'Art des Trois Quartiers, boulevard de la Madeleine

1930: Grand reception hall for Le Cercle de l'Union Interalliée, in collaboration with Delpuech, Marguerite Gros, and Desnos; marketed by Studio 'Athélia'

Bouchet, Léon

Salon des Artistes Décorateurs

1921: Dining room in waxed wild cherry, in collaboration with Brandt (chandelier), J. Luce (glassware), Thomas (printed fabrics), and L. Malclès (sculpture); marketed by Le Confortable

1922: Library in macassar ebony and locustwood, in collaboration with Dinner (cabinetry)

1926: Chiffonnier in amboyna, chaise longe in palisander, *poudreuse* and armchair in sycamore; marketed by G. E. and J. Dennery

1927: Hall in palisander, marketed by G. E. and J. Dennery

1928: Industrialist's study in palisander

1929: Dining room of circular design constructed in a square room; including buffet and table in burl walnut, 8 chairs upholstered in green Moroccan leather, 4 silver cabinets, radiator covers, a panel decorated by Edelmann, and a ceiling fixture by Boris Lacroix; marketed by G. E. and J. Dennery
Smoking-room, comprising a bookcase with wireless set and phonograph, bridge table and 4 chairs, chair, divan, revolving bookcase and light fixtures by Boris Lacroix; marketed by G. E. and J. Dennery

1930: *Grand salon de collections*, comprising a large piece of furniture in jacaranda with pivoting doors and vitrine, commode in ebony with *galuchat* panel, secretary in burl thuya with interior pivoting drawers, vitrine in burl walnut with pivoting glass interior sections, filing cabinet in burl walnut, large settee, 2 armchairs, 4 chairs, 3 carpets by da Silva Bruhns, and a lacquered screen by Jean Dunand; marketed by G. E. and J. Dennery

1931: Storage cabinet, burl thuya with pewter inlay; marketed by G. E. and J. Dennery

1932: Dining room, including buffet in burl walnut decorated with chromed metal fillets, glass and metal table with illuminated central section, leather upholstered chairs; marketed by G. E. and J. Dennery. In collaboration with J. Luce (glass and platinum tableware), Tétard (silverware), Jean Besnard (ceramics), Charles Despiau (sculpture), and Mme Chabert-Dupont (blinds and table linens)
Moderately priced dining room, including oak buffet with mirrored showcase, extension table, 6 chairs, bookcase-desk; in collaboration with J. Luce (ceramics, plates, and glassware), and Jean Besnard (ceramics)
Study and dining room in tabasco wood, marketed by G. E. and J. Dennery

1935: Bedroom for a young mother in collaboration with Louis Jolain (decorator), and Mlle Grabar (painting); marketed by G. E. and J. Dennery

Salon d'Automne

1920: Study in palisander with marquetry, marketed by Le Confortable (4/6/8 rue de Rome)

1921: Bookcase in macassar ebony and locustwood

1922: Dining room in mahogany and zebrawood, marketed by Soubrier; fabrics by Raoul Dufy, marketed by Bianchini-Férier (24 bis, avenue de l'Opéra)
Smoking-room in collaboration with Raoul Dufy, marketed by Bianchini-Férier

1927: Actress's loggia, canapé and dressing table in burl amboyna and palisander

1928: Industrialist's study in palisander

1932: Study and dining room, including buffet, bookcase, table, desk, chair, 6 chairs, and divan, in tabasco wood; marketed by G. E. and J. Dennery

Brandt, Edgar

Salon des Artistes Décorateurs

1919: Metal lamps and objects with sections in glass, iron, and copper

1920: Lamps and objects
Staircase panel in wrought-iron for a ocean liner of La Compagnie Générale Transatlantique, in collaboration with Bouwens de Boijen (architect)

1921: Door of the monument 'Aux morts de Verdun de la tranchées des baïonettes' in wrought-iron, in collaboration with André Ventre (architect)
Small iron-work and lighting fixtures

1922: Radiator cover, in collaboration with Max Blondat
'Les Cigognes d'Alsace': gates in wrought iron

1923: Selection of iron-work

1924: 'Les Jets d'eau' and 'Les Cocardes': wrought-iron doors
'Acanthes': wrought-iron console with marble top
Wrought-iron mirror
'Flambeaux': wrought-iron sconce
'La Force' and 'L'Audace': wrought-iron lamps, in collaboration with Henri Favier (architect)

1926: 'Générosité': wrought-iron table
'Arabesque': wrought-iron doors
'Heraclès' and 'Le Zodiaque': wrought-iron panels with lacquer by Dunand
In collaboration with Henri Favier (architect), and Pierre Lardin and Gilbert Poillerat (metalwork)

Salon d'Automne

1919: Vitrine with wrought-iron objects, lamp

1920: Vitrine with wrought-iron objects
Floor lamp in wrought-iron and marble
Floor lamp in gilt-copper
2 chandeliers in wrought-iron

1921: 'Abondance': console in wrought-iron and marble
'Les Vagues': floor lamp in glass and wrought-iron
Sconces and psyche in wrought-iron
'La Mer', 'Les Vagues', and 'La Cave': vases in glass and wrought-iron
Auguste Denis' cave doors in steel
In collaboration with Mme Chabert-Dupont (lace), Daum (glassware), and Pantin (crystal)

1923: 'Age d'Or': doorway for grand salon
Console, mirrors, lamps, sconces; in collaboration with Henri Favier (architect), and Max Blondat (sculpture)

1924: 'Altesse' and 'Fantaisie': consoles in wrought-iron
'L'Oasis': screen
'Fleurs et jets d'eau' and 'Automne': mirror frames
'Le Cascade' and 'Marguerites': appliques
'Le Lys' and 'L'Elégance': floor lamps

1926: Decoration of a hall in collaboration with Henri Favier (architect), Badory (sculpture), Rodier (striped fabrics), Wormser (lighting), and Poillerat and Petit (designers)

1934: Monumental door in wrought-iron and 'Studal' metal

Burkhalter, Jean

Salon des Artistes Décorateurs

1919: Silver chisels, 2 vases, flower-holder, and 2 boxes; marketed by Heinin & Cie

1920: Projects for a music room in Henri Rapin's ensemble, with silverware and fabric designs

1924: Ensemble for 'La Réception et l'intimité d'un appartement moderne' organized by Chareau, in collaboration with Fau and Guillard (ceramics) and Mme Pernet (carpets)

1926: Architecture presented by Primavera

Salon d'Automne

1920: 5 paintings

1921: Endpapers

1924: Une Place Publique: Boutique #7: 'Pierre Imans', in collaboration with R. Lardeur (stained glass windows), E. Brandt (wrought-iron doors), Jean Booss (fabric designs for dresses), Mme Pernet (carpet), J. and J. Martel (bench), and Fau and Guillard (ceramic vases)

1925: Sketch of an artist's house

Champion, Georges

Salon des Artistes Décorateurs
1923: Dining room for an inn
Hall
Dining room
Smoking room
1929: Dining room in palisander and sycamore, in collaboration with Lallemant (ceramics); marketed by Studio Gué

Salon d' Automne
1924: Furniture for workers and farmers
1926: Dining room for M. Guérin, 14 Faubourg Saint-Antoine, in collaboration with Georges Champion (cushions), and André Fau (ceramics); marketed by Studio Gué
1927: Hall, including dining room, desk, and bar, in collaboration with Sonya Delaunay (cushions and drapes) and Lallemant (ceramics); marketed by Studio Gué

Chareau, Pierre

Salon des Artistes Décorateurs
1922: Desk, canapé, and armchair
1923: Ensemble for children's room
Architectural project for a house
1924: 'La Réception et l'intimité d'un appartement moderne', including a vestibule by Mallet-Stevens, study by Legrain, dining room by Ruhlmann, veranda by Poiret, windows by Tony Selmersheim, carpets and fabrics by Eileen Gray, *nécéssaire* by Burkhalter; paintings and sculpture by Bonnard, Laurens, Lurçat, Maillol, Utrillo, Picasso, Matisse, etc.
1926: Desk and chairs

Salon d' Automne
1919: Study in collaboration with Jean Lurçat (carpets executed by Mme Ch. L'Hote-Lurçat and Marthe Hennebert), and Chana Orloff (wood carving)
1920: Bathroom
Bedroom furniture in collaboration with Jean Lurçat (carpets and cushions)
1921: Dining room
Boudoir, in collaboration with Jean Lurçat (tapestries)
1922: 3 rooms for a villa: 1st in palisander and thuya, 2nd in ash and sycamore, 3rd in mahogany and palisander, in collaboration with Jean Lurçat (carpets and tapestries)
Table for a winter garden in concrete and enamels
1923: Boudoir, bedroom, and dressing room in palisander and straw
Commode in palisander
1924: Cabinet in palisander and macassar ebony
Une Place Publique: Boutique #9: 'Pierre Chareau', in collaboration with Burkhalter and Survage (fabrics), Lurçat (wallpapers), and Dalbet (wrought-iron)
1926: Furniture for a lecture hall, commissioned by the 'Grand Hôtel de Tours'
1927: Bar and smoking room for the 'Grand Hôtel de Tours'
1931: Sketches and model for a House of Glass
1934: Metallic panelling for an ocean liner cabin in Schneider stainless steel

Chauchet-Guilleré, Charlotte

Salon des Artistes Décorateurs
1919: Lacquered dining room, marketed by Primavera
Printed fabrics
1920: Boudoir, in collaboration with Mlle G. Lehmann and Marcel Guillemard (design), and Chassaing (sculpture); marketed by Primavera

1920: Dining room, marketed by Primavera
1921: Entrance hall decoration: painting and furniture, in collaboration with Marcel Guillemard, Henri Tourtin, and Mlle G. Lehmann; marketed by Primavera
1922: Bedroom in palisander and sycamore with boxwood marquetry
Child's bedroom in painted wood, in collaboration with Marcel Guillemard (furniture), and Olesiewicz (decoration); marketed by Primavera
1923: Lady's bedroom in wild cherry, in collaboration with Olesiewicz (decoration); marketed by Primavera
Stoneware
1924: Stoneware, marketed by Primavera

Salon d' Automne
1920: Dining room, marketed by Primavera
Vitrine containing a coupe and inkwell in enamel and gilt-bronze
1921: Bedroom in sycamore inlaid with ivory and ebony, marketed by Primavera
Vitrine containing a coupe, vases, and inkwell in enamel and gilt-bronze
Dining room in smoked oak, executed by Les Usines du Printemps; marketed by Primavera
1922: Man's bedroom, in collaboration with Marcel Guillemard, Olesiewicz, Mlle Claude Lévy, and Toulan, marketed by Primavera
Study, in collaboration with Guillemard and Olesiewicz
Vitrine including vases, coupes, and bowls
1923: Vitrine including ceramics; marketed by Primavera
1925: Vitrine with coupes and vases
1926: 2 exhibition rooms with paintings by Alice Polsterer
1933: Bar and carpet in collaboration with Robert Verly and Colette Guéden, marketed by Primavera

Da Silva Bruhns, Ivan

Salon des Artistes Décorateurs
1920: Wool carpet in point noué
1921: 'Le Cygne' and 'Les Vautours': paintings
1922: Carpets and painted screens for the Dominique stand
1923: Carpets in Dominique and Leleu stands
1924: Carpets for Leleu, Montagnac, and Genet and Michon
1926: Ensemble in collaboration with Leleu
Carpets in Leleu and Fréchet stands
1927: Carpet in Leleu stand
Façade for a carpet shop
1928: Ensemble of carpets in point noué
Carpets in Leleu and Bouchet stands
1929: Presentation stand: carpet in point noué
1930: Hand-woven carpets in Montagnac and Leleu stands
5 carpets for Printz ensemble, one for Atelier Prou, 3 in Bouchet stand
1931: Ensemble of carpets
3 carpets in Leleu stand
1933: Carpets
1934: Carpets and fabrics for Leleu and Blech-Bertrand stands
1935: Carpets for Leleu ensemble and René Prou stand

Salon d' Automne
1920: Carpet in *haute laine au point noué* for Montagnac ensemble
1921: 4 carpets in Montagnac stand
1922: 4 carpet maquettes
1923: 2 carpets
1924: 2 carpets for Leleu and Montagnac stands

1926: Carpets for Montagnac and Glaize
1927: Carpet boutique with da Silva Bruhns carpets
1929: Carpet ensemble in *point noué à la main*
1930: Carpet ensemble
1931: Carpet for His Royal Highness Y. R. Holkar, Maharajah of Indore
1932: Carpets
1933: Carpets for da Silva Bruhns and Leleu stand

De Bardyère, Georges

Salon des Artistes Décorateurs
1921: Large psyche in sycamore with carved decoration
1922: Salon in mahogany, lighting by Georges and Eugène Capon
1926: Salon in mahogany and burl Burmese wood, in collaboration with Genet and Michon (lighting), Sylvestre (bronze low-reliefs), Jean Luce (glassware), and Aubusson (carpets)
1927: Chiffonier in mahogany, palisander, and ivory
Table in mahogany and ivory, marketed by Les Etablissments Marcel Coupé
1928: Studio in amboyna and ivory, in collaboration with Robert Bonfils (wall hangings and silks), Marcel Coupé (carpets), Le Verre Artistique (engraved glass doors), Genet and Michon (ceiling fixture), Schenck (wrought-iron), and Jean Dunand (vase)
1929: Bedroom in palisander in collaboration with Genet and Michon (lighting), Bonfils (wallpapers, bed coverlet, and silk upholstery), Mme Chabert-Dupont (window shades), da Silva Bruhns (carpets), and Bertin and Lapeyre (painting on wood in Stic-B)

Salon d' Automne
1919: Dining-room furniture, light fixtures, *torchère*, vases, and a window shade, in collaboration with H. Pinguenet (pochoirs, paintings, and carpets); executed by La Maison Marcel Coupé
1920: Dining room in mahogany
Vitrine with objects in sculpted wood, in collaboration with Mme P. Rivière (embroidery), H. Pinguenet (mural decoration), and Joseph Bergès (painting)
1921: Ensemble for a boudoir in sycamore and burl ash in collaboration with Marguerite Lehucher and Mlle Méry (window shades), Georges and Eugène Capon (wrought-iron chandelier), and R. Lachenal (ceramics)
1922: Dining room in Cuban mahogany and burl Burmese wood, in collaboration with Marguerite Lehucher and Mlle Méry (blinds), Georges and Eugène Capon (lighting), R. Buthaud (ceramics), and E. Lassé (wallpaper)
1923: Bedroom in mahogany and burl Burmese wood, in collaboration with Mme Pangon (headboard)
Large round table in mahogany and burl Burmese wood
1924: Cupboard in mahogany and amboyna with ivory inlay
1925: Cupboard in mahogany and burl Burmese wood, and a mirror
1926: Ensemble, with molded glass light fixtures by Genet and Michon
1927: Ensemble in jacaranda and synthetic lacquer, marketed by Les Etablissements Marcel Coupé in collaboration with Parayre (coralwood statue), Genet and Michon (lighting), and Claudius Linossier (vases)
1928: Ensemble including a gilt-wood clock, storage cabinet in burl walnut and ivory, table, walnut chair, synthetic lacquered mirror; carpet in point noué, executed and marketed by Marcel Coupé; in collaboration with Feigenheimer, Fils & Cie (wallpaper and silk upholstery)

1929: Commode in palisander with gilt-bronze
mounts
Bedroom in palisander; in collaboration with
Genet and Michon (lighting), Robert Bonfils
(wallpaper, bed coverlet, and silk upholstery),
Mme Chabert-Dupont (blinds), da Silva Bruhns
(carpets), and Bertin and Lapeyre (painting on
wood)
1930: 'Un cosy corner' in collaboration with Genet
and Michon (lighting), Marcel Coupé (carpets),
and Balande (canvas)
1933: Storage cabinet in mahogany and palisander
with marble top, a chair upholstered with red
velvet, a small mahogany table with marble top
Ensemble in palisander and mahogany,
in collaboration with Genet and Michon (lighting)
Circular mirror in chromed metal, 2 vases
1934: Guéridon in mahogany and burl amboyna with
marble top

Desvallières, Richard

Salon d'Automne
1920: Cock in wrought-iron for a monument to the
dead
1921: 'Promethée enchaîné': firescreen in wrought
iron, a shelf and settee in *repoussé* iron, a small
monument for war victims in wrought-iron
1927: Firescreen
1928: Stairwell grill in wrought-iron
1929: Section of a staircase ramp and balustrade,
executed for the chateau of M. Mignot at Sept-
Saux (Marne)
Sword handle presented to M. G. Desvallières
by La Société du Salon d'Automne
1933: Wrought-iron chandelier, sconces, fire-dogs,
and lamp

Djo-Bourgeois

Salon des Artistes Décorateurs
1923: Architectural project for a restaurant in a park
1924: Chimney executed by La Maison Fau et Guillard
1926: Office, bedroom, and bar for a villa on the Côte
d'Azur
1927: Bedroom for a yacht
1928: Fabrics and carpets by Elise Djo-Bourgeois
1929: Entranceway of the 19th Salon of the Société
des Artistes Décorateurs, in collaboration with
Perfecla (lighting)
1930: Study
Waiting room, in collaboration with Perzel
(lighting), La Société Electro-Cable (rubber
carpets), Stic-B (painting)
1931: Dining room ensemble
1932: Exposition Hall, including stands by Paul
Brandt, Léon Leyritz, Perzel, Coquerel, Tétard,
Tardy, Lardin, including sculpture by K. H.
Rosenberg, lighting by Francis Paul, fabrics and
carpets by Les Usines du Nord, metalware by
Métal Aluminium Français, and lighting
equipment by La Compagnie des Lampes
Corner of a room, printed fabrics by Elise Djo-
Bourgeois
1935: Architectural sketch

Salon d'Automne
1923: Dining room: 'Myne', marketed by Studium
Louvre, in collaboration with Léon Leyritz and
J. and J. Martel
Hotel hall, marketed by Studium Louvre, in
collaboration with Léon Leyritz, F. A. Quelvée,
Brégeaux, and Burkhalter
1924: Smoking room in the country, marketed by
Studium Louvre
Une Place Publique: Boutique #4: 'Une entrée
de boutique pour une bijouterie . . .'

1925: Desk in palisander and sycamore
Cupboard in mahogany
1926: Mediterranean villa
1927: Child's bedroom: furniture in cork, carpets by
Elise Djo-Bourgeois
Villa at Hyères
1928: Ensemble
1929: Living room, in collaboration with Elise Djo-
Bourgeois (cushions), Paul Brandt (jewelry),
Jean-Georges and Louis Tétard (silver), and
Louis Tardy (silver)
1930: Exhibition-room for a large hotel, in
collaboration with Elise Djo-Bourgeois (silks),
Paul Brandt (jewelry), Jean-Georges and Louis
Tétard (precious metals), and Valery Bizouard
(silver)
1931: Ensemble
1932: Maquette of a villa
Maquette of the villa's interior
1933: Room in a villa on the Côte d'Azur

Dominique (Domin, André and Genevrière, Marcel)

Salon des Artistes Décorateurs
1922: Lady's study, in collaboration with Puiforcat
(lamp), da Silva Bruhns (carpet), and Redard
(doors)
Studio ensemble
1923: Bedroom in Indian palisander for M. Jean
Borlin
1924: Bookcase in burl walnut
1927: Lacquered furniture, marketed by Dominique
1932: Dining room, marketed by Dominique

Salon d'Automne
1922: Ensemble in amaranth and palisander, with
carpet by da Silva Bruhns; marketed by
Dominique
1923: Piece of furniture in palisander and burl walnut
2 sconces
1933: Small studio in macassar ebony, marketed by
Dominique

Dufet, Michel

Salon des Artistes Décorateurs
1921: Small *salon* with grey maple and gold-lacquered
furniture, and marble pilasters
1922: Dining room, marketed by M.A.M., including a
commode in macassar ebony with marble top
and a small brown lacquered desk
1929: Room marketed by Le Sylve, Bûcheron's art
studio
1930: Living room, marketed by Le Sylve, Bûcheron's
art studio
1933: 4 cabins for Mme Armand Esders' yacht *Aronia
II*
1935: Studio: white and royal blue, including a table
in chromed steel and glass tiles, chairs in
chromed tubular steel, and a large cabinet in
polished palisander and chromed steel;
marketed by Au Bûcheron

Salon d'Automne
1919: Drawing room in silvered lacquer
Dressing room, marketed by M.A.M.
1920: Drawing room in orange lacquer with columns
in marble, the capitals carved by Binquet, the
furniture in amaranth and silver; marketed by
M.A.M.
1921: Bedroom with furniture in lindenwood and
pewter, marketed by M.A.M.
1922: Bedroom in grey birch, mahogany, and silver
lacquer

1926: Cupboard in macassar ebony, ivory, and marble
Portrait of Mrs Eve Francis
1927: Glass lampshades executed by Boris Lacroix
Panel executed by La Société de Tissu Tressé
1928: Editor's desk in maple with metal and copper
inlay, marketed by Au Bûcheron
Dining room *de série*, in sycamore and walnut
1929: Bedroom in metal, glass tiles, and jacaranda,
marketed by Le Sylve, Bûcheron's art studio
1930: Studio in olivewood, palm, and polished metal
1931: Living room including a dining room *de série* in
macassar ebony and polished Duralumin, and a
desk and bookcase in sycamore and polished
Duralumin; marketed by Au Bûcheron
1932: Lady's *salon* in palm, ash, and gilt-metal,
marketed by Au Bûcheron

Dufrène, Maurice

Salon des Artistes Décorateurs
1919: Boudoir in maple, lacquer, and giltwood
Dining room in painted wood
1920: Dining room in mahogany and thuya decorated
with black lacquer and marquetry
Carpet in point noué
1921: *Salon* corner: console, secrétaire, chairs, mirrors,
carpet, and lamps
Painted wallpaper, marketed by Ch. A. Geffroy
1922: Dining room 'Rusticana', in oak, walnut, and
varnished Zingana
Study in carved walnut
Bedroom in varnished sycamore
1923: Dining room in mahogany and amboyna
Study in waxed walnut
Dining room in mahogany and amaranth,
marketed by La Maîtrise
1924: Tea room of Galeries Lafayette, marketed by La
Maîtrise
1926: Apartment, in collaboration with Jean Bonnet,
Henri Brochard, Gabriel Englinger, Suzanne
Guiguichon, Sylvain Guichard, René Lecointre,
including works by Georges Chevalier (faience
and bronzes), Charlotte Perriand (fabrics), Bodio
(lighting), Mlle Coutant (carpets), Chassaing
(faience), Bonifas (ceramics), Adnet (faience),
Hairon (sculpture); marketed by La Maîtrise
1927: Bedroom in violetwood and amaranth, with
mother-of-pearl inlay, including silks by
Charlotte Perriand and carpets by Dubuisson
(executed by Beligant and Fesneau); marketed
by La Maîtrise
Boudoir in maple and palisander, with light
fixture by Englinger, garniture by Raby
(executed by Vasseur and Guilly); marketed by
La Maîtrise
1928: Communal house, in collaboration with Jacques
Meistermann and Israel Tcherniack (furniture
executed by Speich Frères)
1931: Cabinet
Secretary in mahogany and amboyna for a small
salon in L'Hotel de la Société des Gens de
Lettres de France
Vitrine including ceramics, marketed by La
Compagnie des Arts Français
Vitrine including vases in carved agate
1932: Furniture for a lady's office, including a desk,
epistolary, bookcase, and guéridon
Lacquered parchment screen
Furniture in gilt-bronze and burl amboyna with
maple and black lacquered interiors
Carpet in fur, light fixtures, and marble tiles, in
collaboration with Paul Pouchol (design),
Speich and Perrin (cabinetry), Labadie
(bronzes), Dervillé (marble); marketed by La
Maîtrise

1933: Dining room, 'La Comtoise', including furniture in moulded oak, a garniture in red straw, and matt and brilliant black ceramic floor tiling
Red lacquered door and window
Carpet in *point mêche*, faience tableware, printed curtains in crêpe de chine; in collaboration with Paul Pouchel (design), Speich Frères (furniture), Gilardoni (floor tiling), Baudemant (mirrors), Labadie (lighting), Valentine (painting), and Huet (carpets)
1934: Country interior, 'Cantegril', communal hall and bedroom consisting of furniture in French oak; in collaboration with Geneviève Constant ('La Prairie': wall fabric), Pierre Labadie (gouaches), La Maison Niepce (cabinetry), E. Deturche (floor tiling), Stic-B (painting), Baudemant (mirrors), Tringles Kirsch (curtain rods), and La Manufacture de Tapis et Couvertures (carpets)
1935: 'Cordoue', combinable furniture *de série* for a bedroom, dining room, and *salon*, in smoked oak enhanced with red, green, yellow, or white copper trim, in collaboration with Jacques Meistermann (design), Speich Frères (furniture), Brunet and Stic-B (painting), Les Etablissements Olagnier (ceramic and quartz tiling), La Maison Niepce (exhibition stand); marketed by La Maîtrise

Salon d'Automne
1919: Bedroom, in varnished and inlaid mahogany, collection of M. Bienaimé
Bedroom for a young girl, polished maple and palisander with marquetry, collection of Mlle Michelette Mougeot
Dining room, in varnished mahogany and thuya, with marquetry
1920: *Grand Salon*, including 3 panels by Félix Bellenot
Music room and mural decoration
1921: Bedroom, in ebony, palisander, and macassar ebony; marketed by Galeries Lafayette
Vitrine including objects, marketed by Galeries Lafayette
Fountain, marketed by La Système Breveté Labadie
1922: Dining room in oak, collection of Mme Lassudrie, marketed by La Maîtrise
Bedroom, 'L'Orbe', in walnut, mahogany, and Zingana, with marquetry
Office, 'Zola', in amboyna, marketed by La Maîtrise
1923: Library, marketed by Galeries Lafayette
Vitrines including glassware, fabrics, and ceramics
1924: Screen, in collaboration with M. Maingonnat (tapestry)
1926: Dining room, 'Neptune', in collaboration with Gabriel Englinger and Jacques Meistermann (design), and Olivier Desbordes (cabinetry)
1927: Dining room in collaboration with Gabriel Englinger (carpets), and Vasseur and Guilly (cabinetry)
Council chamber
Boutique and tea room
Boutique and hairdressing salon
1929: 3 editions of 'interchangeable and juxtaposable' furniture for multiple usage in a bedroom, dining room, and work area; marketed by La Maîtrise
1930: Office for the President des Gens de Lettres de France, installed in the residence of the Duke of Massa on the Champs-Elysées in 1784 and reconstructed by André Ventre in 1930 in Le Parc de l'Observatoire, in collaboration with Yencesse (bronzes), Jean Besnard (ceramics), and Perrin (furniture)

1931: Cabinet in varnished mahogany, 2 chairs, vitrine, and 6 carpets
1932: 24 photographs of interiors, including 2 cinemas, bedrooms, living rooms, dining rooms, hairdressing salons, offices, and halls; marketed by Galeries Lafayette
1933: Ensemble, including a secretary, table in black palisander, chair, screen in metal and parchment, and carpet; marketed by Galeries Lafayette
1934: Dining room, including murals, furniture in varnished sycamore, wallpaper, and carpets; in collaboration with Marcelle Maisonnier (design), Yencesse (sculpture), Denier (painting), Speich (cabinetry), La Manufacture Tapis et Couverture (carpets), Baudemant (mirrors), and Brunet (painting in Stic-B)

Dunand, Jean

Salon des Artistes Décorateurs
1919: Vases and metal objects
1920: 2 large green copper vases
Metal objects, including ashtrays, powder boxes, and inkwells
Plate and vases in Théodore Lambert's ensemble
1921: Lacquered panel designed by Henri de Waroquier
1922: 'Chasse': lacquered panel designed by Georges Dorignac
Commode designed by Jean Goulden
'Le Chataîgnier': panel by Schmied
1923: Various objects
'Fougères': 4-panelled lacquered screen
'Léopard et Cobra': lacquered screen designed by P. Jouve
1924: Various objects including copper and silver vases, and a gong
'Lac Leman': lacquered screen designed by Bieler
1926: 'Niagara': 4-panelled screen and various objects
1927: 'Afrique': panel in 3 leaves
'Décor geometrique': panel in 8 leaves
'Oiseaux': panel in 4 leaves
'Josephine Baker' panel in 4 leaves
Table and 2 armchairs in brown lacquer
'Grand Carré': 4-panelled screen
1930: Boudoir in crystallized and carved beige lacquer
Vestibule: 4 large lacquered panels on a silver ground: 'Sénégal', 'Maroc', 'Cameroun', 'Indo-Chine'
Two large vases in lacquered gold metal
Vitrine including vases in various metals inlaid with lacquer and silver
Lacquered screen for Bouchet's stand
'Eléphants': lacquered panel
1931: Lacquered screen
Lacquered and inlaid metal objects
1932: 'Herons': 12-panel screen in black lacquer
Incrusted and lacquered metal objects
1933: Lacquered screen
Poster for the 23rd Salon of the Société des Artistes Décorateurs
1934: Screen and decorative panels
1935: 'Les Vagues': panel in carved black lacquer

Salon d'Automne
1919: Vitrine including objects in diverse metals
1920: Vitrine including objects in diverse metals
1922: Vitrine including objects in diverse metals
1923: 'Moustiers Saint-Marie': screen in Japanese lacquer from a design by Henri de Waroquier
1927: Vitrine including objects in diverse metals
1928: Vitrine including objects in diverse metals
1930: 'Biches': screen in silvered lacquer
Vitrine including vases in lacquered and incrusted metals

1931: Lacquered panel and vitrine including vases in incrusted and lacquered metals
1933: 'Religions': lacquered screen
'Christ en Croix': mosaic
1934: 'Biches': 4-panelled brown lacquered screen

Dupas, Jean

Salon des Artistes Décorateurs
1923: Poster and over-door
1924: Painting, poster, and catalogue cover for the 15th Salon of the Société des Artistes Décorateurs
1926: Engravings and paintings
1927: Cartoon for the ocean liner *Ile de France*
1931: 'Le Taureau Noir': watercolour; 'L'Amour et Psyche': sketch
1933: Designs

Ecole Boulle (see also *Fréchet*)

Salon des Artistes Décorateurs
1926: Gallery of students' works, including bronze and steel pieces executed by 2nd, 3rd, and 4th year students, and a screen designed by J. Rothschild and embroidered by the students
1931: Large cabinet in lemonwood with etched gold and silver-inlaid copper doors
Cupboard with marquetry
Commode with chiseled bronze mounts, executed by the students

Englinger, Gabriel

Salon des Artistes Décorateurs
1926: Dining room in palisander, in collaboration with La Renaissance de Meuble
1927: Dining room
1928: Dressing room in burl ash with a carpet in point noué, polished iron gate and alabaster sconces
Vestibule furniture in palisander
1929: Study including bookcase, desk, and swivel desk chair in violetwood and 2 armchairs in palisander, the side of the desk forming bookshelves; with a low table and sconces in frosted glass. Carpets in the study marketed by Hamot Frères & Cie.
Smoking room including a table in tamo and palisander, cigar drawers, cigarette cases, and pivoting liqueur tray, 2 chairs in tamo, divan and hanging bookshelves, marketed by Le Studio Abran
1930: Dining room in varnished walnut, in collaboration with Milleret (sculpture), Stéphan (lighting), Véroni and Larchevêque (cabinetry)
1931: Small *salon* in chestnut and sycamore, carpet in point noué, in collaboration with Cappellin (lamp, chandelier, and bibelots in Venetian glass)
Children's bedroom with lacquered furniture, in collaboration with Raymond Bègue (photography), Mlle Vaquez (wool carpet marketed by La Laine de Cernay)
1935: Cabinet in mahogany and varnished tapelli, presented in an architectural setting, in collaboration with Marguerite Englinger (embroidered panels)

Salon d'Automne
1927: Sketch for a bar, marketed by Galeries Lafayette

Fabre, Auguste-Victor

Salon des Artistes Décorateurs
1921: Wardrobe in zebrawood with boxwood marquetry

1922: Studio in macassar ebony, with maple and silver marquetry
Dining room in ash, in collaboration with M. J. Steeg; marketed by Les Ateliers A. Fabre
1923: Grey maple dining room
1924: Lacquered bedroom

Salon d'Automne
1919: Powder room in collaboration with La Maison Le Décor Mural (wallpaper and carpet)
4 paintings
1920: Boudoir
1921: Ensemble for a studio in macassar ebony, with maple and silver marquetry
White pongee silk printed in blue and red, red silk crêpe de chine, yellow and white pongee silk
1922: Dining room
Furniture for a bedroom in Gabonese rosewood and gray maple
1923: Small *salon* in lemonwood with relief marquetry in mahogany
1924: Dining room in mahogany
1926: Modern bedroom, marketed by La Maison Decaux et Maous
1927: Dining room, marketed by La Maison Decaux et Maous

Follot, Paul

Salon des Artistes Décorateurs
1919: Dining room in sycamore, coralwood, and ebony, with murals
1920: Dressing table and carved, gilt, and lacquered chair
Guéridon and chair in amboyna and palisander
Carved wood armchair and lamps
1921: Bedroom in palisander and amboyna, decorated with gadrooning and marquetry
Carved wood lamp, bed, wardrobe, bedside-table, guéridon, armchair, and chair, marketed by M. Coupé; in collaboration with Schenck (handmade carpet), Mme Follot (paintings), Brandt (sconces), and Cornille Frères (fabrics)
1922: *Petit* and *grand salon*, including a Pleyel piano, in collaboration with Laurent Malclès (ormulu clock)
1923: Study in palisander and marquetry
Drawing room with carved, lacquered, and giltwood furniture
Dining room in carved clear oak
Bedroom in waxed oak, marketed by Pomone
1924: Music room in palisander, macassar ebony, and carved giltwood; in collaboration with Joseph Bernard (sculpture), Cavaille (organ), and Pleyel (piano)
1926: Vestibule and bedroom in amboyna with ivory inlay, in collaboration with Raoul Josset (carpet), and Andre Sebreuil (palisander and *galuchat* desk)
Dining room in walnut with ormolu flambeaux, in collaboration with Albert Guénot (sculpture), René Shils and Germaine Labaye (paintings)
1927: Hall in palisander
Boudoir in maple with marquetry and silver mounts, in collaboration with Savonnerie (carpet), Brugier (silverware, ceramics, and lacquered vases), Mlle Poupelet, and Halon and do Canto (statuettes)
Desk in mahogany, ivory, and amboyna
'Mélanite': wood panelling
1929: Deluxe dining room with lacquered wood panelling, a wrought-iron console and marble chimney, sideboard and table and 12 chairs in carved sycamore and coralwood; in collaboration with Pierre Traverse (Bronze

group: 'Femme à l'Antilope'), La Manufacture de Tapis de Cogolin (carpet), Daurat (silver), Luce (ceramics), and Baccarat (crystal), marketed by Waring and Gillow
1931: Presidential office
1932: Small boudoir, the giltwood dressing table lacquered in cellulose
1933: Stand including an extension games table, 3 armchairs, and a large armchair in lacquered Duralumin and Moroccan leather; the garnitures and guéridon in polished aluminium and mirror; in collaboration with Michel Dubost (curtain and wool carpet in point noué), and La Société Charles Follot (wallpaper), the furniture marketed by Studaz (23 bis, rue Balzac)
1934: *Armoire-chiffonier* in maple and ebony
Armchair in maple and ebony upholstered in satin, in collaboration with Max Beucher (painted wallpaper), marketed by La Société Charles Follot (43 boulevard Diderot, Paris)
1935: Painted wallpaper, marketed by La Société Charles Follot

Salon d'Automne
1920: Dining room in palisander with marquetry
Small *salon* in palisander and amboyna with marquetry and lacquer
1921: Hallway including lacquered and giltwood furniture and a carpet 'Nocturne', in collaboration with Süe et Mare, Ruhlmann, and Brandt (wrought-iron bookcase)
Carpet in the Süe et Mare stand
Carpet in the Ruhlmann stand
Participation in the exhibition of furnishing for the ocean liner *Paris*
1923: Bedroom in jacaranda and burl elm
Dining room in carved mahogany
Vitrine in wrought iron, containing silver tea and coffee services, marketed by Pomone
1924: Bedroom in palisander, amboyna and ivory, in collaboration with Savonnerie (carpet); marketed by Pomone
1926: Bedroom in synthetic lacquered wood, with carpet by Savonnerie, and statue: 'Chasseresse' by Wolkovski
Study in Cuban mahogany with marquetry, in collaboration with Savonnerie (carpet), Lamourdedieu (bronzes), Wolkovski (faiences); marketed by Pomone
1927: Bedroom in carved wood lacquered in 'Duco', in collaboration with Savonnerie (carpet) and Gaudissard (painting); marketed by Pomone
1928: Dining room in carved palisander with wrought iron console, in collaboration with Damas (curtains), Savonnerie (carpet), and Cappelin (table edges in Venetian glass)
1932: Vitrine including a tea and coffee service in silver and ivory, chocolate service in silver and ebony, marketed by Laparra (157 rue de Temple)
3 wallpaper designs, marketed by La Société Charles Follot

Fréchet, André

Salon des Artistes Décorateurs
1919: Country dining room, marketed by Régy Fils
1923: Wardrobe in walnut and carved palisander in collaboration with Louis Malclès (sculpture), marketed by Vérot (3 boulevard Richard Lenois)
1924: Dining room in collaboration with Louis Malclès (sculpture), and Georges Chevalier (glassware); marketed by Vérot

1926: Library, marketed by Vérot
1927: Lady's room in maple and leather, marketed by Vérot, in collaboration with Studium Louvre (fabrics), and Genet and Michon (lighting)
1929: Dining room including a large cupboard, dining table, and 8 chairs; marketed by Vérot
1930: Office including a desk in chestnut with lacquered top, coffee-table, bookcase with metal doors, desk-chair, chairs and lounging armchair in walnut upholstered in red velvet; in collaboration with Paul Fréchet (design), Genet and Michon (lighting), Brunet and Meunie (curtains and carpet), and Maxime Vibert (carpet, marketed by Marcel Coupé); marketed by E. Vérot
1931: Bedroom including a bed, dressing-table, commode, 2 small tables in palisander with chromed copper handles, and chairs and armchairs, in collaboration with Paul Fréchet (design), Jane Bernard ('Clos de la Brèche', 'La Charité', and 'Nievre', carpets), Genet and Michon (lighting), and Massis (cushions and bedcover); marketed by E. Jacquemin
Palisander wardrobe, circular table and 2 chairs, in collaboration with Paul Fréchet; marketed by Vérot
1932: (André and Paul), dining room/studio in varnished walnut with gilt-bronze mounts, marketed by E. Jacquemin
Young girl's bedroom in rosewood, marketed by Jafex
Gallery with walnut panelling, marketed by Jafex
Dressing-table and lady's desk in Cuban mahogany and gilt-bronze, in collaboration with Massis (curtains, furs, and cushions), Genet and Michon (lighting), and Brunet and Meunie (carpet); marketed by Vérot
Installation and decoration of the Jean-Goujon gallery
1933: Powder room including a lady's desk and chair in mahogany, guéridon and chair in silvered mirror and mahogany, palisander chiffonière; in collaboration with Massis (carpet & cushions), and Genet and Michon (lighting); marketed by Verot.
Gallery with a large black cupboard with gilt-bronze mounts, a revolving table, armchairs and chairs in pearwood; in collaboration with La Manufacture Nationale de Porcelaine de Sèvres (vitrine), La Manufacture Nationale de Tapisserie de Beauvais (Charles Martin sketches), H. Sourdet (parquetry floor), G. Poillerat (wrought-iron door), Jean Luce (crystalware), and Massis (carpet and furs); marketed by Jacquemin and Baudet-Donon
1934: (André and Paul): Walnut dining room comprised of a large cupboard/sideboard, table 'à l'Italienne', 6 chairs; in collaboration with Pico (mural decoration), Denis Gélin (sculpture), Jean Luce (crystalware), Véronèse (lighting), Brunet and Meunie (carpet); marketed by Jeanselme
1935: (André and Paul): Study for the Commissioner General of Fine Arts at the 1937 Exposition
Furniture in Cuban mahogany, black wood, and gilt-bronze, chairs in lacquered wood; in collaboration with Louis Leygue (sculpture), Genet and Michon (lighting), Brunet and Meunie (carpet and fabrics); marketed by Jeanselme

Salon d'Automne
1919: Antechamber
1923: Bedroom in walnut and palisander, in collaboration with Edgar Brandt (electrical ceiling fixture), marketed by Jacquemin (44 rue de Vieux Marche-aux-Vins)

1935: Lady's bedroom in lacquered wood, gilt
  canework, and varnished pearwood, in
  collaboration with Louis Leygue (bust), Paule
  Manot (fabrics), and Gilon-Bayet and Chasles
  (iron gates); marketed by Jeanselme

Gabriel, René

Salon des Artistes Décorateurs
1919: Painted wallpaper: colour projects
1920: Ensemble for a little girl's bedroom with
  printed wallpaper
1921: Dressing room and small desk in maple and
  ebony
  Printed wallpaper
1922: Bedroom in *pylma* and grey sycamore
1923: Dining room in wild cherry and burl elm
  Poster project
  Wallpaper
1924: Commode in *pylma* and mahogany
  Bookcase in maple and ash, 2 chairs in *pylma* and
  grey sycamore
  Embroidered curtains and wallpaper
1927: Part of a studio in waxed oak, in collaboration
  with Perzel (lighting)
1928: Poster for the 18th Salon of the Société des
  Artistes Décorateurs
1929: Ensemble in bubenga, mahogany, and nickel, 2
  armchairs in palisander and leather, coffee table
  in palisander and burl walnut, 2 steel chairs,
  garniture in rubber
1930: Study in sycamore and chromed-metal;
  marketed by Viacroze-Décoration, porcelain
  executed and marketed by Haviland & Cie,
  Limoges
  Poster and catalogue cover for the 20th Salon of
  the Société des Artistes Décorateurs
  Wallpapers
1931: *Coin de repos* for the *Ile de France* executed in
  'Salubra' fabric, and steel furniture; marketed
  by Viacroze-Décoration
1932: Small apartment
1933: Apartment with 6 rooms
1934: Study in an inexpensive house
1935: Dining room and bedroom

Salon d'Automne
1919: 'L'Ile de France': wallpaper
  2 chairs and a reading table
1929: Communal hall, marketed by Viacroze-
  Décoration

Goulden, Jean

Salon des Artistes Décorateurs
1924: 3 frescoes
  Champlevé enamelware
1929: Various objects
1930: Coupe in silvered-metal and champlevé enamel
  Panel in silvered-metal and champlevé enamel
  Coffret in red enamel and gilt metal
  Coffret in green enamel and gilt metal
1931: Plaques, cup, and boxes in champléve enamel
1935: Enamelled panel

Gray, Eileen

Salon des Artistes Décorateurs
1919: 'La Nuit': lacquered panel
1923: Studio in Monte Carlo including a black
  lacquered bed, door and desk, a mahogany
  armchair, screens and carpets
1924: Carpets and curtains
1933: Presentation of furniture and chairs for a hall
  Photographs and architectural models

Salon d'Automne
1922: Ensemble including a commode in an exotic
  wood with lacquered maroon top
  Lacquered panel
  Carpet in point noué
  Fabric with blue, white, and black stripes
1923: Furniture

Groult, André

Salon des Artistes Décorateurs
1920: *Petit salon*, in collaboration with M. J.
  Laboureur (wallpaper)
1921: Bedroom in *galuchat*
1922: Bedroom in *galuchat*
  Dining room in cherry
  Library in grey wood
1928: Chinese lacquered screen, straw paper screen,
  aluminium table and bergère: giltwood
  sculpture by Zadkine
1930: Small *salon* including furniture and wall-
  covering in straw paper, in collaboration with
  Baguès (lighting)

Salon d'Automne
1921: Modern furniture
1928: Screen in Chinese lacquer, decorated by Ossip
  Zadkine
1934: Chinese lacquered panel, decorated by Sergé
  Férat (67 bis, boulevard Saint-Jacques)

Guiguichon, Suzanne

Salon des Artistes Décorateurs
1928: 2 carpets in Dufrène exhibit
1930: Study in macassar ebony (pink, green, and
  white), harmonious colour theme, in
  collaboration with Henri Brochard; marketed
  by Speich Frères (230 Faubourg Saint-Antoine)
  Maquettes of a boudoir, studio, and
  hairdressing salon
  Photographs of a dining room, bedroom, and
  studio
1931: Studio and dining room in black varnished
  pearwood, wall panelling in white scyamore,
  green seats; marketed by Speich Frères, in
  collaboration with Flexwood, Chicago (mural
  covering)
1932: Powder-room corner in burl ash, the chairs
  upholstered in peach velvet; marketed by
  Speich Frères
  Photograhs of 2 interiors: a studio and a dining
  room
1933: Studio corner including a secretary-bookcase in
  jacaranda with sycamore interior, the chairs
  covered with yellow fabric, and a hand-woven
  carpet
  Maquettes of a bedroom, studio, boudoir, and
  dining room
1934: Living-room for two people
1935: Studio for a young man or woman including
  white oak furniture, the chairs covered with
  hand-woven linen

Salon d'Automne
1922: *Bonbonnière* in cloisonné enamel, silks and scarfs;
  marketed by La Maîtrise
1929: Bedroom in sycamore
  Maquette for a dining room and study,
  marketed by Speich Frères
1930: Bedroom in varnished sycamore, marketed by
  Speich Frères

Guillemard, Marcel

Salon des Artistes Décorateurs
1923: Study in mahogany with marquetry, in
  collaboration with Olesiewicz; marketed by
  Primavera

1924: Studio in collaboration with Olesiewicz
  (carpet), and Thomas (painting)
  Dining room in collaboration with Olesiewicz
  (painting)
1926: Dining room in collaboration with Chassaing
  (sculpture)
  Smoking room in collaboration with Boivinet
  (armchairs)
  Studio marketed by Primavera
1927: Bedroom in sycamore, marketed by Primavera
1929: Metal chairs, part of Sognot's ensemble;
  marketed by Primavera
1930: Hall in collaboration with Henri Boulanger
  (furniture), Colette Guéden (carpets), and Alice
  Polsterer (screen); marketed by Primavera
1933: Lady's desk, metal chair, and bookcase;
  marketed by Primavera

Salon d'Automne
1923: Dining room in cherry, in collaboration with
  Olesiewicz (paintings), and Chassaing
  (sculpture)
1924: Hairdressing salon, marketed by Primavera
1927: Hall, marketed by Primavera

Hamanaka, Katsu

Salon des Artistes Décorateurs
1932: Screen in Japanese lacquer
  Footed tray in lacquer
  Box in lacquer
1933: Japanese lacquer screen
1934: Japanese lacquer screen
1934: Japanese lacquer screen
  Tabletop in Japanese lacquer
1935: Screen and tabletop in Japanese lacquer

Salon d'Automne
1929: Screen in lacquer
1930: Vitrine including a tray in Japanese lacquer and
  eggshell
1931: Table in Japanese lacquer
  Screen in Japanese lacquer
1933: Table in Japanese lacquer
  Screen in Japanese lacquer
1934: Table in Japanese lacquer
  Screen in Japanese lacquer

Herbst, René

Salon des Artistes Décorateurs
1922: Living room in collaboration with Madeleine
  Vionnat, Tassmari and Chatel (silks), and
  Boudin (interior); marketed by the Musée de
  Crillon
1924: Dining room for M. R. L. Roubaix, in
  collaboration with M. Yung (floor lamps)
1926: Shop façade, interior, and dress designs by
  Lanvin; marketed by the Siègel
1927: Illumination for the Compagnie des Lamps
  Contreplaquées de Luterma Français, marketed
  by Siègel
1928: Smoking room in steel, varnished wood, and
  velvet, in collaboration with Djo-Bourgeois,
  Perriand, Sandoz, and Fouquet

Salon D'Automne
1921: Furniture for a *coin de repos* at the Musée de
  Crillon, in collaboration with Francis Paul
  (wallpaper), and Tassmari and Chatel (silks)
1922: Office ensemble in ash and mahogany
1924: Une Place Publique: boutique for Siègel
1926: Study in concrete with tubular desk and chairs
  upholstered in leather, for La Société Electro-
  Cable
  La Boutique Siègel, in collaboration with La
  Compagnie des Lampes (lighting)

La Boutique Ducharne, in collaboration with Ducharne (silks), and La Compagnie des Lampes (lighting)

1927: 'Les Parfums Isabey', interior design 'Magasin Siègel', interior design in collaboration with Vigneau and Décor

1928: Dining room furniture in steel Study with metal furniture, in collaboration with A. Salomon (lighting), and Hélène Henri (fabrics)

1929: Office with metal furniture, in collaboration with A. Salomon (lighting), and Hélène Henri (fabrics)

1931: Dining room in nickelled steel, leather, and mahogany, chaise longue in chromed steel, in collaboration with Hélène Henri (fabrics)

1933: Presentation of furniture, in collaboration with Hélène Henri (fabrics and carpets)

1934: Ocean liner cabin in steel, in collaboration with Carlu, Cassandre, and Bernard (posters) Ocean liner cabin in steel in collaboration with Hélène Henri (fabrics), A. Salomon (lighting), Etablissements Paul Bres (metal furniture), and Etablissements Krieg & Zuwy (metallic furnishing; 4, avenue Rodin), under the patronage of O.T.U.A. (Office Technique pour l'Utilisation de l'Acier)

Iribe, Paul

Salon des Artistes Décorateurs

1932: Sketches

Jallot, Léon-Albert and Maurice-Raymond

Salon des Artistes Décorateurs

1919: Dining room in sculpted oak Bedroom in lacquered oak, marketed by La Maison Régy

1920: (Léon) furniture ensemble

1921: Buffet with carved panels inlaid with ebony Living room in amaranth and camphorwood with marquetry

1922: Dining room in burl wild cherry, in collaboration with La Maison Coupé (carpet), Coudyser (windows), and Bonfils (printed fabrics)

1923: Bedroom, bed and table in collaboration with Mme Chabert-Dupont (bedcover) and Paul Vera (tapestry)

1924: Bedroom in palisander, in collaboration with Mme Chabert-Dupont (blinds and bedcover) Dining room in macassar ebony

1926: (Léon) living room marketed by Favre

1927: (Léon) dining room in palisander (Maurice) studio smoking room in walnut, *galuchat*, and macassar ebony

1928: (Léon) powder room including lacquered screen and furniture in *galuchat* and ormolu, in collaboration with Favre (Maurice) dining room in walnut, in collaboration with Favre, Subes (wrought iron), Lalique (tea-service), and Tétard Frères (silverware); marketed by Grand Dépôt

1929: Powder room including a lacquered table with wrought-iron legs by Subes, lacquered settee, lacquered commode, varnished macassar ebony and *galuchat* table, palisander armchairs, lacquered panels, carpet in point noué, and showcases with vases by Jean Dunand and Raoul Lachenal

1930: (Léon) studio-library with a lady's desk in macassar ebony and ivory, including chairs, armchair, eggshell coffee-table and a circular carpet

(Maurice) hall including a console, iron gate, writing-table with parchment top, armchairs and a large cabinet; in collaboration with Subes (wrought iron)

1931: Waiting room with macassar ebony commode, lacquered armchair, stainless metal and glass table, chairs in leather and palm; in collaboration with Jean Besnard (vases), Rodier (window shades), and Mme Chauvel (flowers)

1933: (Léon and Maurice) rotunda including a commode in parchment with silvered tile top and crystal handles Cupboard in palisander and metal with crystal handles Cupboard with lacquered sculpture, 2 large wrought iron doors; one large ceramic vase and 2 projects by Jean Mayodon & Cie; in collaboration with Durand (cabinetry), Meunié de la Roussière (fabrics), Subes (wrought iron) and Hagenauer (mirrors)

1934: (Léon & Maurice) dining-room in oak with lacquered gold wall panelling, in collaboration with Labouret (floor tiles), Perzel (lighting), Jean Luce (glassware), Mme Chabert-Dupont (lace), Jean Tétard (silver), Mayodon (ceramics), Sangouard (furnishings), L. Raynaud (sculpted plaster), Besnard (painting), Rault (window shades), and Subes (wrought iron)

Salon D'Automne

1919: Oak dining room Lacquered oak bedroom, marketed by La Maison Régy

1922: Commode in painted wood Macassar ebony table

1924: Furniture

1926: Ensemble

1927: Furniture

1930: Toulon: 'Le petit yacht'

1931: Interior

Jaulmes, Gustave-Louis

Salon des Artistes Décorateurs

1919: Garden 'Gloriette' with painted furniture and concrete vases; in collaboration with Rambouillet (canvas)

1921: Poster for the 12th Salon of the Société des Artistes Décorateurs

1923: Tapestry design for La Manufacture des Gobelins: 'The Rivers of France: The Seine, Rhône, Loire, and Garonne'

1924: Cartoons for tapestries

1929: Pieces of porcelain, executed and marketed by Haviland & Co., Limoges

1933: Tapestries executed by La Manufacture des Gobelins: 'The Seine, Rhône, Loire, and Garonne'

1934: Cartoons for tapestries

Salon d'Automne

1919: Cartoon for a tapestry depicting the departure of the American troops, offered by the French State to Philadelphia, to be executed by La Manufacture des Gobelins Cartoons for a tapestry for the Hotel Biron (Museé Rodin) Screen in tapestry, by Marie-Georges Jaulmes Back of an armchair, by Marie-Georges Jaulmes

Joubert (René) et Petit (Philippe)

Salon des Artistes Décorateurs

1919: Powder room, in collaboration with André Rivaud (door handles), da Silva Bruhns (carpets), and Montagnac (lacquer)

1920: Boudoir, in collaboration with André Rivaud (door handles), da Silva Bruhns (carpets), and Montagnac (lacquer)

1921: Wardrobe with interior mirror Dressing table in amaranth, gray maple, and silvered bronze Carpet in point noué In collaboration with Pinchon (silvered bronze), marketed by D.I.M.

1922: Dining room in walnut, in collaboration with G. Mouveau, marketed by D.I.M.

1923: Cupboard in satinwood and palisander Psyche in walnut and padouk Furniture for 'Radiola' Lady's desk and armchair in white maple Piano in oak for Pleyel

1924: Cupboard in palisander, marketed by D.I.M.

1926: Cupboard in palisander and walnut Living room in palisander and walnut

1927: Living room and dining room

1928: Bedroom in silver and crystal Powder room with an Electrophon piece of furniture Vitrine with objects made of Venetian Lava glass

1929: Bedroom, including the crystal and silverware dressing-table Boudoir furniture in Electrophon Elecson Vitrine of objects in Venetian Lava glass, marketed by D.I.M.

1930: Study in walnut and metal, chimney in polished aluminium and parkerized steel; carpet by V. Boberman, terra cotta by Vadim Androusov, vases by Mme Dem

1931: Dining room and lady's bedroom

Salon d'Automne

1919: Dining room

1921: Dining room buffet in mahogany and satinwood

1922: Piece of furniture for a dressing room in palisander and satinwood, marketed by D.I.M.

1923: Dressing-table and armchair in palisander

1924: Dressing table and armchair in palisander

1926: Entrance hall

1927: Carpet boutique, in collaboration with Ekman, marketed by D.I.M.

1928: Coffee shop in New York, in collaboration with Marcel Bouis, marketed by D.I.M.

Jourdain, Francis

Salon des Artistes Décorateurs

1919: Dining room

1920: Furniture in *bois gris*

1921: Dining room

1922: Dining room in sycamore and maple

1923: Dining room in oak and zingana, marketed by Francis Jourdain

1924: Piece of furniture

Salon d'Automne

1919: Studio in collaboration with La Maison Laplante (carpet), and Edouard Schenck (radiator cover)

1920: Nursery Study in macassar ebony, in collaboration with Vuillard (painting)

1921: Country dining room Furniture in *bois gris*

1922: Dressing-table Office

1924: Une Place Publique, Boutique # 2: Les Editions Cres & Cie

1927: Façade for Helena Rubinstein's beauty clinic

Kinsbourg, Renée

Salon des Artistes Décorateurs
1927: 'Navire' and 'Printemps': carpets
1928: Screens composed of 2 and 3 leaves
1929: Corner of a hotel hall, in collaboration with Jacques Martel (lighting), marketed by Les Arts de France
1931: Carpet for F. and G. Saddier

Salon d'Automne
1921: Lady's bedroom with a palisander and lacquered cupboard, in collaboration with Les Arts de France
1924: Ensemble in wild-cherry and sycamore, marketed by Cotte
1926: Smoking room, including a console with marble top, ebony table, macassar ebony sofa-bed, and a lacquered corner piece
1927: Lady's room in palisander and lacquer, marketed by Les Arts de France
1928: Transatlantic cabin, marketed by Les Arts de France
1931: Fountain with stone low-reliefs, marketed by Antony and Calo Séailles

Kiss, Paul

Salon des Artistes Décorateurs
1926: Table with marble top; console with marble top; mirror; chandelier, sconces and lamp in alabaster
Gate in wrought-iron, 6 chairs in wood, leather, and iron in collaboration with Paul Feher
1927: Console table, lustre, sconces, and gate in wrought-iron, in collaboration with Paul Feher

Salon d'Automne
1926: Wrought-iron ensemble
1927: Modern study in collaboration with Paul Feher (glasswork), and Mlle Lardeur (carpets)

Klotz, Blanche–J.

Salon des Artistes Décorateurs
1934: Lady's desk in collaboration with Pierre and Jacques Lardin (engraving on glass)

Kohlmann, Etienne

Salon des Artistes Décorateurs
1924: Dining room in mahogany and oak, in collaboration with Meslin (sculpture); marketed by Studium Louvre
1926: Dining room and desk in mahogany, in collaboration with Léon Leyritz (sculpture); marketed by Studium Louvre
1927: Bedroom in sycamore, in collaboration with Mlle Max Vibert (carpets and curtains)
Powder room in limewood, in collaboration with Suzanne Mazoyer (carpets)
Study in varnished palisander
1928: Lady's room in pearwood and burl ash, marketed by Studium Louvre
1929: Lady's apartment:
 1. Gallery including walls in black zapon, in collaboration with Simone Godquin (varnished pearwood furniture), Max Vibert (nickelled mouldings)
 2. Bedroom including silk wall, violet wood and metal furniture, and a carpet in point noué, in collaboration with Mme Mazoyer (drawings)

3. Small *salon* including silk walls, burl walnut and green lacquered furniture, carpet in point noué, in collaboration with Max Vibert (mural designs); marketed by Studium Louvre
1930: Private apartment:
 1. Lady's bedroom including burl ash furniture, carpet, and bedcover
 2. Boudoir including ash furniture and lacquered wood chairs, upholstered in velvet
 3. Man's room, including palisander furniture, black mirror, and nickelled metal; in collaboration with Max Vibert (carpet)
 4. Study in palisander, including a desk, bookcase, bridge-table, game archchair, in collaboration with Mme Mazoyer (cartoon for a carpet in point noué), Fontayne (painting), and Simone Godquin (drawing); marketed by Studium Louvre
1931: Architecture for a tea room and bar with a flower presentation, in collaboration with Max Vibert (mosaics), Mme Philippe de Vilmorin (flower arrangement) marketed by Emaillerie de Saint-Maurice (wall covering), La Pépinière (curtains), Alnet (mosaics), Etablissement Puech & Cie (plain and engraved mirrors), L'Irradiance (glass vases), Société Monolampe (lighting), Balas (plumbing), E. Thierry (painting), La Société Parisienne de Décoration (bar stools and chairs), and Collas (flowers)
1932: Sales manager's office of La Société Le Stic-B, in collaboration with Max Vibert (mural paintings), Marguerite Lehucher (curtains and window shades), Francis Paul (lighting), Stic-B (painting); marketed by Brunet-Meunie and Brunet de la Roussière & Cie
1933: Lady's room in violetwood, in collaboration with Max Vibert (taffeta curtains and bedcover and carpet in point noué), François Ganeau (plaster sculpture); marketed by Studium Louvre
1934: Dining room in varnished wild cherry, including straw chairs, in collaboration with Max Vibert (ensemble), and P. Juget (lighting), marketed by Studium Louvre
1935: Furniture for a country house:
 1. Bedroom with lacquered furniture, chairs upholstered in white linen, painted wallpaper designed by Max Vibert and sculpture by François Ganeau
 2. Dining room including furniture in natural oak, chairs decorated with 'Rabanne' fabric, and painted walls; in collaboration with Max Vibert and François Ganeau (sculpture); marketed by Studium Louvre

Salon d'Automne
1923: 'Cendrillon' bedroom in pearwood with ivory and ebony marquetry; 'Léo' study in violetwood, burl thuya and ebony, in collaboration with Dubau; marketed by Studium Louvre
1924: Library in *gaiac* and pearwood
Carpet, 2 alabaster sconces; marketed by Studium Louvre
1925: Ebony dressing-table in violetwood and burl thuya, marketed by Studium Louvre
1926: Luxurious apartment for La Compagnie Générale Transatlantique
Room with a carpet by Max Vibert
Living room by Suzanne Mazoyer
Hall for a villa
1927: Country dining room in green waxed oak, in collaboration with Max Vibert (silks) and Jean Lévy (chandelier); marketed by Studium Louvre
1928: Living room in walnut and burl walnut
Boudour in burl amboyna and giltmetal, in

collaboration with Matet (chairs), Max Vibert (carpet and silhouette)
Dining room in walnut and burl walnut
1929: Study and smoking room including furniture in satinwood and black lacquer, in collaboration with Simone Godquin (commode), Max Vibert (carpet and curtains), and Sebastien Gab. Simo (sculpture); marketed by Studium Louvre
1930: Dining room, smoking room and bedroom in collaboration with Miss Godquin (furniture), Max Vibert (carpets), and S. Sebastian (terracotta)
1931: Boudoir in burl ash and giltmetal with gold mosaic walls
Furniture *de série*: enamelled stainless sheet-iron table and chairs, maquette of a terrace with furniture in mosaic of enamels by Briare, in collaboration with Max Vibert (metal animals), Miss S. Godquin (small table), and Suzanne Mazoyer (window blinds); marketed by Studium Louvre
1932: Boudoir and winter garden in collaboration with Max Vibert (murals)
1933: 'Minima', apartment including a dining room, bedroom, and study, the oak furniture inlaid with metal, in collaboration with Max Vibert (design); marketed by Studium Louvre
1934: Skier's chalet in Oregon pine including a living room in collaboration with Max Vibert (fabrics), Holophane (sconces), Gigou (mounts of a commode)
Dining room in Oregon pine, including a large table convertible into 2 bridge tables, in collaboration with P. Juget and Holophane (lighting)
Entrance hall in Oregon pine, marketed by Studium Louvre
1935: Child's bedroom with white lacquered furniture and a rubber floor, in collaboration with Max Vibert (fabrics)
Games room including a table in lacquered sheet metal and a rubber floor
Boudoir with painted walls, desk in leather and chromed metal, a console in lacquered and chromed sheet metal, an armchair covered in silk, and a work-table, in collaboration with Max Vibert (fabrics), and Holophane (lighting)

Lahalle (Pierre) et Lévard (Georges)

Salon des Artistes Décorateurs
1921: Entrance hall
Palisander chest of drawers inlaid with amboyna and ivory
Giltwood frame, in collaboration with L. Malclès (sculpture)
1922: Dining room in smoked oak; in collaboration with L. Malclès (sculpture)
Young girl's bedroom
1923: Lacquered cabinet and objects
1924: Lady's desk in burl walnut and lemonwood, armchair upholstered in silk with wood and ivory marquetry
3-leaf screen in Coromandel lacquer
1929: Young girl's bedroom furniture in grey sycamore and amaranth
1930: Small *salon*, including a *revêtement* in Coromandel lacquer; a burl walnut and walnut print cabinet, and a sofa upholstered in silk; in collaboration with Genet and Michon (chandelier), and Marguerite Lehucher (curtains)
1931: Screen in Coromandel lacquer
1934: Screen in Coromandel lacquer
1935: 4-panel screen

Salon d'Automne
1919: *Coin de salon*, in collaboration with Maurice Lucet and Dhomme (murals and ceramics), Louis Malclès (sculpture), Deltombe (tapestry), Hamot Frères (carpets), and Goddio (cabinetry)
1920: Lacquered cabinet
1921: Bedroom executed by Mme P. Lahalle; bed embroidered by Mme Fréchet, bedcover by La Maison François Tédésco
1922: Bedroom at 'Bon Marché' in lemonwood with marquetry; in collaboration with Edmond Lassé (wallpaper)
1923: Dining room in smoked oak and marquetry; in collaboration with Mlle de Puygaudeau (window shade: 'La Corbeille'), Subes (chandelier), Jean Luce (tableware)
Wood screen with lacquer and tapestry executed by the National School of Aubusson
1924: (Lévard only) swimming pool for a villa on the Côte d'Azur; in collaboration with Sognot (boudoir), Guillemard (hairdressing salon), Claude Lévy and Meyer and Tavarnier (carpet), Thomas and Sognot (drapes), and Mme Sougez (glassware)
1927: *Chiffonier* in palisander and amboyna with ivory marquetry
Picture frame in giltwood by Laurent Malclès
1928: Boudoir in Coromandel lacquer
Dressing-table in sycamore and silvered-bronze
Wrought-iron gate executed by Morand & Cie, in collaboration with Rodier (fabrics)

Lalique, René

Salon des Artistes Décorateurs
1922: Decorative ensemble and glassware
1926: Glassware
1927: Oval glass table
1928: Tableware
1929: Door in glass and chromed metal
Tables in engraved crystal
Chandelier, sconces, and objects of art
1930: Room in sycamore and glass
Fountain in white marble and glass
Glass table and centrepiece
1931: Crystal doors
Two vitrines containing glass objects
1932: Intimate dining room

Salon d'Automne
1928: Chandeliers and sconces
Liquor bar
1929: Small living room
1931: Large illuminated glass table
Chapel doors (2 faces)
1933: Ensemble
1934: Table in glass
Chandeliers and crystal service
1935: Screen in glass and sycamore
Two vitrines containing glassware

Le Corbusier and Jeanneret, Pierre

Salon d'Automne
1922: Diorama of a contemporary town and plans for 2 types of buildings
1923: Architectural urban art
1924: Photographs of completed buildings
1927: Standardized windows; marketed by Les Manufactures de Saint Gobain
Photographs of completed buildings
1929: Furnishings for a home with the collaboration of La Maison Thonet (serial furniture), Charles Blanc (kitchen fixture), and L'Etablissement Saint Gobain (sun tiles)
1931: Architecture

Legrain, Pierre

Salon des Artistes Décorateurs
1921: Bookbindings and dressing-table, marketed by Louis Vuitton
1922: Filing cabinet, lacquer by Jean Dunand
1923: Table with lacquered top
1924: Library in collaboration with Edouard Degaîne, Czaky and Miklos (sculpture)
1926: Bookbindings

Leleu, Jules

Salon des Artistes Décorateurs
1922: Living room; in collaboration with J. Calliet (cabinetry), E. Letessier (chairs), and Gigou (metalware)
1923: Bedroom in burl walnut, rosewood, and ivory
1924: Dining room in macassar ebony
1926: Ensemble in collaboration with da Silva Bruhns (carpet)
1927: Living room in walnut; in collaboration with Gobert, da Silva Bruhns (carpets), and La Maison Cornille (fabrics)
1928: Cupboard in palisander, 2 armchairs
1929: Dining room in Caucasian burl walnut; in collaboration with Hamot Frères (tapestry from cartoons by J. Beaumont)
1930: Living room with bookcase and sofa in ebony, chairs upholstered in leather
Dining room with table in burl walnut; in collaboration with da Silva Bruhns (carpet), and A. Kasskoff (leather)
1931: Living room including a sofa in silk and velours, games-table in jacaranda, armchairs covered with tapestry by A. Kasskoff, marketed by Hamot Frères, desk in jacaranda, several chairs upholstered in silk, low table in Chinese lacquer, lacquer screen; in collaboration with da Silva Bruhns (carpet)
1932: Ensemble
1933: Living room
1934: Lady's bedroom and powder room, in collaboration with A. Kasskoff (leather)
1935: Dining room including a cupboard, circular table, chairs and armchairs, in collaboration with da Silva Bruhns (carpet), Bastard (furniture ornamentation), and Paz-Silva (lighting)

Salon d'Automne
1922: Dining room including a cupboard, console table, chairs, and table
1923: Living room furniture
1924: Library including a bookcase in macassar ebony and 2 chairs
1927: Buffet for a dining room in burl walnut with silvered mounts, walnut dining-chair
1928: Bedroom in *galuchat* and macassar ebony, including a bed, small table, dressing-table, 2 chairs, and a walnut commode
1929: Studio corner
1932: Desk and chair in palisander
1933: Chairs and desk for Dr Roussel's library
1934: Large cupboard for a dining room

Lévy, Alfred (see Majorelle biography)

Salon des Artistes Décorateurs
1926: Furniture ensemble: Majorelle Rétrospective 1910–25, in collaboration with L'Atelier Majorelle
1929: Bookcase and secrétaire in palisander
1931: Cabinet and secrétaire in varnished jacaranda with silvered-iron feet; in collaboration with P. Majorelle; marketed by L'Atelier Majorelle

1934: Ensemble in French oak and ash, including a living room, reading room, and bedroom; marketed by Rémon and L'Atelier Majorelle
1935: Cupboard in palisander and burl ash, in collaboration with Frederik Stiner (sculpture); marketed by L'Atelier Majorelle

Salon d'Automne
1927: Palisander hall, marketed by L'Atelier Majorelle

Lurçat André

Salon des Artistes Décorateurs
1924: Project for a house

Salon d'Automne
1923: Maquette for a house for M. X, Paris
1924: Maquette in scale, for the house of a factory manager
1925: Photographs and plans for 5 *hôtels particuliers* built in Paris
1927: *Hôtel particulier* for M. Walther Guggenbuhl

Majorelle, Louis and Pierre

Salon des Artistes Décorateurs
1923: Dressing room
1924: Bedroom in collaboration with A. Lévy
1925: Coral smoking room in collaboration with A. Lévy (architecture), Janin (windows), and Francin (carpet)
1926: Retrospective
1927: 1900–1925 Retrospective: Orchidées and Algues (1900). Coral smoking room (1925)
1933: (Pierre) dining room in burl walnut and walnut, marketed by L'Atelier Majorelle, Nancy

Salon d'Automne
1919: Studio ensemble
1920: Silverware cabinet for a dining room; in collaboration with A. Lévy
Glassware with wrought-iron mounts
1921: Dining room ensemble in collaboration with A. Lévy
1922: Bedroom ensemble and sideboard in amaranth and macassar ebony
1926: Retrospective: desk and chair 'Aux Nénuphars' in mahogany and locustwood (1900 Exposition)
Buffet in amaranth, macassar ebony, and American walnut (1922 Salon d'Automne)

Mallet-Stevens, Robert

Salon des Artistes Décorateurs
1923: Pavilion for an exhibition
Bathroom, marketed by Les Etablissements Richard Lenoir

Salon d'Automne
1920: Small hall for the film company Diamant (decoration for a cinema), in collaboration with Charles Hess (decorative panels), Binquet (sculpture), and Maurice Lombart (cushions)
1921: Small hall in collaboration with Fabre (furniture), Baguès (lighting), Niepce and Fetterer (cabinetry), Lombart (cushions), Cottineau (paintings), and Leblanc (electricity)
'Un fond de jardin' in collaboration with Binquet (sculpture), Niepce and Fetterer (cabinetry), Leblanc (electricity), Cottineau (painting), and Hannu (electric pump)
1923: Bathroom sconces, marketed by Les Etablissements Ch. Blanc
Bookshop, in collaboration with Dreyfus-Stern (decorative panels)
A park for Art Urbain

1925: Maquette for a refueling depot for aircraft
1934: Steel cabin for an ocean liner, tourist class, in collaboration with Les Etablissements Flambo (furniture), Les Etablissements Perfecla (lighting) and Hélène Henri (fabrics)

Martine School (see Poiret)

Matet, Maurice

Salon des Artistes Décorateurs
1924: Bathroom in collaboration with J. and J. Martel (sculpture), marketed by Studium Louvre
1926: Bedroom, in collaboration with Max Vibert (panels); marketed by Studium Louvre
1927: Lady's bedroom with furniture in wild cherry Lacquered dining room including chairs in burl ash with velvet, in collaboration with Max Vibert (carpet, marketed by La Maison Coupé), Brunet, Meunie & Cie (fabrics), Thonet Frères (bookcase, marketed by Studium Louvre); marketed by La Maison Saddier et ses Fils
1928: Boudoir in burl amboyna and pigskin
1929: Lady's bedroom in burl wild cherry; chairs in burl ash and velvet, marketed by La Maison Saddier et ses Fils; in collaboration with Max Vibert (carpet marketed by La Maison Coupé), and Brunet, Meunié & Cie (fabrics) Bookcase marketed by Thonet Frères

Salon d' Automne
1923: Work study: 'Leo', in violetwood and thuya with ebony and ivory marquetry Bedroom: 'Cendrillon', in *gaiac* and pearwood with ivory and ebony marquetry, in collaboration with Dubard, marketed by Studium Louvre
1924: Hall in collaboration with Mlle M. Bec (engravings), marketed by Studium Louvre
1926: Architecture and decoration of the gallery of the Studium Louvre Furniture in palisander, ebony and mother-of-pearl, in collaboration with Max Vibert (carpets), and Léon Leyritz (sculpture)
1927: An engraved glass curio table, marketed by Studium Louvre
1928: 2 chairs in pearwood and velvet, guéridon in amboyna and brass; marketed by Studium Louvre

Mère, Clément

Salon des Artistes Décorateurs
1921: Objets d'art
1922: Objets d'art

Mergier, Paul

Salon des Artistes Décorateurs
1928: Vases and engraved objects, marketed by Bernard Lyon
1934: Various objects
1935: Paintings and vases in enamel-on-copper

Salon d' Automne
1925: 'Nessus': screen in lacquer, with black, gold, and silver relief, incrustations in pewter, mother-of-pearl, and eggshell
1926: Vitrine containing metalwork
1927: Vitrine with copper objects inlaid in precious materials Objects in copper with enamel and silver applications
1928: 'Neptune': screen in embossed and *repoussé* copper inlaid with silver and gold 'Bacchante': enamelled copper bust
1929: Copper door inlaid with silver and metals

1930: Piece of *salon* furniture in palisander, the doors in copper inlaid with silver, lead, pewter, and gold
1932: Vitrine including objects in precious metals and enamel-on-copper 'Deux Aigles': *repoussé* copper panel incrusted with silver and other metals, from a design by W. Wuilleumier
1933: Vitrine including objects in dinanderie and enamel-on-copper
1934: Vitrine including paintings and vases in enamel-on-copper

Montagnac, Pierre-Paul

Salon des Artistes Décorateurs
1921: Panel for a dining room Tapestry cartoon and watercolour
1922: Commode in palisander and ebony, marketed by Le Confortable
1923: Furniture, marketed by Robert Sangouard for an ensemble including a table, chair, table-desk with armchair, and a carpet by Bouix
1924: Bedroom in African lemonwood, coral, and mahogany Palisander cupboard with carved edges, marketed by Sangouard
1926: Dining room, marketed by Sangouard
1927: Cabinet in palisander Boutique for Daum
1928: Cupboard and chairs Rotunda for a drawing room
1929: Study in collaboration with da Silva Bruhns (carpet)
1930: Small *salon*, in collaboration with Subes (wrought iron), da Silva Bruhns (carpet), Marguerite Lehucher (curtains), Pleyel (piano); marketed by Etablissement Sangouard
1931: Architecture and decoration of a library and reading room, in collaboration with Mme Chabert-Dupont (curtains), Subes (illuminated glass), G. Daniel (sculpted plaster), H. Beaud (electricity), Genet and Michon (lighting), Etablissements Borderel (illuminated vases), Cornille & Cie (fabrics), and Sangouard (tables)
1934: Ensemble with furniture and carpet in collaboration with Perzel (lighting), Subes (ironwork), and Albert Guénot (sculpture: 'Bacchante et l'Enfant')
1935: Office ensemble

Salon d' Automne
1919: 'Faune et Nymphes': painting
1920: Ensemble including a dining room and 2 paintings
1921: Ensemble including a bookcase, 3 chairs, table, cupboard, and mirror
1922: Furniture ensemble including a tapestry by l'Ecole Nationale d'Art Décoratif d'Aubusson Dining room furniture manufactured *en série*, marketed by Robert Sangouard, (116 avenue des Batignolles, Saint-Ouen)
1923: Games-table in oak with carved chairs, executed by Sangouard Cane chair, marketed by Marceau
1924: Bookcase and 2 chairs in jacaranda, marketed by Robert Sangouard
1926: Library, including a desk, bookcase, and filing cabinet
1927: Boudoir, in collaboration with Bastard, Daum, da Silva Bruhns, and Subes
1928: Smoking room, marketed by Robert Sangouard
1931: Bedroom in sycamore, in collaboration with A. Marque (sculpture), Demarcq ('Tapinoué' carpet, Cornille et Cie), Perzel (lighting); the furniture marketed by Robert Sangouard
1932: Bookcase-cabinet

Moreux, Jean-Charles

Salon d' Automne
1924: *Hôtel particulier* for M. X, Saint-Germaine-en-Laye Houses *en série*

Nathan, Fernand

Salon des Artistes Décorateurs
1919: Commode in palisander with gilt and chiseled bronzes Mirror in carved giltwood
1920: Small bedroom
1921: Coin de salon including a settee, armchair, guéridon, and carpet
1922: Study including a bookcase, desk, armchair, and guéridon
1923: Dining room including a commode, mirror, and curtains; marketed by Primavera
1924: Living room including a settee and silk curtains
1932: Architectural project of a tourist hotel in the Var

Salon d' Automne
1919: Salon in palisander and sycamore with marquetry and lacquer, light fixture in silk, *torchères*; in collaboration with Joseph Bernard (bronzes and watercolours), Henri Ottmann (paintings), Mme Ottmann (carpet), and Avenard and Mayodon (faiences)
1920: Dresser in ash and palisander, chairs in ash, carpet and wallpaper; marketed by Nathan
1921: Living room, in collaboration with Evelyn Wild (carpet), and Robert Bonfils (curtains); marketed by Bianchini
1922: Dining room in collaboration with Jensen (silver), marketed by Galeries Lafayette
1923: Dining room, marketed by La Maîtrise
1924: Une Place Publique: Boutique #6: 'Lina Mouton'
1927: Living room furniture, in collaboration with Evelyn Wild (carpet), Robert Bonfils (curtains), and Dhomme (faiences); marketed by Bianchini
1931: Carpet in 'Basse-lice' by Aubusson, marketed by Marcel and Gilbert Petit (37 rue de la République, Puteau (Seine))

Pascaud, Jean

Salon d' Automne
1933: Chest of drawers in satinwood and mirror
1934: Cupboard and secrétaire in ebony and mirror
1935: Decorative ensemble, panels by Léon Lang

Perriand, Charlotte

Salon des Artistes Décorateurs
1926: Room in palisander and burl amboyna, in collaboration with Mlle Clouzot (tapestry)
1928: Dining room

Salon d' Automne
1927: Bar underneath a roof
1929: Interior equipment of a home in collaboration with Le Corbusier and Jeanneret

Petit, Pierre

Salon des Artistes Décorateurs
1927: Shop window for a shirt boutique
1928: Wardrobe in palisander
1930: Bedroom
1931: Bedroom in collaboration with J-K. Ray (glass window), and Malbranche (bedcovers)

1932: Dining room in waxed oak, in collaboration
with J-K. Ray (glassware), Straub and Vagniat,
(lacquered furniture and murals), and Gigou
(door mounts)
1933: Dining room in waxed oak, in collaboration
with Dieupart (lighting)
1934: Small drawing room with sycamore table; in
collaboration with Mme Mondragon (carpet
and fabrics), and Henri Rapin (silvered metal
panel)
1935: Ensemble in mirror, glass, marbrite, and
opaline: 'Repos, Cote d'Azur'; in collaboration
with Pico (map and engraved motifs), La
Société Industrielle des Glaces de Bobigny
(gravure and moulding), Marguerite Lehucher
(curtains), Marie Chauvel (glass flowers);
marketed by le Comptoir Général de Vente des
Manufactures des Glaces de Saint-Gobain

Salon d'Automne
1926: Industrialist's desk, marketed by Siègel
1927: Advertising material for a hotel hallway,
marketed by Siègel
1928: Dining room in collaboration with Seailles (wall
covering), and J-K. Ray and Chauson (stained
glass)
1934: Dining room

Poiret, Paul
Salon des Artistes Décorateurs
1924: Veranda for Chareau's Reception, marketed by
Martine

Salon d'Automne
1920: Lamp-shade fabric, 2 pieces of furniture,
bibelots
1921: Grand piano and upright piano
1922: 10 carpets, including: 'Les Liserons', and
'Pommes de Pins'
1923: Dining room for a hunter's rendezvous
5 carpets
1924: Une Place Publique: Boutique #8, in
collaboration with Ronsin (painting), Martine
(cushions, carpets, and bibelots), and Rosine
(perfumes)
1926: Bedroom
1927: Ensemble including a lacquered table with
incrustations, 3 carpets, light fixture; marketed
by Martine

Porteneuve, Alfred
Salon d'Automne
1930: Installation of the Exhibition Hall at the 20th
Salon of the Société des Artistes Décorateurs, in
collaboration with E.-J. Ruhlmann
1935: *Coffret* in Chinese black lacquer, red Moroccan
leather, and giltbronze, the interior lined in
blond oak

Printz, Eugène
Salon des Artistes Décorateurs
1926: Bedroom in rosewood, in collaboration with
Bezault Frères (locks), Emile Auzet and Jean
Dunand (vases), Germaine Schroeder
(bookcover), and Veguet (carpet)
1927: Bedroom in kekwood, in collaboration with
Jean Dunand (vases), Evelyn Wild (carpet),
Hélène Henri (fabrics), and Monville and
Beaufils (scales)
1928: Library in chestnut; in collaboration with Emile
Auzet and Jean Dunand

1929: Dining room with wood panelling, furniture in
palm, cupboard with folding and sliding metal
doors; with central cupola (lighting by indirect
light); in collaboration with René Seyssaud
(painting), Jean Dunand (lacquered panel),
Evelyn Wild (carpet), and Jean Sala (glassware)
1930: Sections of a private apartment: *Le salon, La
chambre, La salle d'habillage*; in collaboration with
Anna Bass, Marie Laurencin, Marguerite
Lehucher, Germaine Schroeder, G. Wittkowski,
Emile Auzet, Maurice Daurat, Jean Dunand,
Raoul Dufy, Auguste Guénot, Albert Laprade,
Henri Matisse, François Pompom, Jean Sala,
René Seyssaud, Ivan da Silva Bruhns; marketed
by L'Atelier Printz, Germaine Montereau,
Louis Brocard, Paul Desseroit, Rault & Cie, and
Auberlet and Laurent
1931: Large vestibule including indirect lighting,
black marble tiling, a screen-shaped black
wooden door, clear glass console, carpet in
point noué
1932: Section of a small *salon*, including architectural
lighting, cupboard in jacaranda with marquetry
in Indian horn and metal, 2 small tables, a couch
with cushions, carpet in point noué, bergère,
glass window by Marguerite Lehucher, and
painting in Stic-B
1933: Section of a living room, including architectural
lighting, a dining-table in Chinese lacquer and
metal, a chest of drawers in jacaranda and metal,
chairs in Chinese lacquer, a carpet in point noué,
velvet curtains, and windows by Marguerite
Lehucher
1934: Section of a small apartment including chairs
upholstered in satin and 'Lutetia' velvet, mural
fabrics in satin, curtains in satin; in
collaboration with Poirier Frères (fabrics),
Marguerite Lehucher (window curtains), Bertin
and Lapeyre (painting in Stic-B)
1935: Ensemble for a study in jacaranda, and dining
room in polished walnut; in collaboration with
Mayodon (ceramics), da Silva Bruhns (carpets),
Marguerite Lehucher (stained glass), and Vinay
(fabrics)

Salon d'Automne
1927: Polished kekwood cabinet with metal doors
decorated by Jean Dunand; the interior lined in
polished palisander and silk (Hélène Henri)
1928: Palm furniture with lacquered doors by Jean
Dunand, the interior lined with jacaranda; metal
chandelier; in collaboration with Auguste
Guénot (sculpture), Hélène Henri (fabrics), and
Evelyn Wild (carpets)
1929: Commode in palm with marquetry and metal
base; in collaboration with Jean Dunand
(vases), and René Seyssaud (painting); marketed
by Paul Desseroit (18 rue des Petits Champs)
1930: Section of a woman's apartment, including 2
corner cabinets, a glass and metal table, a palm
bookcase, an armchair, lighting by reflection,
and 2 carpets in point noué
1931: Hall for a *hôtel particulier* with furniture in
Chinese lacquer and carpet in point noué
1932: Furniture and chairs, carpet in point noué
1933: Bookcase in 3 parts, of which 2 are mobile
1934: Palm cupboard on a metal base
1935: Cupboard in Jacaranda, and a carpet in point
noué

Priou, Gaston
Salon des Artistes Décorateurs
1922: Black lacquered dressing-table
Panel
1928: Screen in lacquer
1933: Screen sections

Salon d'Automne
1927: Lacquered screen
1932: Tray in lacquer and eggshell
Maquette: part of a decoration in lacquer and
eggshell, marketed for de luxe cabins on the
ocean liner *S.S. Felix-Roussel*

Prou, René
Salon des Artistes Décorateurs
1923: Perfume shop, carved and polished wood
façade; marketed by R. Finkel & Cie, Saint
Maur
1924: Piano in palisander and ebony
Dining room for the ocean liner *De Grasse*
1927: Murals for a drawing room
Lady's desk and bergère in palisander, chair in
sycamore, and a lamp
1928: Small lady's *salon* for a palace; in collaboration
with A. L. Guénot (low table), Jacques Tissèyre
(tea table), and D. Louvet (carpet)
1930: *Grand salon de réception* in gold, white, and red;
marketed by Pomone
1931: Linen room and powder room, marketed by
Pomone
1932: Installation and decoration for Jean Goujon
rotunda
1933: Living room for a villa on the Cote d'Azur, with
fireproof metal furniture, including a metal bed,
armchairs, chairs, table, small table, lighting,
showcase; marketed by Société Studal
1934: Commode in pink tortoise shell with giltiron
foot
1935: Bedroom at Antibes including cane beds,
commode in marquetry, chairs lined with
decorated canvas, carpet; in collaboration with
Henri Martin, Adrien Eckman, Genevrière, da
Silva Bruhns, Lauer, Taroudgi, and Le Fibre
d'Acier

Salon d'Automne
1919: First-class cabin for the ocean liner *Paris*;
furniture executed by Schmit & Cie
1920: 3 paintings and a watercolour
1921: Inside door in wrought iron by Yung (32 rue
Merlin-de-Womille, Suresnes)
1922: Rooms for an ocean liner, in collaboration with
Leglas and Simon (drawing room), and Billard
and Rousseau (smoking room)
1923: Silverware display case in amaranth and carved
malachite
1924: Secrétaire in *bois des îles*, lacquered chairs
upholstered in silver fabric, giltwood bergère,
tapestry, and ebony chairs upholstered in velvet
1926: *Salon* furniture in violetwood, metal, amaranth,
and ebony; in collaboration with Denise Louvet
(sculpture)
1927: Armchair, table, and a 7-panelled screen
1928: Section of an apartment in collaboration with
Albert Guénot (dining room), Jacques Tissèyre
(smoking room), Lucie Besnier (smoking
room), and Henri Martin (bedroom); marketed
by Pomone
1929: Smoking room and card room; marketed by
Pomone
Grand stairway for an ocean liner of the
Compagnie Générale des Transportations,
marketed by Pomone
1930: Commode in blue Chinese lacquer with silvered
foot, marketed by Pomone
1932: Ensemble in collaboration with L'Etablissement
Lever
1933: Ensemble of furniture inlaid with *galuchat* and
blue mirrors, 2 armchairs in gilt Duralumin; in
collaboration with Aubusson (tapestry),

Georges Lepape (cartoons for tapestry), and Sèvres (blue porcelain vase)
1935: Third-class train coach for P.L.M. (Compagnie de Chemin de Fer)

Rapin, Henri

Salon des Artistes Décorateurs
1929: Cabinet in palisander and carved and silvered wood; in collaboration with Charles Hairon (sculpture), and Georges Capon (ironwork)
Decorative painting for Jacques Rapin's ensemble
Presentation of Gaudin and Simonnet's stand
1930: Swimming pool, in collaboration with H. Bouchard (sculpture), J. Gaudin (mosaic in glass and cement), Andre Ballet (ceramic tiles), marketed by Les Marbres Français, Bacle and Moulin (mosaic), Etablissement Levalois (lighting), Stic-B (painting)
Organisation of *Salle de Livre* at the 20th Salon des Artistes Décorateurs
Presentation of an ensemble of porcelain vases and objects in faience by La Manufacture Nationale de Sèvres
1931: (Henri and Jacques) large armoire-bookcase
1935: Large bookcase and 2 chairs

Salon d'Automne
1923: Ensemble for the apartment of the group of L'Habitation Franco-Americaine, marketed by Evrard Frères
1924: Models for an edition of carved wood frames; in collaboration with Le Bourgeois

Renaudot, Lucie

Salon des Artistes Décorateurs
1923: Project for a rest room, in collaboration with Paul Simon (stone and marble sculpture)
1926: Dining room, marketed by Dumas (24 rue Nôtre-Dame-des-Victoires)
1927: Man's bedroom, marketed by Dumas
1928: Apartment including a dining room and bedroom, marketed by Dumas
1929: Smoking room, marketed by Dumas
1931: Bedroom and boudoir in Provence, marketed by Dumas
1932: Study for Mme Lapeyre at Château des Fontenelles, Nanterre, in Stic-B
Two painted wallpapers, marketed by Dumas
1933: Decoration of the reception hall rotunda of the exhibition, in collaboration with Bertin and Lapeyre (painting in Stic-B)
1935: Table

Salon d'Automne
1919: Boudoir
1920: Girl's bedroom and country living room
2 watercolour sketches
1921: Dining room and children's bedroom, marketed by Paul Dumas
1922: Ensemble including a study and living room in mahogany and burl thuya
1923: Dining room in mahogany and amboyna
1924: Bedroom in mahogany and ebony

Renouvin, Georges

Salon des Artistes Décorateurs
1930: Section of a gallery in varnished maple and leather, in collaboration with Soudbininne (ceramics 'grand feu')
1932: End section of a gallery in varnished maple and leather, in collaboration with Soudbininne (ceramics)

Ruhlmann, Emile-Jacques

Salon des Artistes Décorateurs
1919: Dressing-table
1920: 'Vide poche' piece of furniture, in amaranth with ivory and ebony marquetry (2 versions: one with mahogany interior, the other with sycamore interior)
1921: Carved macassar ebony table with ivory and ebony marquetry
1922: Precious furniture in macassar ebony with ivory marquetry
1923: Cylindrical desk in macassar ebony with ivory marquetry and coral interior
1924: Mahogany commode with silvered-bronze mounts
Chiffonier in bronze with ivory marquetry
1926: Reception desk for a collector in collaboration with Porteneuve, La Manufacture Nationale de Sèvres (vase), Fontayne (carpets), Bernard (sculpture), Decoeur (ceramics), Degallaix (watercolours), Dunand (dinanderie), Janniot (decorative panel), Legrain (writing pad), Prouve (wrought iron); the cabinetry by Berger with metal mounts by Delion
1927: Games room and galleries for the ocean liner *Ile de France*, in collaboration with Dupas (games-room sketches), Boileau and Cabrière (designs of glass), Prouve (wrought iron), Dunand (lacquered dressing-table, screen), La Compagnie des Lampes (lighting)
1929: Studio for the Heir Prince, Viceroy. . . . at the Cité Universitaire, in white lacquer and chrome, in collaboration with Degallaix, Utrillo, and Vlaminck (painting); Bernard and Janniot (sculpture), Picaud (map), Mayodon (ceramics), Rodier (fabrics and curtains), Pleyel (piano), Braquenie (carpet in point noué), Fontaine (decorative key furniture), Berger (cabinetry), Ragon (plaster), Compagnie des Lampes (indirect lighting), Siègel (illuminated ramps), and Moral (electrical installation)
Woman's Art studio for the 19th Salon of the Société des Artistes Décorateurs, in collaboration with A. Porteneuve (architecture)
1930: Loggia for Jacqueline Francell, in collaboration with the architect A. Porteneuve, and Daurat (precious metals), Degallaix (painting), Janniot (sculpture), Denise Sourzac (carpet in point noué), Faille and Reinhardt (coloured and adjustable lighting), Mme Leroy (Max Furs), Rodier (shades), Auberlet and Laurent (plaster), Berger (cabinetry), l'Etablissements Ruhlmann et Laurent (painting and glasswork), and Fontaine (decorative locks)
Installation of the exhibition gallery at the 20th Salon of the Société des Artistes Décorateurs, in collaboration with A. Porteneuve
1932: *A Rendez-vous for a Trout Fisherman*
In collaboration with A. Porteneuve (architect)
Objects lent by Baron Jacques de Neuflize, President of the Casting Club of France
Collaborators: Degallaix (painting), Janniot (sculpture), Le Bourgeois (sculpture), Marchegay, vice-president of Casting-Club de France (sculpture), Picard Le Doux (painting), Paul-Emile Pissarro (painting), F. Pompom (animal sculpture), Jean Besnard (ceramics), Jean Dunand (lacquer), Gentil and Bourdet (tiles and chimney), Jean Luce (glass), Mayodon (ceramics), Pico (carpet in point noue and map), Rodier (linens and coverlet), Denise Sourzac (carpet in point noué), J. Tétard, (silverware), Aciers Profilés et Glacés (Etablissements Borderel et Robert, and Etablissements Rel), Berger (carpentry and cabinetry), Etablissements Rel (painting), La Maison Hardy Brothers (seat caning and house utensils), Milde

(lighting), La Maison Radio-Walda (Radiophone), 'Vivarium' (aquarium and exotic fish), and Fontaine (chromed hardware)
1933: Lady's desk in violetwood with Moroccan leather, the interior in macassar ebony with writing surface in lizard; with chromed metal mounts and special key furniture by La Maison Fontaine, stamped 'Progrès'
Chair in violetwood upholstered in Moroccan leather, lighting by La Compagnie des Lampes (29 rue de Lisbonne) in collaboration with A. Porteneuve (architect)
1934: *Retrospective Exposition*: silver cabinet in macassar ebony with gilt-bronze mounts, collection of Mme Van Beuningen (1930)
Fall-front in amaranth, *galuchat*, and ivory, the leather interior by Legrain, collection of Mme E.-J. Ruhlmann (1927)
Fall-front secretary in violetwood with gilt-bronze mounts, collection of Mme E.-J. Ruhlmann (1931)

Salon d'Automne
1919: Furniture ensemble and maquettes
1920: Cupboard in amboyna, ivory, and silvered-bronze, the central medallion by Foucault entitled 'La Nuit et Le Jour'
1921: Hall ensemble with furniture in macassar ebony, in collaboration with Paul Follot and Süe et Mare; marketed by Etablissement Ruhlmann et Laurent
1922: Precious furniture in macassar ebony with ivory marquetry
1923: Desk in amboyna with ivory marquetry and *galuchat* top (Fr9900)
Chair in amboyna with ivory marquetry and velvet upholstery (Fr2200)
1926: Collector's cabinet in macassar ebony, the doors inlaid with ivory, the interior lined with grey suede and goffered gold
1932: Three design projects for the stage set of *Christine* by Paul Geraldy of the Comédie-Française

Saddier, Fernand and Gaston

Salon des Artistes Décorateurs
1926: Mahogany dining room, marketed by Saddier et ses Fils
1927: Bar in moiré silk, in collaboration with Jean Luce (glass)
1928: Dining room
1931: Palisander dining room, in collaboration with Raymond Quibel (decorative panel), Renée Kinsbourg (carpet), Mlle Cettier (mural draperies marketed by Brunet, Meunie & Cie), Marguerite Lehucher (glass panel), Sabino (lighting), Marcel Goupy (tableware marketed by Rouard)

Salon d'Automne
1926: Bedroom in mahogany and velvet sapele, marketed by Saddier et ses Fils, in collaboration with Marianne Clouzot (pastels), Dunaime (chandeliers), Marcel Coupé (carpet), and Marguerite Lehucher (panel)
1928: Feminine interior in precious woods, in collaboration with Marguerite Lehucher (curtains), Mongermon (chairs); marketed by Saddier et ses Fils
1930: Living room in burl wild cherry

Sognot, Louis (in collaboration with Charlotte Alix)

Salon des Artistes Décorateurs
1924: Bedroom, marketed by Primavera

1926: Living room including carpets by Henri
Boulanger, painting by Claire Forque and Mme
Sougez
Powder room including paintings by Jean
François Thomas, and futon by Mlle Gatelet
1929: Tea room, including paintings by Colette
Gueden, marketed by Primavera, architecture
and general decoration by Sognot, metal and
glass buffet, metal tables, garden tables,
adjustable metal chairs; in collaboration with
Guillemard (metal chairs), Colette Gueden
(mounted objects)

Salon d'Automne
1923: Man's bedroom, marketed by Primavera
1924: Dressing and powder rooms, marketed by
Primavera
1926: Man's bedroom in collaboration with Henri
Boulanger (carpet) and Brieu (radiator)
Woman's bedroom in collaboration with Alice
Polsterer (carpet) and Brieu (radiator)
1927: Bar and smoking room; marketed by Primavera
1928: Double-faced psyche and 2 chairs
1929: Double-faced psyche and 2 chairs
'Fighting Eagles': design for a screen
1930: Plans for a *salon de repos* in a colonial habitat, in
collaboration with La Société Duralumin
1931: Furniture for Y. R. Holkar, Maharajah of
Indore; in collaboration with Hélène Henri
(fabrics), and da Silva Bruhns (carpet)
1932: Bedroom ensemble in lacquer for Mme U. G., in
collaboration with Charlotte Alix
1934: Ensemble including a piece of glass furniture
and an armchair; in collaboration with Gimond
(sculpture), Brianchon (watercolour), and
Cloisonna (walls)

Subes, Raymond-Henri

Salon des Artistes Décorateurs
1919: Glass chandelier, portable lamp, and floor lamp;
marketed by Maison E. Borderel
1920: Interior gate, 2 sconces, 1 bedside lamp, all in
wrought-iron
1921: Bronze lustre with wrought-iron animals
1922: Coffin doors, staircase ramp, radiator cover, 2
sconces, 1 chandelier, 1 lamp, a vase in iron and
blown glass
1923: *Desserte* in wrought-iron and marble
2 interior gates, a mirror, and lamps
1924: 2 radiator covers, a console and mirror, 2
sconces in alabaster, one interior gate in M.
Rapin's ensemble
1926: Wrought-iron guéridon with marble top
Lamp sconces, fire screen, and mirror
1927: Entrance door for a bank
1928: Vestibule gate, screen in aluminium and
patinated copper, lamps in chromed wrought-
iron
Gate for a building and school
Screen and radiator cover in Roux-Spitz's
ensemble
Balcony and lamps, marketed by Grand Dépôt
1929: Console with marble top
Interior wrought-iron gate
1930: Large entrance gate for a bank, in collaboration
with Letrosne and Marrast (architects)
Polished steel door for a vault, in collaboration
with Valensi (architect)
Console table, door, and ventilator grill in
chromed steel in the Jallot and Subes exhibits
1931: Wrought-iron gate
2 consoles with marble tops
2 X-shaped chairs with leather upholstery
2 reflector vases
1932: Ensemble including 2 small gilt-iron gates, a

wrought-iron console table and mirror frame in
lacquered Duco by Les Ateliers Rep, 2
illuminated vases on black lacquered stela
Gate for the Eglise Saint-Pierre de Roye, in
collaboration with Duval and Gonse (architects)
Gate designed for a ballroom; in collaboration
with Chappey (architect)
1933: Wrought-iron gates for the city hall of Puteaux
Wrought-iron gates for the Biarritz
Oceanographical Museum; in collaboration
with Hiriat, Lafaye, and Lacourreye (architects)
Wrought-iron decorative motif for a garden; in
collaboration with Bassompierre, de Rutte, and
Sirvin (architects)
Large gate in gilt wrought iron for the ocean
liner *Normandie*
2 consoles with marble tops, 2 chairs
upholstered in leather, 2 reflecting vases in
repoussé metal
1934: Grill and communion gate for the 'Chapelle des
Scouts', in collaboration with Hiriart (architect)
Ensemble including the entrance gate of the
Town Hall of the 14th *arrondissement*, in
collaboration with Sébille (architect)
Communion gate and balustrade for the Basilica
of Notre-Dame de Saint-Omer; in collaboration
with Huignard (architect)
2 small gates in Montagnac's stand
Polished iron console in Maurice Jallot's stand
1935: Large bronze door for the dining room of the
ocean liner *Normandie*, in collaboration with
Patout and Pacon (architects)
Gilt-bronze console with marble top
2 polished stainless steel doors
Gilt-copper and *repoussé* vase
Entrance door for the 25th Salon of the Société
des Artistes Décorateurs

Salon d'Automne
1920: Floor lamp in wrought-iron and bronze
1921: Portable lamp in wrought-iron
Lamp in bronze with wrought-iron base
1922: Wrought-iron console with marble top,
wrought-iron psyche
1923: Oak and iron furniture, 2 floor lamps with
alabaster shades, portable lamp, balcony in
wrought-iron, in collaboration with Alleman
(architect)
1924: Dining room table with marble top
2 benches in wrought-iron, covered with leather
stripes
Floor lamp in wrought-iron with alabaster
shade
Mirror with wrought-iron frame
1925: Wrought-iron cross for the Eglise Saint-
Quentin; in collaboration with Emile and
marketed by Brunet
1926: Balustrade in wrought-iron for the ocean liner
Ile de France
1927: Table in wrought-iron with marble top
1928: Wrought-iron gates for a garden crypt, fire
screen, and mirror frame, in collaboration with
Tournon (architect)
1929: Entrance door for a bank
Entrance gate for a house in Provence
1930: Wrought-iron gate with gilt decoration for Le
Musée Permanent des Colonies
1931: Wrought-iron gate for the Ministère de la
Marine Marchande, in collaboration with André
Ventre (architect)
Wrought-iron grill for an architect's office, in
collaboration with Viret and Marmorat
(architects)
1932: Gate for the Chapel at St Joseph's Hospital,
sculpture by C. Villandre
1933: Wrought-iron gate, console, and 2 small grills
1934: Entrance gate for the cemetery at Passy, in
collaboration with Berger (architect)

Building gateway, in collaboration with Mme
Bodecher
1935: 2-part door in patinated steel
2-part door in steel and leather
Maquette for the C.P.D.E. building

Süe (Louis) et Mare (André)

Salon des Artistes Décorateurs
1919: Furniture *en série*
1921: Bedroom, marketed by La Compagnie des Arts
Français
Printed fabrics by Süe and P. Vera, marketed by
Charles Stern
1922: Settee with tapestry by Aubusson, marketed by
Maurice Laver in collaboration with Samara (tea
service)
Dining and powder room, piano marketed by
Gaveau
1927: Sideboard and chair
1932: (Süe) Small *coiffeuse* and chair
1933: (Süe) Bedroom and cupboard
1934: (Süe) Music stand
1935: Music stand in macassar ebony

Salon d'Automne
1919: Mahogany dining room
Cupboard and bergère in collaboration with P.
Vera (bronzeware and clock), and Bisson
(bronzeware)
1920: Furniture, curtains, and objects; marketed by
La Compagnie des Arts Français
1921: Grand piano in palisander and burl walnut,
marketed by La Maison Gaveau (45 rue la
Boétie)
Music cabinet in palisander and burl walnut
Piano stool, circular carpet, in collaboration
with P. Follot and Ruhlmann
Vitrine containing key furniture, marketed by
Fontaine and Vaillant (181 Faubourg Saint-
Honoré)
Vitrine with toiletry items, marketed by La
Maison Christofle (33 boulevard des Italiens)
1922: Centrepiece in gilt-bronze and crystal, marketed
by La Maison Christofle, table belonging to B.
Boutet de Manel, marketed by La Compagnie
des Arts Francais
1924: Silverware and furniture
Cupboard and chairs
1925: Model of an aeroplane refuel depot
1927: Cupboard and chair
Gas station

Suisse, Gaston

Salon d'Automne
1926: Vitrine including boxes in red lacquer and
eggshell
1927: Vitrine including lacquered boxes, and étuis
1928: Vitrine including lacquered boxes, and étuis
1929: Vitrine including lacquered boxes, and étuis
Study for a screen
1930: 'Jaz': 4-panelled lacquered screen
'Paysage': 2-panelled lacquered screen
1931: Lacquered screen, marketed by Straub and
Vagnat
1933: Sketch of a lacquered screen and panels
1934: 2 lacquered panels

Szabo, Adelbert

Salon des Artistes Décorateurs
1920: Ironwork
1921: Wrought-copper chandelier
Clock for the façade of the newspaper *Le Temps*
building

Photographs of chandeliers for a movie theatre
1923: Photographs of ironwork
1924: Wrought-iron chandelier and stained glass by Matisse
1926: Wrought-copper ceiling light
1928: Wrought-iron sconces
1929: Wrought-iron radiator cover
1930: Wrought-copper and bronze ceiling light, firescreen, collection of Mme Alexandre
1931: Elevator door and section of a staircase ramp for La Banque de l'Union Parisienne
1932: Wrought-iron ramp for La Banque de l'Union Parisienne, in collaboration with Audoul (architect)
Small radiator cover in wrought-copper, property of M. Weill, in collaboration with La Maison Vialatoux (stucco)
1933: Entrance door in wrought-iron for a studio
1934: Mirror frame in polished steel

1935: Door panel for the First-Class dining rooms on the ocean liner *Normandie*
2 sections of the great door of the First-Class dining room on the *Normandie*, in collaboration with Pacon and Patout (architects)

Vera, Paul

Salon des Artistes Décorateurs
1920: 'Le Baigneuses' and 'Hirondelles et Papillons': wallpaper
'4 seasons' and 'Divinites champêtres' printed fabrics marketed by La Compagnie des Arts Français
1921: Tapestry cartoons
'4 seasons': panel
1922: 'L'Enfance d'Orphée': screen

1924: Watercolour
Decoration of a garden house (photograph)
1927: 'Orphée': screen in tapestry

Salon d'Automne
1919: 'Orphée et l'Enfant': cartoon for a tapestry
1920: 'Les Deux Pigeons': tapestry screen, exhibited in the ensemble of La Compagnie des Arts Français
2 paintings
1921: 'L'Eté': bas-relief, executed by Martin
'L'Automne', executed by Martin, marketed by Süe et Mare
1922: Screen in tapestry, executed by l'Atelier de Tissage de l'Ecole Nationale d'Art Décoratif d'Aubusson, with a wood frame by Louis Süe
Screen for a dining room: 'Le Pain, Le Vin, Les Fruits, La Viande', marketed by La Compagnie des Arts Français

BIBLIOGRAPHY

Une Ambassade française (Exposition internationale des arts décoratifs et industriels modernes, Paris, 1925), organized by the Société des Artistes Décorateurs, Paris 1925
L'Amour de l'art, July 1929
Les Années '25', catalogue by Yvonne Brunhammer, 2 vols., Paris 1966
Art Deco, Katherine McClinton, New York 1972
Art Deco, Finch College Museum of Art, 1971
Art et décoration, 1919 to 1935
L'Art décoratif français 1918–1925, Léon Deshairs, Paris 1926
L'Art décoratif français en 1929, Pierre Olmer and Henri Bouche-Leclercq, Paris 1929
L'Art français depuis vingt ans: Le mobilier, Emile Sedeyn, Paris 1921
Le Arti d'Oggi, Roberto Papini, Casa Editrice d'Arte Bestetti e Tumminelli, Milan 1930
L'Art vivant
Les Arts de la maison,
    Autumn and Winter 1923
    Spring and Summer 1924
    Autumn and Winter 1924
    Winter 1925
    Spring 1926

'Bureaux secrétaires pays divers XXème siècle', *Art et décoration*, January–June, 1928

'*Bureaux secrétaires pays divers XXème siècle A-Z*, 1928

The Connoisseur
Croquis de Ruhlmann, Leon Moussinac, Paris, n.d.

Decorative Folding Screens, J. W. Adams, London 1982
Décors et ameublements au goût du jour, Gaston Fleury, Paris 1926
DIM, Exposition générale de ses oeuvres (catalogue of the firm: D.I.M.), 1926
'Dunand Screens in the Modern French Spirit', *Arts and Decoration*, May 1928

Les Echos d'art, Jan. 1932
Les Echos des industries d'art, Jan. 1927, June 1926
Encyclopédie des métiers d'art, Vol. 1, Paris, n.d.
Ensembles choisis, Paris
Ensembles mobiliers (Exposition internationale des arts décoratifs et industriels modernes, Paris 1925) 3 vols., Paris 1925–1927
Ensembles nouveaux, Paris, n.d.

Exposition internationale des arts décoratifs et industriels modernes, 1925, Yvonne Brunhammer, Vol. 1, New York 1976
Exposition rétrospective E.-J. Ruhlmann, Musée des Arts Décoratifs, Paris 1934 (exhibition catalogue)

Femina
La Ferronnerie moderne (Exposition internationale des arts décoratifs et industriels modernes, 1925), H. Clouzot, 4 series
Feuillets d'art

Galerie Edgar Brandt, 1924 (gallery catalogue)
La Gazette des beaux-arts

Harmonies intérieurs de Ruhlmann, Paris, n.d.
L'Hôtel du Collectioneur, Groupe Ruhlmann (Exposition internationale des arts décoratifs et industriels modernes, 1925) Paris 1926

L'Illustration
Intérieurs, Frantz Jourdain, Paris, n.d.
Intérieurs – I-VI, Léon Moussinac, Paris, n.d.
Intérieurs au Salon des Artistes Décorateurs, J. Hiriart, Paris 1931
Intérieurs d'aujourd'hui, Waldemar George, Paris 1928
Intérieurs de Süe et Mare, Paris 1924
Intérieurs en couleurs (Exposition internationale des arts décoratifs et industriels modernes, 1925) Léon Deshairs, Paris 1925
Intérieurs français, Jean Badovici, Paris 1925
Intérieurs français au Salon des Artistes Décorateurs, P. Follot, Paris 1927
Intérieurs modernes, Henry Delacroix, Paris, n.d.
Intérieurs modernes, Albert Novi, Paris, n.d.
Intérieurs présentés au Salon des Artistes Décorateurs, Henri Rapin, Paris 1930

Jean Dunand, Jean Goulden, Galerie du Luxembourg, 1973 (exhibition catalogue)

Le Luminaire (Exposition internationale des arts décoratifs et industriels modernes, 1925), Guillaume Janneau, 3 series, Paris 1926–1931
Luminaire moderne (Exposition internationale de 1937), Gabriel Henriot, Paris 1937

Maison et jardin
Meubles du temps présent, Paris, n.d.
Meubles et objets d'architecture dans les années 1925, Galerie Maria de Beyrie, 19 November–31 December 1976 (exhibition catalogue)

Le Meuble français moderne, Léon Moussinac, Paris 1925
Meubles modernes en métal, Pierre Pinsard (Librairie des Artistes Décorateurs)
Meubles nouveaux, Guillaume Janneau, Paris 1937
Le Mobilier français d'aujourd'hui (1910–1925), Pierre Olmer, Paris 1926
Mobilier et décoration, March, May, Nov., 1926; May, June, 1927; Dec., June, 1929; Dec. 1930; July, Dec., 1933; June 1934
Mobilier et décoration d'intérieur; June, July 1924; June, July, August 1925
'Modern Interiors in Europe and America', *The Studio*, Herbert Hoffman, 1930

Nouveaux Intérieurs français, 4 series (?) (?–1936)

L'Oeil

Plaisir de France
Paris 1928, Antoine Roche, Paris 1928
Petits Meubles du jour, Paris 1929
Petits Meubles modernes, Paris 1929
Pierre Chareau, édition du Salon des Arts Ménagers, U.A.M., Paris 1954

Quand le meuble devient sculpture, 1930 (exhibition catalogue)
'Quelques ensembles de Pierre Legrain', *L'Amour de l'art*, 1924

La Renaissance, Paris 1928
La Renaissance de l'art français et des industries de luxe, 1925
Répertoire du goût moderne I-V, Paris, n.d.

Le Salon des Artistes Décorateurs, Paris 1930
'Le Salon des Artistes Décorateurs', *Art et décoration* (special issue), Paris 1927
Sièges contemporains, Paris, n.d.
The Studio
Le Style 1925, Yvonne Brunhammer, Paris, n.d.
Le Style moderne dans la décoration intérieure, Henri Clouzot, Paris 1921

25 années U.A.M., René Herbst, Paris 1956

Wendingen, no. 6 of the 6th series, Amsterdam 1924

INDEX